821.4
W11t

84224

DATE DUE			

Thomas Traherne.

Thomas Traherne.

By Gladys I. Wade,

WITH A SELECTED BIBLIOGRAPHY OF CRITICISM,

BY ROBERT ALLERTON PARKER.

1969

OCTAGON BOOKS

New York

Printed in U.S.A. by
TAYLOR PUBLISHING COMPANY
DALLAS, TEXAS

To C. W.

who shared the Adventure.

ACKNOWLEDGMENTS.

IN gathering the material for this book, I have benefited by the courteous cooperation of many people, to whom my thanks are due. I have to acknowledge with gratitude the access to the Traherne manuscripts which Mr. P. J. Dobell has always afforded me; and for his permission to quote from them and from his publications. Part of my research has been done in Herefordshire; and for facilities to examine the manuscripts in the possession of the Corporation of Hereford I am indebted to Mr. Feltham, Town Clerk of Hereford. I have also to thank Canon Bannister and all the many clergy of Herefordshire and Gloucestershire who permitted me to search their parish registers. Canon Fletcher of Salisbury and the Reverend D. M. Taylor of Hinton Martel supplied me with interesting and valuable particulars about Philip Traherne. The Bursar of Brasenose, Mr. Cox-Hill, afforded me generous assistance during my stay in Oxford to inquire into Traherne's period of residence at that College. The Probate Officers at Gloucester and at Llandaff gave me every facility for searching the seventeenth-century wills in their custody. To them, as to the officials of the Bodleian and the British Museum Libraries, at the Record House and at Somerset House and elsewhere, from whom I have received most courteous help, my thanks are due.

I should also like to express my gratitude to the two far-asunder universities which have fostered this research of mine— the University of London, where Miss Edith Batho of University College has given me the benefit of her advice and criticism; and the University of Western Australia, to which, by its award to me of a Hackett Research Studentship, I owe the opportunity I have had to undertake and carry through this work. It is an odd coincidence that it is the Press associated with yet a third university in yet a third continent that publishes the result of that research! Finally, my grateful thanks are due to a fellow Traherne-enthusiast, Mr. Robert Allerton Parker of New York, for unfailing encouragement and for his preparation of the manuscript for publication; and for permission to include his valuable bibliography of modern critical commentary on Traherne.

Sydney, 1942.   G.I.W.

ℵOTE TO THE SECOND PRINTING.

The Rev. F. E. Hutchinson, D.Litt., F.B.A., of All Souls College, Oxford, whose special field of study has long been the seventeenth century in English Literature, has carefully checked all my quotations and references. He realized that access to original sources was impossible for me now in Australia. I am grateful to him for a long labor voluntarily undertaken; and have gladly made use of the notes he forwarded to me to remove many inexactitudes. If any remain, it will not be the fault of Dr. Hutchinson, whose scholarly net is fine enough to catch even the erring comma and the misplaced capital.

Sydney, 1946.   G.I.W.

CONTENTS.

PART FOUR: THOMAS TRAHERNE THE "DIVINE PHILOSOPHER"

APPENDIX

PART ONE.

The Ending of an Eclipse.

"The lid of ignorance or inconsideration interposing, they are oftentimes eclipsed, or shine only through some crannies."—CENTURIES IV, 86.

CHAP. I.

The Discovery.

IN the middle of the seventeenth century, there walked the muddy lanes of Herefordshire and the cobbled streets of London a man who had found the secret of happiness.

He lived through a period of bitterest, most brutal warfare and a period of corrupt and disillusioned peace. He saw the war and the peace at close quarters. He suffered as only the sensitive can. He did not win his felicity easily. Like the merchantman seeking goodly pearls or the seeker for treasure hid in a field, he paid the full price.

But he achieved his pearl, his treasure. He became one of the most radiantly, most infectiously happy mortals this earth has known.

Some little measure of fame he enjoyed even in those troubled times when party leaders, successful generals, a king and his mistresses, held the stage. He would have frankly enjoyed an honorable renown; the lack of it troubled him not at all. For he was concerned only to savor and to communicate his own dazzling ecstasy.

Fortunately for us, not all that communication was oral and personal. Fortunately for us, he was impelled to bestow on some of it the more abiding form of the written word. And so it was he wrote from time to time poems like this:

News from a forrein Country came,
As if my Treasure and my Wealth lay there:
So much it did my Heart Enflame!
Twas wont to call my Soul into mine Ear.
Which thither went to Meet
The Approaching Sweet:
And on the Thresh hold stood,
To entertain the Unknown Good.

It Hoverd there
As if twould leav mine Ear.
And was so Eager to Embrace
The Joyfull Tidings as they came,
Twould almost leav its Dwelling Place,
To Entertain the Same.

But little did the Infant Dream
That all the Treasures of the World were by:
And that Himself was so the Cream
And Crown of all, which round about did lie.
Yet thus it was. The Gem,
The Diadem,
The Ring Enclosing all
That Stood upon this Earthy Ball;
The Heavenly Ey,
Much Wider then the Skie,
Wher in they all included were
The Glorious Soul that was the King
Made to possess them, did appear
A Small and little thing![1]

And prose like this:

Your enjoyment of the world is never right, till every morning you awake in Heaven; see yourself in your Father's Palace; and look upon the skies, the earth, and the air, as Celestial Joys: having such a reverend esteem of all, as if you were among the Angels. The bride of a monarch, in her husband's chamber, hath no such causes of delight as you.

You never enjoy the world aright, till the Sea itself floweth in your veins, till you are clothed with the heavens, and crowned with the stars; and perceive yourself to be the sole heir of the whole world, and more than so, because men are in it who are every one sole heirs as well as you. Till you can sing and rejoice and delight in God, as misers do in gold, and Kings in sceptres, you never enjoy the world.

Till your spirit filleth the whole world, and the stars are your jewels; till you are as familiar with the ways of God in all Ages as with your walk and table; till you are intimately acquainted with that shady nothing out of which the world was made; till you love men so as to desire

---

[1] "On News," *Centuries* III, 26.

their happiness, with a thirst equal to the zeal of your own; till you delight in God for being good to all: you never enjoy the world.[2]

He died at the age of thirty-six, that strange young man who had learned to "enjoy the world aright" with so intense a quality of joy. And as the years went by, he passed from living memory. He had published little; and that little anonymously. His anonymous manuscripts were inevitably dispersed.

That might have been the end of his story. Thomas Traherne and all his works might well have passed beyond all recall into the countless legions of forgotten men and forgotten writings.

But it was not to be so. Something, Chance or Providence, that withheld him from his own day and generation, has given him again to ours; and the story of the recovery of those long-hidden, miraculously preserved writings, and the rediscovery of the personality of their author, is surely one of the strangest tales in all the history of literature.

The first chapter, the actual human life and the writings that flowered from it, belong as I have said to the middle of the seventeenth century—the period from 1638 to 1674.

The next chapter began two and a quarter centuries later, in 1895.

It began when a certain lover of books, William T. Brooke, was engaged in the pleasant pastime of turning over the contents of a secondhand bookbarrow in the Farringdon Road, London. Every one of us who has had the chance has succumbed to that lure. The long dingy street, the rough homemade barrows, the coster-owner with his indomitable cheeriness, the wares piled high, all the flotsam and jetsam of the book world halting a space before final consignment to the paper mills. Who knows what may lie at the bottom of the pile? Some rare first edition, maybe; one of the missing first folios of Shakespeare; some oddity or curiosity of literature worth perhaps a fortune, worth

---

[2] *Centuries* I, 28-30.

certainly the twopence or sixpence asked for it. The combination of books, bargains, and treasure-hunt is too much for human nature to resist.

And this was to be William T. Brooke's lucky day. For he happened on two old manuscript volumes in perfect preservation; one a folio, one a small octavo. Brooke was of course too wily a bargain-hunter to betray his interest; and when he walked off with the two manuscripts under his arm, he was the poorer by only a few pence.

Two Traherne manuscripts, after who knows what hair-breadth escapes from destruction, had made at that instant the first step out of the oblivion of two and a quarter centuries.

Mr. Brooke knew a good deal about seventeenth-century verse, and so it was the first half of the folio volume that attracted him. The second half of the folio had been used to hold classified prose extracts, and was obviously a student's notebook. The octavo volume was filled with short prose passages, with just a little verse here and there. But the first half of the folio contained a considerable quantity of poetry, fine in itself, and new to Mr. Brooke. He studied it carefully, with a mounting conviction that he had happened upon something unusually good. He saw at once the strong resemblance between these new poems and the known work of Henry Vaughan. Like Vaughan's, these were deeply religious in tone, and they, too, treated childhood and nature in a manner rare in the seventeenth century. A hitherto unknown collection of poems by the well-known poet, Henry Vaughan, would certainly be a "find."

A prominent personage in the literary life of London at that time was Dr. Alexander Grosart. Dr. Grosart was one of those indefatigable people who faithfully edit enormous "collections" of writings. He had edited one set running to 39 volumes, another of 38, a trifle of 14 volumes, and another of 33. His special field was rare Elizabethan and Jacobean material; and it was natural that William T. Brooke should seek him out with his recently acquired manuscript and his theory of Vaughan authorship.

Dr. Grosart was at once interested. He studied the new poems, concurred in Brooke's ascription of authorship, and bought the two manuscripts from him. He decided on the strength of it that he would edit a new and very elaborate edition of Henry Vaughan's poetry, in which he would incorporate this new material. He had not succeeded in carrying out this project, however, when he died in 1899.

This was fortunate; for if Dr. Grosart had repeated with Traherne manuscripts the similar error of Dr. Hickes—of whom more later—he would have set up a new barrier. Students of the poetry would have had first to detect and then to refute the wrong ascription of authorship before they and we could have arrived at the truth.

That barrier was fortunately avoided by the difficulties which arose to delay Dr. Grosart's project.

In the meantime, William T. Brooke had naturally told the story of his exciting find to many literary friends; and among them to Bertram Dobell, another well-known figure in London at the close of the nineteenth century.

The name of Bertram Dobell will always be closely associated with that of Traherne; for to him more than to any other human agency we owe the rediscovery of Traherne. Bertram Dobell was an interesting personality. With little or no formal education, he became a man of letters and a critic of acute insight. Born in humble circumstances, he began life as an errand boy. The bookbarrows and stalls attracted him, and he began to collect books. Many years later, with a capital of £10 he opened a bookseller's business; in 1887 he moved to the shop in the Charing Cross Road which he made famous, and which still bears the family name. It was he who befriended the poet James Thomson when he sorely needed a friend; it was he who edited Thomson's poems in 1895. He wrote verse himself, and some sound critical work on Shelley and Charles Lamb; and finally, in the first decade of this century, he entered the story of Thomas Traherne.

After Dr. Grosart's death, his library was sold. Charles Higham, a well-known bookseller, purchased it. Higham and Dobell were friends; and Dobell, interested in the supposed Vaughan manuscript from Brooke's account, was given the opportunity by Higham to study it carefully. Dobell, like Brooke and Grosart, was keenly interested in its contents; he made a deal with Higham and became the owner of the folio containing the poetry and also of the companion octavo with the prose extracts.

He bought the poems, of course, with a view to publishing them; and commercially, they would have been of considerable value as additions to the work of a recognized major poet. As such, they would attract on publication a widespread interest in literary circles; and this interest would redound to the profit as well as the prestige of the publisher.

But the more Bertram Dobell studied these manuscript poems, the more he was convinced that something was amiss with the judgment of Brooke and Grosart. It was true that this new collection dealt exclusively with religious topics, as did Vaughan's poems; it was true that in vocabulary and in verse-forms there were marked resemblances; it was true that both venerated childhood in a peculiar way; it was true that both saw in childhood and in nature a special religious symbolism.

Yet in spite of these strong similarities, the differences appeared to Dobell so profound that he was reluctantly driven to the conviction that these poems were none of Vaughan's. It seemed to him that in the poems of Vaughan and in these manuscript poems two fundamentally different personalities found expression; that the quiet, restrained, slow-moving Vaughan could never be the author of verse so fiery, so joyous, so abounding in energy.

But if Vaughan were not the author, who could be?

Which left Dobell with an anonymous manuscript, and the whole vast field of seventeenth-century religious verse to search for some connecting clue. The proverbial needle in a haystack might not offer a more hopeless quest.

But Dobell was not lacking in determination or in energy; and once again William T. Brooke came into the story. Dobell and he discussed this new critical angle; and Brooke remembered that he had once used in an anthology a poem that had a similar joyous ring to it. He had found this poem in an anonymous little book in the British Museum, a book called—with typical seventeenth-century prolixity—*A Serious and Pathetical Contemplation of the Mercies of God, in several most Devout and Sublime Thanksgivings for the same*, a book written in a kind of free verse, interspersed with poems in more regular rhythms. It was one of these poems that Brooke had used in his collection; and all of these poems he now copied out for Dobell. Dobell read them; and knew at once, beyond all argument, that they came from the same pen as his unidentified manuscript. To his critical judgment the tone, the energy, the radiance, the whole expression of personality, were unmistakably one.

But such a purely personal conviction was no proof. Nor was he at that stage much nearer to naming the author of either set.

But the little book with the long name afforded one clue; its Preface stated that the author had been "to the service of the late Lord Keeper Bridgman as his Chaplain."

Sir Orlando was soon traced as a prominent personage of the reign of Charles II and, for a period, holder of the high office of Lord Keeper of the Seal. Further research revealed that Sir Orlando had had a chaplain whose name was Thomas Traherne.

Once a name emerges, inquiry always becomes easier. The seventeenth century has its modest equivalent of the *D.N.B.* for its more famous men; and in Anthony à Wood's *Athenae Oxonienses*—a sort of *Who's Who* of the Oxford University men—appeared the following paragraph:

Thomas Traherne, a shoemaker's son of Hereford, was entered a Commoner of Brasen-nose College on the first day of March, 1652; took one degree in Arts, left the House for a time, entered into the sacred function; and in 1661 he was actually created Master of Arts. About that time he became Rector of Credenhill, commonly called Crednell, near to the city of Hereford; . . . and in 1669, Bachelor of Divinity.

His authorship of two published books, *Roman Forgeries* (1673) and *Christian Ethicks* (1675) was soon established. Both were searched minutely by Dobell for any clue that might link the anonymous work in the manuscript to these. And at last came the moment when Dobell's long search was triumphantly ended; the exciting moment when he found, casually imbedded in the prose of *Christian Ethicks*, a passage of verse that was also to be found in one of his precious manuscripts.

So it came about that Dobell gave to the world in 1903 the first edition ever to be printed of the poems of Thomas Traherne; and in 1908 the second manuscript of prose passages, which he named *Centuries of Meditations*. And in so doing, he gave back to the modern world something rare and beautiful which had been hidden from men's eyes since the seventeenth century.

Each of these publications contained a thoughtful and well balanced evaluation by Dobell of Traherne as a writer and a thinker; and in the first to appear, the Poems, was given a brief account of the discovery of the manuscripts and of their identification as Traherne's.

Dobell's researches and that of interested friends brought to light a few further biographical scraps. We learned the date of Traherne's death and the place of burial. His odd little will was unearthed. We found he had had a brother named Philip. Another manuscript volume, *Poems of Felicity*, was discovered in the British Museum by Dr. Bell and published by him in 1910.

The whole story of this modern recovery of a forgotten poet and prose-writer, and of the romantic survival of his manuscripts, aroused widespread interest. Many articles were published in literary journals; Traherne has his place in today's *Encyclopaedia Britannica*, and since 1911 in the *Cambridge History of English Literature.* Extracts from his prose appear in modern anthologies.

Nevertheless, few people today are familiar with his writings; the great majority of well educated people have never even heard of him.

Thomas Traherne, in fact, has yet to come into his own. For Thomas Traherne was a truly great man, with a message we peculiarly need. He has only partially emerged from the utter darkness of his eclipse. He stands in peril of slipping back into the mists.

The reason for this is, I am convinced, that only a few devoted Traherne enthusiasts have seen Traherne as a man. To the world at large he is at best only a disembodied voice, coming thinly across the centuries. The biographical facts are bare bones, lacking the flesh and blood of life. His rare jewels of idea and inspiration seem but ghostly moonshine; they cannot win our acceptance, they seem too far sundered from the harsh realities of our daily life.

It is my ambitious purpose in the ensuing pages to take you back to those green fields of Herefordshire and the muddy streets of Restoration London, and to a chapter of history as dark as our own; and to recreate as best I can the child, the youth, and the man who lived and loved and suffered as we do, yet found—as, alas! we too often fail to do—the secret of triumphantly happy living; a man who became the Friend of God.

PART TWO.

Thomas Traherne the Man.

"And when all secrets shall be revealed, all hidden things brought to light, his life shall be seen in all its perfection."
—CHRISTIAN ETHICKS.

Background.

Homas Traherne, as Anthony à Wood stated in his biographical note, was born "a shoemaker's son of Hereford."

The exact date of his birth still eludes discovery. Bertram Dobell and other searchers, including myself, have explored carefully all the likely parish registers in Herefordshire; but without result. However, the record of his entry into Brasenose College, which I discovered in an old Record of Admissions at Oxford, fixes the period of it fairly narrowly. This record is not the original, but any error is very unlikely. It informs us that Traherne was fifteen on March 1, 1652. That would be 1653 by modern reckoning, as the new calendar year then began on March 25. So if Traherne was in his fifteenth year on March 1, 1653, he must have been born between March 1, 1637, and February 28, 1639.

In the subsequent chapter I shall have something to say of his home and parentage. But first we have to explore the significance of the date and the place of his birth, the city of Hereford.

The county of the same name, of which Hereford is the capital, lies far over to the west of England, bordering on Wales. It is a sort of transition county, half English, half Welsh. Today, as in Traherne's time, it has no industrial centers, no ironworks or collieries. As in Traherne's time, it is a land of timbered farmhouses, of orchards famous for apples and cider, of woods and clear streams and little hills. One can stand in the fourteenth-century porch of Traherne's little church at Credenhill and see substantially the same picture—to the west the hills of Wales, to the south and east a wide panorama of fields and orchards and gently rolling meadowland. Masefield, who was also of Herefordshire, once wrote of it: "Whenever I think of Paradise, I think of parts of this country; for I know no land more full of the beauty and the bounty of God than these red ploughlands and these deep woodlands so full of yew trees, and these apple orchards and lovely rivers and running brooks."

By accident of birth in Herefordshire, Traherne was thus in his earliest years surrounded by natural beauty such as this; and he has himself told us of the passion of his early love of nature. He could remember in manhood when and where he first saw a living tree, and the tumult of feeling then aroused. "The green trees when I saw them first through one of the gates transported and ravished me, their sweetness and unusual beauty made my heart to leap and almost mad with ecstasy, they were such strange and wonderful things," he wrote in the *Centuries*; and that he became in manhood a poet of nature and a nature-mystic is, I believe, in no small measure due to the loveliness of the place of his birth.

Yet unchanged as Herefordshire still is in some respects, in others it is enormously different from its seventeenth-century self. It requires today, with all our modern developments in transport and communication, a real effort of the imagination to conceive how isolated was Traherne's native city, how cut off from the great centers of business and of political and intellectual activity. Hereford City was then off the beaten track of trade. Bristol to the south, Worcester and Shrewsbury to the north, had direct and fairly easy access to London. Hereford, hampered by difficulties of communication, neither bought nor sold to any considerable extent. It produced and consumed its own commodities; and sent the inconsiderable surplus of its products to Bristol. It had no mines, and no important manufactures; it imported very little coal, and very little of anything else. It quite definitely did not desire any expansion of trade; for when a scheme was mooted for opening the Wye to navigation, the people of Herefordshire strongly and successfully opposed it, declaring that the trade it would bring would do "no good at all, but rather hurt, by the importation of wines, fruits, sugar, spices, and such unnecessary commodities which are better spared than had."[3] The prosperous, fertile county was self-sustaining and quite self-satisfied. " 'Tis a county exceeding fertile," wrote a seventeenth-century topographer[4]; "for wheat, wool, and water it yieldeth to no county in England. . . . The City [of Hereford] is no less pleasantly than commodiously situated, amongst delightful meadowes and rich corn-fields, and almost encompassed with rivers . . . over which are Two Bridges." Another contemporary of Traherne, a Parliamentary officer during the Civil Wars, has also given us a graphic picture:

"Saturday our squadron watched at St. Owen's Gate, which day I took an opportunity to view the city, which is well scituate, and seated upon the river Y, environed with a strong wall, better than any I have seen before; with five gates, and a strong stone bridge of six arches over the river, surpassing Worcester. In the city there is the Statelyest market-place in the Kingdome, built with collumnes . . . the Minster every way exceeding that of Worcester, but the city in circuit not so large. The inhabitants are totally ignorant of the waies of God, and much addicted to drunkenness and other vices, but principally to swearing, so that the children that have scarce learned to speake doe universally swear stoutlye."[5]

To Bristol they sent for remarketing in London and elsewhere a certain amount of this famous wheat and wool, and some of their even more famous cider, product of the Redstreak apples of their orchards. But the local markets and fairs were the chief centers of business—and provided the chief relaxation of most of the people. In the great farmhouses, many of which had been held in unbroken succession since the Conquest, they brewed their ale, dipped their candles, spun their flax and their wool, and pressed their cider. These farms were isolated even from each other during certain parts of the year by the terrible state of the

---

[3] Webb, *Memorials of the Civil Wars in Herefordshire.*
[4] Blome, *Britannia* (1673).
[5] "Letters of a Subaltern," *Archaelogia*, Vol. XXXV, p. 332.

roads; Herefordshire roads were proverbial for badness even in the seventeenth century, when no roads were particularly good if judged by modern standards. But in Herefordshire they were mere ditches, deep forest lanes, overhung with trees, and trodden down by centuries of wear till they were deeper than the head of horse and rider. Such roads as these were never free from mud, even in midsummer: and in winter were often impassable. Bridges, also, were very few, and the fording of such a river as the Wye usually difficult and often dangerous. These factors of difficult communication, prolonged for generations, had their inevitable effect on the habits and characters of the people of Herefordshire, perforce absorbed in the narrow interests of the farm and the parish. Traherne himself did not entirely escape the effects of environment, as his later history will show.

The social habits of the Herefordshire people largely determined their reaction to the forces which cleft the nation into warring factions—forces already at work before Traherne was born. Isolated geographically off the beaten routes of trade, and further isolated by local difficulties of communication, they remained for a considerable time untouched by events happening in London.

And this brings us to the implications of the other fact, the date of Traherne's birth. For Traherne was but in his fifth year when the long-smoldering quarrel of King and Parliament broke into the open flame of the Civil Wars; and, as the conflagration ran its course, turned the Eden of lovely Herefordshire into a pretty imitation of Hell.

To the great mass of the common people of England, the Civil Wars were wars for religious principles. The leaders of the Parliamentary side might know they were fighting as well for the political rights of the House of Commons; Charles I and his advisers might know they were fighting to keep for the Crown privileges the Tudors had exercised unquestioned. But in the eyes of their supporters the Parliamentary leaders were fighting against "Popery," against a return to the horrors of that reign of "Bloody Mary" which was still recent history; while to the rank and file of the Royalists the King was fighting to save the "true Protestant religion" from the disorderly sects of Brownists and Anabaptists and the like. The political propaganda of both sides played deliberately upon these fears; and it was because the fear of "Popery" proved stronger than the fear of "Schismaticks" that Parliament won to its cause the great mass of the nation. With a Roman Catholic queen on the throne, with Roman Catholic priests and laymen not only tolerated but even favored at court, with the illegal Mass once more openly said, with a papal legate openly received, with Archbishop Laud making changes and "Popish" innovations in the churches, it is easy to understand the widespread uneasiness that took hold of the people.

But all the general fear, all this bitter religious passion working elsewhere in England, found scant response in Herefordshire. Hereford folk for a while went indifferently about their daily work. In 1637 Laud himself said—and Laud was not easy to satisfy—"For Herefordshire, I find not much amiss."

Yet conflict was inevitable. The whole nation was rapidly dividing itself into two hostile camps, each determined on sweeping changes.

By January 1642 the national temper was heated; London shops were shut, Londoners thronged the streets shouting, "Down with the Bishops!"; angry mobs were bursting into churches, pulling down the new communion rails and making bonfires of them. News of these disorders penetrated even to Herefordshire, and gave rise to a "Petition to the Lords and Commons"—a petition wholeheartedly Royalist in sympathy. This was the first of such documents to bring Hereford into bad odor with the Parliamentarians; another was the bold "Declaration of the County of Hereford," sent when hostilities were known to be inevitable. This latter caused considerable stir in the House of Commons, which passed a resolution "That this is a most scandalous and infamous paper," and ordered the punishment of its publishers and printers.

Before the close of 1642, when Traherne was a child of five, Hereford City had its first experience of actual war.

Earlier in that year, the King in preparation for hostilities had appointed his Commissioners of Array for Herefordshire as elsewhere; by August these commissioners had raised the militia and sent £3,000[6]—nearer fifty thousand dollars in modern money—to the King. When the King took up his quarters in Shrewsbury, valuable supplies came to him from Bristol via Hereford; and therefore Essex, the Parliamentary General, decided to cut this line of communication.

Hereford then possessed fairly strong walls, surmounted by sixteen towers; there were gates, a moat, and a drawbridge. But in the long years of peace these had fallen into partial decay. In 1642 the citizens thus had these defenses, such as they were, and a magazine. They probably had no guns; and certainly had no efficient organization. They learned only by bitter experience the need to be up and doing in their own defense. The first capture of Hereford by the Parliamentary forces was ludicrously easy. In the contemporary *Letters of a Subaltern* we have an account of the operation:

> In this poore condition cominge to Hereford, the gates were shut against us, and for two hours we stood in dirt and water up to the middle legge; for the city were all malignant, save three, which were Roundheads. . . . But the Roundheads in the city, one of them an Alderman, named Lane, persuaded the silly Mayor (for so he is indeed) that His Excellency [i.e. Essex] and all his forces were at hand; whereupon he opened unto us. And so we entered the city, but found the dores shut, many of the people with their children fled, and had enough to do to get a little quarter. But the poor Mayor (seeing he was so handsomely cozened) was not a little angry. . . .

Thus Hereford was captured; and the Earl of Stamford was appointed by Essex to govern it for the Parliament. Hereford

---

[6] All contemporary money quoted needs to be reckoned at four or five times the amount to approximate to present-day value.

received from Stamford its first lesson in Puritan rule; and for a
while—till the time should come when Cavalier and Puritan
were equally hated—Hereford became through its sufferings
more ardently Royalist than ever. It had to endure insolent
interruptions of its cathedral services—our subaltern has told us
of some incidents of the first Sunday of occupation:

> Sabbath day, about the time of morning prayer, we went to the Min-
> ster, where the pipes played and the puppets sang so sweetly that some of
> our soldiers could not forbear dancing in the holy choir; whereat the
> Baalists were sore displeased. The anthem ended, they fell to prayer, and
> prayed devoutly for the King, the bishops, etc.; and one of our soldiers
> with a loud voice saide, "What! never a bit for the Parliament?" which
> offended them much more. Not content with this human service, *we*
> went to divine . . . and went to hear Mr. Sedgwick, who gave us two
> famous sermons. . . .

And there were darker deeds, deeds of wanton cruelty, such
as that done to the household of the country rector, Thomas
Swift, grandfather of the famous dean. Because of rumors that
he had been active in the Royalist cause, Thomas Swift was
stripped of property to the value of £200,[6] his house plundered
to the bare walls, his children and servants left with hardly a
garment to cover them at the beginning of winter, and anyone
who showed them charity threatened with severe penalties. The
contemporary chronicle runs:

> Ransacking every corner of the house, that nothing might be left be-
> hind, they [Stamford's troopers] find a small pewter dish in which the
> dry-nurse had put pap to feed the poor infant. . . . The nurse intreats, for
> God's sake, that they would spare that, pleading that it was all the suste-
> nance that was or could be provided to sustain the life of the child. . . .
> Throwing the pap to the dogs, they put up the dish as lawful prize.

Stamford held Hereford for two and a half months; then, in
consequence of the battle of Edgehill, the major armies moved
far from Herefordshire, and he was obliged to leave and retire
to Gloucester.

Hereford was once more its own master; and after a brief
period of retaliation on those suspected of too great friendliness

toward their late masters (the "silly Mayor" among them) the whole county enjoyed a return to tranquillity.

But not for long. In April of the next year, Hereford was besieged by Waller. Cave did his utmost to hold the city for the King, but it proved indefensible against guns; and he was also seriously hampered by the inertia of the citizens. He simply could not get them to organize or carry out obvious defense measures; even when left on guard they melted away and went home to bed. Hereford surrendered after a brief experience of gunfire, though most of its chief citizens had already vanished unobtrusively across the river. Not a heroic tale.

So for the second time the city was in the hands of the Parliamentarians; and as this time it had been taken by force, it had to pay £3,000[6] to be exempted from plunder. Waller, its new master, was fortunately a merciful man. But his stay, like Stamford's, was brief; military duties called him elsewhere, and the Puritan forces were withdrawn.

During the years 1644-1645, the war everywhere took on an aspect of increased savagery and brutality. Both sides were recruiting by press gangs. The unfortunate peasants so "pressed" naturally deserted at the first opportunity; floggings and hangings ensued. Men began to avoid the garrison towns for fear of these press gangs; and we have ample evidence that they were active in Herefordshire as elsewhere.

The disaster of Marston Moor, and the subsequent lesser defeats, loosed bands of roving Cavaliers all over England. Many of these found their way into Herefordshire; and the unhappy people suffered more from their depredations than from any other single cause in the war. For the desperate, starving troopers plundered friend and foe alike with utter recklessness and often with wanton cruelty. Even the remotest places knew the misery they could inflict. In bitterness at this, and also in fear of the sequestrations that now began wherever Parliament was strong enough to enforce them, many a Royalist laid down his arms and "compounded."

Rupert, Gerrard, and other Royalist leaders, who from time to time marched across Herefordshire or the neighboring counties, brought further odium upon the Royalists by savage brutalities to their foes and equally savage insolence to their friends. When I first read those contemporary records, I found them almost incredible; but the Gestapo and the concentration camp prove that man indeed can do such things to man. I quote two to illustrate the kind of thing the child Traherne could scarcely have escaped seeing. One is an account of the behavior of Royalists:

> The barbarous and cruel enemy drive away our cattle, rifle our houses to the bare walls. All provision of victuals where they come, carried away or destroyed. Divers villages and country towns, being neither garrisons nor any annoyance to the enemy, burnt down to the ground. The standing corn they burn and destroy. All sexes and degrees stripped naked by the enemy; the aged, and unarmed persons, inhumanly murdered in cold blood; and others half-hanged, and afterwards stigmatised, and their flesh burnt off their bodies to the bare bones; and yet suffered in great torture to live.[7]

The other describes the behavior of Puritans, and is even more horrible in that it is written by a Puritan with obvious complacency. It is Colonel Michael Jones sending in his report:

> By the blessing of God the army is safely returned with (as I conceive) 6,000 sheep and 500 cows. A gentleman's house near Hollywell was fired, for that it had soldiers in it that killed a man of yours. The widow Hanmer's house near Hollywell that did us much prejudice is taken, fired, and all the refused quarter (viz. 12) put to the sword, 9 whereof were roasted.[7]

We begin to see now why to Traherne his England seemed "a den of thieves, and those of blood," a "general.Bedlam."

In 1645 there was a serious rising in Herefordshire. The sorely tried patience of a patient people suddenly broke, and between fifteen and sixteen thousand men marched to Hereford to see the governor, Scudamore, and demand some redress. They

[7] Both quoted by Webb, *op. cit.*

could not keep together long enough to achieve anything; but that people once too inert to build a breastwork to save their capital could rise in such numbers and show such spirit, is eloquent proof of the bitterness of their sufferings.

The Royalist armies suffered another great defeat in the second battle of Newbury; and after it there were again stragglers all over the countryside, raiding and ravaging. Charles I, fleeing to South Wales, stayed for twelve days in Hereford. He endeavored to recruit, but unsuccessfully; Rupert's two marches across Herefordshire would account for that reluctance to serve. Yet, in those twelve days, the little county raised £5,000[6] for his obviously hopeless cause.

The King went on his way. Then came tidings to Herefordshire of the advance against them of the dreaded Scottish Army. We can well imagine with what sick hearts the people waited for what the days would bring. They could not look to their King for any help whatever—he was himself a fugitive. But in Scudamore they had a capable and energetic governor, in Philip Traherne an indomitable mayor; and at last, under the spur of such terrible danger as this, they gave them active help. They "strengthened the old ramparts, scoured the ditches, silenced the bells, stopped the clocks, burned the suburban houses, even to an almshouse, cleared away trees and hedges"—perhaps those very trees outside the city gates that had so moved the childish heart of Traherne!

So the Scots found a city grimly determined to sell itself as dearly as possible.

The siege lasted six weeks. Six weeks of stormings and sallies; of breaches made in the walls, to be as quickly stopped up by the citizens with timber and woolsacks, the women of Hereford working side by side with their menfolk at this dangerous task. Six weeks of mining and countermining; and of sallies from within in which even the small boys of Hereford—and just possibly Traherne himself—took part. Scudamore wrote of that later: "A notable sally was made at St. Owen's gate with great execution . . . at which time little boys strived which should first carry torches and faggots to fire their works. . . . We countermined, and employed our boys by day and by night to steal out and fire their works." Many and many a year later Nathaniel Salmon heard the ladies of Hereford retell by their firesides their adventures and exploits in the famous Scottish siege.

The Scottish Army never took Hereford. They were recalled before they had accomplished their purpose.

But, again, the country round had suffered terribly. For though the Scots were merciful to the lives and persons of the people, and very kindly to children, they were obliged to live upon the occupied country. They had had no pay for seven months; they lacked the simplest necessities; and so the ragged, half-starving army rifled Herefordshire with a thoroughness that, in spite of all that had previously happened, it had not known before. Later it was computed that in these thirty-six days of occupation the value of their plunder was £31,700[6] in contemporary money.

Royalist rejoicing over the defense of Hereford was shortlived. All over England the Parliamentary forces were sweeping everything before them. The fall of Hereford was only a question of time. It came at last, suddenly and ignominiously—by treachery within. It was just at Christmastime. The weather was bitterly cold and the snow lay thick. Some, warned in time, escaped across the frozen Wye. Others, the majority, woke one morning to find their city in the hands of the dreaded Puritans. A sad Christmas it must have been for every man, woman, and child in the doomed city.

From that time until the Restoration in 1660, Parliament was the undisputed master of Hereford; and a hard master. The usual confiscation of church properties followed; the usual sequestrations; the usual heavy fines on "delinquents" and "malignants." These totaled in Herefordshire £44,000,[6] apart from rents and confiscated estates. A good many of the old clergy were left in peace, provided they kept quiet.

Herefordshire had very little to do with the final phases of the war. When the Prince of Wales came to Worcester to make one more desperate bid for victory in the field, and the streets of "The Faithful City" ran blood in his cause, Herefordshire stood aloof. It had had enough. Individuals such as Richard Hopton and Hopton's future wife—of whom we shall hear more later— might risk their lives as secret Royalist agents; but the mass of the people were too exhausted for further effort. As speedily as might be, they adapted themselves to the conditions imposed by the victors; as speedily as might be, they turned once more to their old avocations, to the cultivation of their wasted lands. And in time, to such as were not prominently obnoxious to those in power, a certain measure of prosperity returned.

But it was an uneasy peace. Most of them believed that the beheading of an anointed king was a sin against God; most of them believed that this abolition of bishops and suppression of the old Church was essentially wicked. Most of them would feel that this long period of supremacy of evil forces was a dreadful punishment from God Who for His own mysterious purposes thus permitted the wicked to flourish. The hope of the ending of that punishment never died. It would be ardently prayed for in secret.

An uneasy peace, shot through with passionate longing for the restoration of old ways, for a king and a national church as of old; and with an imperishable hope that this would some day in the mercy of God come to pass.

And in those twenty years of brutal warfare and uneasy peace, twenty years of disorder, of bloodshed, of unimaginable misery and of rebellious submission, Thomas Traherne passed from childhood to adolescence, and from adolescence to manhood. He was in his twenty-third year when Charles II came back to the throne.

CHAP. III.

The Cottage and the Inn.

IN the preceding chapter has been sketched the broad background of Traherne's early life, the environment of nature and of men he knew from his birth until that March of 1653 when he went up to Oxford; a background of exquisite natural beauty and of darkest human suffering that must inevitably have had on so sensitive a spirit an indelible effect. As we shall see, Traherne was never to escape the consequences of having been born in Hereford, and in that time.

But let us now turn for a space from geography and history to Traherne's own niche within the vaster framework—to the child Traherne as a member of a family and through it, of a social group.

In tracing this personal history, I am accepting as literal facts Traherne's own references and allusions in his *Centuries of Meditations* and in the two autobiographical cycles in his poems. For while it is true that he uses these personal experiences as illustrating universal truths, and is almost solely concerned with their spiritual implications, yet every reference we can check from other sources has been found to be literally true. For instance, he discusses in the *Centuries* his studies at a university, and we have proof of his long stay at Oxford.

There is a wealth of personal allusion in Traherne's writings. No one so far has collected them or examined their value as biography; but, because of them, something approaching a picture of his life does become possible.

I have also accepted the chronological order of events and personal experiences given by Traherne. I have combined his information with a considerable amount of material from other sources; and though definite dates are few and documentary evidence is practically non-existent, particularly for the earliest period, what emerges is, I believe, substantially true as well as most enlightening.

In reconstructing those earliest years, our chief information comes from that note by Anthony à Wood, who told us Traherne was "a shoemaker's son of Hereford"; from a paragraph in a gossip-writer; from old records and registers of Hereford and adjoining counties; and most important, from Traherne's own statements.

The gossip-writer to whom I refer was John Aubrey, who published in 1696 *Miscellanies upon Various Subjects*. One section of these *Miscellanies* gave a collection of vouched-for anecdotes of ghosts and apparitions, one of which Aubrey said he had heard from Thomas Traherne. I shall quote his somewhat confused paragraph in full, though the ghost part is quite irrelevant. What is relevant is the repetition of the statement that Traherne's father was a tradesman, and the added information that he was a master craftsman employing two apprentices. Traherne's reputation as "learned" will concern us later. Thus Aubrey:

Mr. Traherne, B.D. (chaplain to Sir Orlando Bridgman, Lord Keeper), a learned and sober person, was son of a shoemaker in Hereford; one night as he lay in bed, the moon shining very bright, he saw the phantom of one of the apprentices sitting in a chair in red waistcost and headband about his head, and strap upon his knee; which apprentice was really in bed and asleep with another fellow-apprentice, in the same chamber, and saw him. The fellow was living, 1671. Another time, as he was in bed, he saw a basket come sailing in the air, along by the valence of his bed; I think he said there was fruit in the basket; it was a phantom. From himself.

Traherne's own allusions also show that his parents were of humble status, and that he was born in a city. He recalls the time, when "the gates were at first the end of the world"; he remembers seeing "boys and girls tumbling in the streets"; he has played in the dirt, and to his mind "the dust and the stones of the street were as precious as gold." In his first infant awareness of the world, "the city seemed to stand in Eden . . . the streets were mine, the temple was mine." A little later in his history, he recalls a time when he was

> Remov'd from Town,
> From People, Churches, Feasts, and Holidays,
> The Sword of State, the Mayor's Gown,
> And all the Neighb'ring Boys.

In Hereford he would find all those things—a city bounded by walls and gates; trees beyond those gates; even a splendidly be-gowned mayor, preceded on state occasions by sword and mace. That reference to the mayor is interesting. Is it just a little boy in a crowd recalling the city's chief citizen? Or has the little boy seen very close Philip Traherne, mayor of Hereford in 1642 —seen him as close as one would a relative? Watched from a corner the family fuss as the old man was helped into his splendid robes?

There is no reference in Traherne's writings to his father's trade; but there are plenty to his family's poverty. And to something more than poverty. I give you the chief allusions from the *Centuries* (from which the above prose quotations were also taken; the verse is part of the poem "Solitude"):

> I who in this life am born to mean things according to the world.
> How can I believe that He gave His Son to die for me, Who having power to do otherwise gave me nothing but rags and cottages?
> Once I remember (I think I was about four years old when) I thus reasoned with myself, sitting in a little obscure room in my father's poor house. . . . How comes it to pass therefore that I am so poor? Of so scanty and narrow a fortune, enjoying few and obscure comforts?
> As for the pleasures that were in great men's houses, I had not seen them.

That the home was poor, with a poverty that pressed even upon the child in that home, seems abundantly clear. The Civil Wars with all their disorder and interruption of the normal ways of life might have accounted for that. But Traherne tells us pretty plainly that there was more to it. He tells us that in that home of his infancy there was vice, and quarrels, and tears; that there was sickness and death; that there was also, as we would expect, difficulty in finding the money both for the war taxes and for bread. He tells us that he was not aware of it at the time; he was too young, and rapt away in the young child's blissful world of its own. These are his words: "I dreamed not of poverties, contentions, or vices; all tears and quarrels were hidden from mine eyes. . . . I knew nothing of sickness or death or rents, or exaction either for tribute or bread."[8]

The point for us at the moment is not that he was unaware of them, but that these things were actually there.

Alongside of all that picture suggests, I want to place Traherne's few significant references to his parents; and his significant silences.

To understand these fully, one must realize that in Traherne's philosophy the infant, the "little child" who symbolizes in the New Testament membership in the Kingdom of God, is spiritually perfect; Traherne, long before Wordsworth or Blake, believed that for most men the process of growing up is the closing in on the soul of "shades of the prison-house." Traherne viewed as tragic the corruption of natural goodness in the child by its exposure to a corrupt world. Traherne does not use words lightly; yet the evil to which he personally was subjected by the adult world of his childhood was such that he says that spiritual murder was committed; that they were foes, pulling down his temple to the ground. Those phrases occur in his poems[9]; they are matched by the more sober statements of his prose: "Those things which my nurses and parents should have talked of, there [i.e. at Oxford] were taught to me." "It is not our parents' loins so much as our parents' lives that enthrals and blinds us."

I have referred to his significant silences. Traherne was one of the most ardently grateful of mortals; he poured out fervent thanksgivings to God constantly—no one has left us thanksgivings more detailed, wide embracing, and rapturous than his. The social ties, the manifold forms of human love, his personal friendships have their constant place in them; so have minute things which remind us of St. Francis, little things like the sound of wind in grass, the "soft delicates" of butter and honey.

Yet you will not find a single thanksgiving for the nurture and care of his parents!

I think it is beyond argument that Traherne had for his parents neither love nor respect.

Or at least for his father. I think his mother may have died when he was very young; probably at the birth of Philip. That is guesswork, but we have certain facts which strongly suggest it. One is the reference to "sickness and death" already quoted as happening in his childhood home; another is the small family of two in an age of very large families; another is the fact that the baby Philip was sent away to nurse, that is, to a wet-nurse, at Lugwardine, a little town about nine miles from Hereford where there were relatives, and only returned to Hereford when he could walk and talk[10]; yet another is the fact to which I shall come soon, that Thomas himself was transplanted when a child into a more prosperous household. The death of Traherne's mother and the ne'er-do-well character of the father would account very naturally for all these.

Little more can be said of Traherne's father than what I have already given. Dobell was shown an old record which proved that a John Traherne living in Hereford at this time was a shoemaker; he inferred that this would be Thomas Traherne's father. But I know from a good deal of local research that all through the seventeenth century there were many Trahernes living in Hereford engaged in that trade. John Traherne the shoemaker may have been the father; but Charles Burney once wrote positively that the father of Philip was named Thomas. I have given the full story of this in the note below[11]; here all I want to say

[10] See the poem "To the Same Purpos."

[11] Philip Traherne, the brother of Thomas, on his return from Smyrna brought back a valuable Greek manuscript of the New Testament which is known to scholars as the *Codex Ephesius*. This manuscript Philip presented to the Archbishop of Canterbury, together with a list of all the variant readings from the Oxford

is that Burney was a reliable person with a fund of information.
Under the circumstances he is likely to be correct.

Of more importance is the name of Traherne's brother, Philip;
for it points to certain family connections.

Philip was not a popular baptismal name in seventeenth-
century England. People had not forgotten that "Bloody Mary"
had married Philip of Spain. The name brought associations of
rack and fire, of Armada, of the Inquisition, of national terror. A
small English boy of those days was about as likely to be called
Philip as one of the 1940's would be to be called Adolf! Only if
it were a "family" name would it recur, under pressure of the
intense family conservatism of the time. Those Traherne family
trees I have investigated will show you Thomases as plentiful as
blackberries, and John and Richard and William appearing generation after generation. But in all the parish registers I have
searched, I have met the name Philip Traherne only at St.
Peter's, Hereford, and at Lugwardine.

It is fairly certain on this alone that young Philip, and therefore his brother Thomas, were connected not only with the
Lugwardine branch but also, as they lived in Hereford, with the
various Philip Trahernes of St. Peter's Church. Of these, the
outstanding figure is the patriarch, Philip Traherne the innkeeper, twice mayor of the city.

If this old warrior holds, as I believe, the key to the problem

Greek Testament of 1675. A second copy of these readings he retained for himself.
This copy passed into the hands of Charles Burney (along with sundry other
Traherne manuscripts). Burney himself was a great scholar, with an extraordinary
fund of knowledge; he was so interested both in the *Codex Ephesius* and in this
collection of notes that he copied into the front pages of the notebook references to
the codex in various critical editions of the Greek New Testament. A point that
annoyed Burney was that three scholars had said that it was *Thomas* Traherne who
had brought the codex from the East. To the first of these erroneous ascriptions,
that in John Mills's edition of 1707, Burney appended the note: "For Phillip
Traheron, Thomae filius", and at the end he added the acid reproof of such inac-
curacy, "Huius codicis lectiones minima cura adscripserant Tres Magni Editores.
C.B." (Burney MS. 24. B.M.) I think it very unlikely under these circumstances
that Burney could be in error in saying that Philip was the son of a Thomas
Traherne.

of Traherne's excellent schooling and his university education, and to that new and wealthy environment into which he was suddenly transplanted in boyhood, he must loom large in any picture of Traherne's personal world in his earliest years.

The Hereford Corporation Manuscript and the State Papers provide an abundance of material about him. Born in 1566, he emerged into the public life of Hereford in 1619 as leader and spokesman in a certain dispute between the citizens and the mayor in office. He suffered disfranchisement, imprisonment, and trial in London before the Privy Council; but in the end he won his case. His courage, a pugnacity, independence, and obstinacy are plainly revealed in the records. He stood high with the clergy and with the local justices; and as for the citizens, they made him mayor in 1622. From then on he was a leading citizen. He was chief assessor before and during the Civil Wars, and he grew increasingly prosperous. No doubt the business of the inn benefited from the popularity and prominence of its host.

When the Civil Wars broke out, and Hereford was seriously threatened, we see Philip Traherne again active in service, a fervent Royalist. (He would not be one to approve those tavern-closing Puritans!) At the time of greatest peril, the siege by the Scottish Army, he shouldered the responsible and dangerous office of mayor; and he was then seventy-nine. He lived long enough to rejoice in the successful resistance of Hereford to the Scots; and died in the autumn of the same year, in time to escape the bitterness of the final collapse of the Royalist cause. A memorial, erected after the Restoration, pays tribute not only to his political zeal, but to his "friendly and affectionate behaviour in conversation."

Yes, he would be a good innkeeper, at home and happy in its world of robust animal well-being, with its feasting and drinking, its music, cards and dice, its busy bustle, and its secret fringe of sordidness and vice. There was not likely to be any particle of the mystic or the contemplative in such a man as Philip Traherne the innkeeper; we have evidence that he was not even conventionally religious if it conflicted with his business interests. He was in fact at one time in some trouble with the authorities for failing to observe Lent, and for supplying his customers with "suppers of flesshe upon Friday nighte."[12]

I said that we have evidence that Traherne as a child was transplanted into a new and wealthy environment, a lonely and rather bewildered little boy. There are also several references to taverns and tavern life. These add up pretty clearly to the fact that Thomas Traherne's second home was the inn of his wealthy relative, Philip Traherne.

Here are the most striking of the relevant allusions.

Traherne was giving his reader the reasons why his first infant awareness of the Divine was deadened in him; and said it was because he was overwhelmed by an "impetuous torrent of wrong desires in all others whom I saw or knew"; and that he was helpless against the torrent because "I was a stranger and unacquainted with them; I was little and reverenced their authority . . . ambitious also, and desirous to approve myself unto them."

These new people who now had authority over him, and whose approval had to be won by the child, were kindly folk, and generous; indeed, they "obtrude their gifts," and made little Thomas come to believe "a ribbon or a feather" well worth having.

> O fine!
> O most divine!
> O brave! they cry'd; and shew'd
> Som Tinsel thing whose Glittering did amaze,
> And to their Cries its beauty ow'd;
> Thus I on Riches, by degrees,
> Of a new Stamp did learn to gaze.[18]

"So I began among my play-fellows to prize a drum, a fine coat, a penny, a gilded book. . . . So that the strange riches of man's invention quite overcame the riches of Nature," he recalls.[14]

---

[12] Hereford Corporation MSS. [18] "The Apostacy."
[14] This and other quotations are from *Centuries* III.

The fine clothes, the ribbons and feathers of the gallant of the day, the gilded books and the money to spend, clearly belong to another social stratum than the "rags and cottages," the stark poverty of the beginning.

The most illuminating and the clearest of the allusions to the child Traherne and the inn itself is the following stanza from his poem "Poverty," with its picture of the inn parlor or dining room, and the lonely child in the inglenook.

> As in the House I sate
> Alone and desolate,
> No Creature but the Fire and I,
> The Chimney and the Stool, I lift mine Ey
> Up to the Wall,
> And in the silent Hall
> Saw nothing mine
> But som few Cups and Dishes shine
> The Table and the wooden Stools
> Where Peeple us'd to dine:
> A painted Cloth there was
> Wherin som ancient Story wrought
> A little entertain'd my Thought
> Which Light discover'd throu the Glass.

Where people used to dine! Would such a phrase be used of a private room in a private home? Does not every word suggest the ever-prepared dining room of an inn, the table and the stools and cups and dishes set in readiness for the arrival of "people"? The little child, sitting there on his stool in the fireplace of the temporarily deserted room, so conscious of being "alone and desolate," is a stranger; for the painted arras cloth above the chimney piece is not something he has always known, but something whose novelty, as he tries to make out its pictured story by the light from the diamond-paned windows, can a little distract his sad heart.

There are many other passing references to taverns in Traherne's writings which now take on a heightened significance; as for instance, when he names among the things that drowned his first felicity,

> Swearing and Roaring Boys,
> Shops, Markets, Taverns, Coaches . . .

And still speaking of happiness:

> In Taverns, Houses, Feasts and Palaces,
> I sought it, but was still deny'd.

The most significant is the following, where he sums up the whole frustration of this period of his life:

> And strove in vain to meet
> That Eas of Mind
> Which all alone I long'd to find:
> A common Inn doth no such thing betray . . .

These last quotations also bring out what will be true all through Traherne's biography, namely, that there is an inner as well as an outer history to record.

The outer history for this earliest period is, as we have seen, one of advancement, of escape from miserable poverty to wealth and indulgence. But the inner history was one of deterioration, of loss. Traherne's own words are clear:

The first Light which shined in my infancy in its primitive and innocent clarity was totally eclipsed: insomuch that I was fain to learn all again. If you ask me how it was eclipsed? Truly, by the customs and manners of men, which like contrary winds blew it out. . . . All men's thoughts and words were about other matters. They all prized new things which I did not dream of. . . . And finding no one syllable in any man's mouth of those things, by degrees they vanished, my thoughts (as indeed what is more fleeting than a thought?) were blotted out; and at last, all the celestial, great, and stable treasures to which I was born, as wholly forgotten, as if they had never been.

Traherne describes the same experience in his poetry:

> Drown'd in their Customs, I became
> A Stranger to the Shining Skies,
> Lost as a dying Flame.

The interaction of material prosperity and deep indefinable inner restlessness continued to determine the course of Traherne's life for many years to come.

Philip Traherne the innkeeper died in 1645, when Traherne was in his eighth year; but his business would go on. Philip had several sons, among them a Philip and a John who had to pay heavy fines when the sequestrations were in force. The will of the old Philip would have been illuminating, I feel sure; but I did not succeed in tracing it. Possibly he never made one; possibly it has not survived the disorders of the Civil Wars. It might well account for Thomas Traherne's possession of those five cottages in Widemarsh Street—cottages he forgot all about when he was making his will, though he remembered his "best Hatt"! Certainly someone made possible the excellent education of both Thomas and Philip, and a prolonged stay for Thomas at Oxford. Who more likely than the one well-to-do Traherne of the day, the generous, hot-tempered old pagan whose inn I suggest afforded a home for a period to a "sad and desolate" little boy?

CHAP. IV

The First Crisis.

AS to most men, much that was of permanent importance to Traherne happened in the stormy years in which he passed from infant to schoolboy, from schoolboy to adolescent, and finally went up, a "man" of fifteen, to Oxford University.

Much of this personal history remains shadowy; but certain great peaks of experience stand out clearly. And just as research has given us back the anxious minds and suffering bodies of the community in which Traherne lived as a child, and has given us a clear enough picture of the still medieval city whose streets he knew, with its winding narrow thoroughfares, tall half-timbered houses that overhung them, the handsome market square onto which the chief tavern doubtless opened, its glorious Norman minster, its dirt and smells and visitations of plague, its swarming children and their unnatural precocity—just as research recaptures for us all this essential part of Traherne's childhood and youth, so it will, if we allow it, cast an illuminating ray or two on Traherne's schooldays.

There was in Traherne's day an excellent grammar school attached to Hereford Cathedral; and this grammar school had the right to "present"—that is, nominate to free scholarships certain of its boys to Brasenose College, Oxford. That Traherne went to Brasenose suggests at first sight that this was the way of it. But it was not so. Traherne entered Brasenose as a "commoner," and paid the usual fees. Moreover, the rolls of the grammar school, extant for at least part of the period of Traherne's schooling, do not contain his name or his brother's.

There are also other facts which suggest that neither Thomas nor Philip went through the general academic mill of the time, and so escaped by a miracle what Milton, who among other things was an educational reformer, has stigmatized as "that asinine feast of sow-thistles and brambles, which is commonly set before them as all the food and entertainment of their tenderest and most docible age."[15] Traherne has told us of his wide-awake curiosity in these school years, of his active brain and his desire to fathom problems. Incidentally he has told us something of his course of studies. "When any curious cabinet, or secret in chemistry, geometry, or physic was offered to me," he wrote, "I diligently looked into it, but when I saw it to the bottom . . . I despised it."[16]

How extraordinary it was that he, a child of that age, should have had the chance to use his wits on problems of chemistry or geometry one can realize fully only by a study of contemporary education. Perhaps this following passage will serve to show what I mean. It was written by a would-be reformer, John Each-

<hr />

[15] *Tractate on Education.*   [16] *Centuries* III, 25.

ard, in 1670—twenty years later—and provoked strenuous opposition. Here is Eachard's plea for a more liberal curriculum:

And first, as to the *Ignorance* of some of our Clergy, if we would make a search to purpose, we must go as deep as the very beginnings of Education; and doubtless may lay a great part of our misfortune to the old-fashioned Methods and discipline of Schooling itself. . . . And first of all, it were certainly worth the considering, whether it be unavoidably necessary to keep lads to sixteen or seventeen years of age, in pure slavery to a few Latin and Greek words? Or whether it may not be more convenient . . . to mix with those unpleasant tasks and drudgeries, something that in probability might not only take much better with them, but might also be much easier obtained? As suppose, some part of time was allotted then for the reading of innocent *English* authors; where they need not go every line so unwillingly to a tormenting Dictionary. . . . Or, suppose, they were taught (as they might much easier be than what is commonly offered to them) the Principles of *Arithmetic, Geometry* and such alluring parts of learning? As these undoubtedly would be much more useful, so much more delightful to them, than to be tormented with a tedious story how Phaeton broke his neck? [17]

Eachard also mentions the harshness of the discipline, the "fifteen or twenty well laid on lashes" that were the schoolboy's fate for "letting a syllable slip too soon"; and ends by the argument that the dullness and the harshness can have only one result —to make the child hate forever everything to do with books and learning.

It was this that Traherne escaped; and the explanation seems to be a private tutor of unusual caliber—possibly one of the cathedral clergy evicted by the Puritans. We do not know that. We only know that he did not attend the city school, and that he was extraordinarily well and widely taught. The same is true of Philip, who never went to a university but became a Greek scholar of great capacity and a student of oriental languages. Whoever Traherne's unknown masters were, the quality of his adult intellectual power, the depth of his religious thought and

[17] John Eachard, *The Grounds and Occasions of the Contempt of the Clergy . . . Enquired into* (1670). This provoked *An Answer to the Enquiry,* where the proposed reforms are strenuously opposed.

experience, owes them not a little. The sense of wonder, the eager desire to know and to find it out for himself "to the bottom" which was fostered in him as a boy, is the power which made him in later life an original thinker and a mystic. For cannot the mystic be defined as one who, in the field of religious experience, is a persistent seeker after firsthand knowledge?

Two other important experiences belong to Traherne's mental development in his schooldays. One was the discovery of the joy of intense visual imagination; and the other was the fascination and the explosive power of the "New Philosophy."

The man, looking back on this period, remembered how vividly the child had conjured up worlds of imagination, how real these were, how brilliant the images. Every lonely child thrown on his own resources for amusement and for escape from the present has something of this power of dramatization; every poet has it all his life; and Traherne was both a lonely child and a poet. In his lonely childhood were developed those powers of the inner eye which were to make his most visionary and rapturous dreamings so actual to his readers. All through his life, whatever he sees, he sees clearly; as did the schoolboy when the pages of history and geography and Scripture were slowly unfolding before his eager eyes. "When I heard of any new kingdom beyond the seas," he recalls, "the light and glory of it pleased me immediately; it rose up within me, and I was enlarged wonderfully. I entered into it, I saw its commodities, rarities, springs, meadows, riches, inhabitants, and became possessor of that new room, as if it had been prepared for me, so much was I magnified and delighted in it. When the Bible was read, my spirit was present in other ages. . . . I saw the land of Canaan, the Israelites entering into it, and ancient glory of the Amorites, their peace and riches, their cities, houses, vines and figtrees. . . . I saw all and felt all in such a lively manner as if there had been no other way to those places, but in spirit only. . . . Anything when it was proposed, though it was a thousand ages ago, being always before me."

Such a desire to see clearly, so eager a curiosity, would naturally not exclude matters of faith from its field of inquiry; and
thus in due course Traherne was caught by an eddy of the "New
Philosophy," which, as Donne had bitterly experienced, "calls
all in doubt."

Traherne was now approaching one of the blackest periods in
his existence. When it began, we do not know; nor even when it
ended. Probably, like most such things in life, it was some years
gathering head and some years working itself out. All we can
infer from Traherne's accounts was that the explosion it provoked, that experience I have called his first spiritual crisis, happened before he went to the university.

We have only hints to guide us in Traherne's repeated accounts of this phase of psychological strain and stress. But three
main elements seem to stand out clearly.

One was the result of an unconscious resistance to the materialism of his present way of life. Outwardly he had completely
surrendered to the tavern and its standards. But somewhere deep
down there was a "desire" unsatisfied, a "thirst" unquenched.
Outwardly he was finding his pleasure in

> Masks, Stages, Games and Plays,
> That then might suit my yong Desires,
> Feathers and Farthings, Holidays,
> Cards, Musick, Dice.

He turned against school and study; he sought an anodyne
in sport and physical activity, and in amusement. In time he
wanted more exciting sensations, and amusements not so innocent. Sex was awake; and there we have the second element in
his unrest.

Traherne speaks with reticence of this adolescent indulgence;
nevertheless it is quite clear that it happened. He tells us that
the "limpid stream" of his life was "fouled with mud." He tells
us that there had been a time when

> I had no Thoughts that were impure;
> Esteeming both Women and Men
> God's work, I was secure;[18]

but that that time is past. He used of himself the strong seventeenth-century word, "wantonness"—

> But Wantonness and Avarice got in. . . .
> A House, a Woman's Hand, a piece of Gold,
> A Feast, a costly Suit, a beauteous Skin
> That vy'd with Ivory, I did behold;
> And all my Pleasure was in Sin.[19]

This passionate, headstrong youth, curious and eager and unhappy, was certainly a "ship of too light ballast" for the seas of adolescent awakening. In manhood he remembered and wrote once, "Affections are but winds, perhaps too great for such a ship as mine, of too light a ballast: pleasures, yea, all these, are but witches that draw and steal us away from God: dangerous allurements, interposing screens, unseasonable companions, counterfeit realities, honied poison, cumbersome distractions. *I have found them so.*"[20] And I think he was also remembering his own youth when again he wrote what I think is too firsthand for mere academic discussion: "That violence wherewith sometimes a man doteth upon one creature, is but a little spark of that love, even towards all, which lurketh in his nature. We are made to love, both to satisfy the necessity of our active nature, and to answer the beauties in every creature. . . ." Then he changes the subject abruptly, but returns with a new vigor: "Suppose a curious and fair woman. Some have seen the beauties of Heaven in such a person. It is a vain thing to say they loved too much. . . . They loved it not too much, but upon false causes. . . . They love a creature for sparkling eyes and curled hair, lily breasts and ruddy cheeks. . . . And so, being defective to other things, perish by a seeming excess to that."[21]

Who this girl was that troubled the lad with her white skin

---

18 "The Apostacy."
20 *Centuries* IV, 89.
19 "An Infant Ey."
21 *Centuries* II, 66-68.

and the touch of her hands we do not know. A notebook of his
university days has come to us with a girl's name penned half-a-
dozen times at the foot of a page—"Elinor."[22] But we do know
that Traherne was to look back on the whole episode with aversion.

The third element in the disharmony of the period was a
conscious scepticism in matters of faith and religion.

What he had seen of war in Herefordshire would partly account for that. It was not easy to believe in an overruling Providence or in a God of Love in days like that. "How can I believe
that He gave His Son to die for me Who having power to do
otherwise gave me nothing but rags?" he cried, rebelliously.
And then the questing, eager mind came to doubt the authenticity of the Bible; and from that, the Christian creed. In those
days of general unquestioning acceptance, to be conscious of
doubt, to be unable to accept with one's fellows, was in itself a
torturing experience. And only the essentially honest faced and
fought it.

A record of this phase of Traherne's scepticism is placed by
him in his *Third Century* between his account of school and
adolescence and that of his life at Oxford. It is veiled and
guarded, yet, once we have a clue, quite luminous. I refer to
Meditations 27 to 35. At a first reading they are an unattractive
group; indeed they appear puerile. They relate how it was an
ardent wish of his at the time that an angel would bring him
personally a book from Heaven; and then show at tedious length
how he came to see that this would have been an unsatisfactory
proceeding. Read them, however, as an allegory of a desire for
incontrovertible proof, for rational conviction, and they are far
from childish. The naïve parable served well enough to explain
to his simple friend for whom the account was written the reality,
a state of disbelief and desire, and at the same time avoided all
risk of any disturbance to her own beliefs. One brief quotation

[22] Burney MS. 126. B.M. See Appendix.

will serve to show both the veiling of the fact and the fact itself of his scepticism (the italics are mine):

This put me upon two things: upon enquiring into the matter contained in the Bible, and into the manner wherein it came unto me. In the matter I found all the glad tidings my soul longed after in its desire of news. . . . In respect of the matter, I was very sure that Angels and Cherubims could not bring unto me better tidings than were in the Scriptures contained, *could I but believe them to be true; but I was dissatisfied about the manner, and that was the ground of my unbelief.* For I could not think that God being Love would neglect His son, and therefore surely I was not His son, nor He Love: *because He had not ascertained me more carefully that the Bible was His book from Heaven.* Yet I was encouraged to hope well, because the matter was so excellent, above my expectation. And when I searched into it, I found the Way infinitely better than if all the Angels in Heaven had brought it to me. . . . *Many other enquiries I had considering the manner of His revealing Himself.*

The diligent study of the Scriptures and the parallel study of the ideas of various philosophers which Traherne describes in the verse account of the same experience (*Poems of Felicity*) must have belonged to the phase of his life which was to follow immediately—his period at Oxford.

This whole unhappy time we have been considering, with its lack of direction, its materialism and youthful wildness, its scepticism and despair, is wonderfully summed up for us by Traherne in a passage of moving sincerity and simplicity, every word of which should be weighed:

Being swallowed up therefore in the miserable gulf of idle talk and worthless vanities, thenceforth I lived among dreams and shadows, like a prodigal son feeding upon husks with swine. A comfortless wilderness full of thorns and troubles the world was, or worse, a waste place covered with idleness and play, and shops, and markets, and taverns. As for Churches they were things I did not understand; and schools were a burden: so that there was nothing in the world worth the having, or enjoying, but my game and sport, which also was a dream, and being passed wholly forgotten. So that I had utterly forgotten all goodness, bounty, comfort and glory.[23]

Then, something happened. Something that set again on a settled course the little ship of too light a ballast which so long had been the prey of the currents.

The young Traherne had been sent away from Hereford into the country. Perhaps because of the financial worries of his relatives during the sequestrations; the boy himself was certainly concerned about earning his board. Perhaps because of that love affair.

Whatever the reason, he found himself out in the utterly quiet country fields just as night was drawing on; the sky was overcast with a threat of storm; and he was absolutely alone.

But the storm that broke first was the storm within. It burst on him like a flood. He was afraid—afraid to the depths of his being. Afraid of the vastness of the universe and his own puniness; conscious to the point of horror of his own desolation. Conscious, too, that there was another plane of living and that in sheer desperation he must find it.

So intense was this experience that he never forgot it. It supplied dynamic sufficient for the first difficult years of reorientation.

He has left us two accounts of this spiritual crisis. The more elaborate and suggestive is found in his poem "Solitude," which is too long to quote here. I shall include a few lines of it after the briefer account in his *Centuries*, where he wrote as follows: "In a lowering and sad evening, being alone in the field, when all things were dead and quiet, a certain want and horror fell upon me, beyond imagination. The unprofitableness and silence of the place dissatisfied me; its wideness terrified me; from the utmost ends of the earth fears surrounded me. . . . I was a weak and little child, and had forgotten there was a man alive in the earth." And in "Solitude":

[23] *Centuries* III, 14.

How desolate!
Ah! how forlorn, how sadly did I stand
When in the field my woful State
I felt! . . .

I do believ,
The Ev'ning being shady and obscure,
The very Silence did me griev,
And Sorrow more procure:

Ye sullen Things!
Ye dumb, ye silent Creatures, and unkind!
How can I call you Pleasant Springs
Unless ye eas my Mind!

Will ye not speak
What 'tis I want, nor Silence break?
O pity me, and let me see som Joy;
Som Kindness shew to me, altho a Boy.

They silent stood;
Nor Earth, nor Woods, nor Hills, nor Brooks, nor Skies,
Would tell me where the hidden Good,
Which I did long for, lies. . . .

Though at the heart of that experience lay a perception, dim
and amorphous, of another way of life, its strongest immediate
content was revulsion—strongest possible revulsion against the
scale of values and outlook of the town-gallant which he had
come to adopt:

Mens Customs here but vile appear;
The Oaths of Roaring Boys,
Their Gold that shines, their sparkling Wines,
Their Lies,
Their gawdy Trifles, are mistaken Joys:
To prize
Such Toys I loath'd. My Thirst did burn;
But where, O whither should my Spirit turn!
Their Games, their Bowls, their cheating Dice
Did not compleat, but spoil, my Paradise.
On things that gather Rust,
Or modish Cloaths, they fix their minds,

Or sottish Vanity their Fancy blinds,
Their Eys b'ing all put out with Dust.[24]

Never again could Traherne be satisfied with the externals of things, however fair. Never again could he be content with the merely sensuous. He knew his own poverty in terms of the riches that abide. Under the shock of the knowledge he made a right-about turn and faced the grim steeps of Truth's high hill. As in the history of most saints and mystics, as with Saul on the Damascus road, the experience was involuntary, and sudden, and painful. And with Traherne, as with them, it marked the first beginning of the long journey that ends in strange and shining places which we who have not visited them scarcely believe exist.

CHAP. V.

The First Period at Oxford.

ON March 1, 1653, Thomas Traherne was "entered a Commoner of Brasen-nose College," as Anthony à Wood records, and as the College Registers confirm. On the following April 2, he was matriculated. The fee for matriculation was eightpence, and for admittance to "the Schooles," half a crown; both of which fees he duly paid.

He had doubtless, like all the other poorer country freshmen, traveled up from Hereford "sitting upon the top of the Pack in the Carrier's cart," as a contemporary record tells us was usual. He was in his fifteenth year, and in many ways mature beyond his age; and he came into an environment completely new. The University was not usually for such as he, a shoemaker's son; he had taken a step in life which was to prove of the most far-reaching importance for his social advance no less than for spiritual and mental development. The old eager curiosity of his childhood now was to find countless new worlds to explore; and how

[24] "Dissatisfaction."

it leapt into the adventure with the ardor of a fine intelligence long denied its rightful food, the tale of the *Centuries* makes plain.

The eager intensity of the study of these years stands in strong contrast with that period of schoolboy idleness and boredom which preceded it. He won for himself in the next three years not only his bachelor's degree and the additional high qualifications for ordination, but the necessary foundation of scholarship on which he built his later original research in a difficult field of ecclesiastical history. His whole heart must have been in his work for this to be possible; and the change of attitude seems explicable only if we link it to his spiritual awakening. The new passion for learning was, I believe, another consequence of that shattering conviction of poverty—poverty seen as intellectual as well as spiritual and physical. He probably had to overcome a good deal of family opposition to get to the University at all. His kinsfolk were farmers and tradesmen, not likely to sympathize with such aspirations. Thomas Traherne was in fact the very first of the family ever to go to a university. But someone, probably the elder Philip Traherne, had already given to the two brothers an education above their station; and possibly his estate made it possible for the family to supply the £20 a year then sufficient to maintain an undergraduate. That by 1653 England seemed to have entered upon a period of stable government may also have had something to do with it. Certainly somehow, in some way, Thomas Traherne achieved the new world of Oxford and all that that implied.

By the time Traherne came up to Brasenose the University had recovered from the complete disorganization of its life that had ensued when Oxford became a garrison and the King's headquarters; and also from the disorder and disorganization incident upon carrying out the "reforms" decreed by the victorious Parliament, and enforced by their appointed "Visitors." The whole institution of the "Committee for the Reformation of the Universities" and of the "Visitations" had been a party triumph of the Presbyterians; with Cromwell in power the rigor of their enactments ceased. From April 1652 to June 1653 the committee itself was dissolved, and in consequence the Visitors in Oxford were unable to act; and when Cromwell, himself now Chancellor of Oxford University, reappointed the committee, its function was no longer to carry out expulsions or institute new measures of reform, but merely to enforce the late regulations.

Brasenose College, which had put up a long and determined fight against the Parliamentary Visitors, was quite settled and peaceable by 1653, well and strictly governed by its Puritan principal, Dr. Greenwood. Dr. Greenwood was appointed by the Visitors, and there was another, Yate, who had been more legally elected by the Fellows: but Yate lived peaceably in London till the Restoration ousted Dr. Greenwood. In the meantime, Brasenose grew and flourished, its principal respected by Royalist and Puritan alike. In the ten years of Dr. Greenwood's rule, the numbers in residence at Brasenose grew from 20 to 120; Cromwell spoke of him as a man "of ability and zeale" and "of integrity, care and vigilancy"; and even to the Royalist Anthony à Wood, he was "a severe and good Governor."

It was in this sober and serious Oxford that Traherne's undergraduate days were spent; and in one of the most thoroughly Puritan of her colleges. In Brasenose, if anywhere, the orders of the Visitors would be faithfully obeyed; Dr. Greenwood, who was so vigilant and zealous, would see to it as directed that "every Tutor . . . at some convenient time between the houres of seven and tenne in the evening" did "cause their Pupills to repair to their chambers to pray with them"[25]; and that all bachelors of arts and undergraduates "every Lord's Day" gave "an account . . . of the sermons they have heard, and their attendance on other religious exercises on that day."[26] Though Traherne's natural bias from his upbringing and environment would be, one must

[25] *Visitors Register*, July 1653.   [26] *Ibid.*, June 1653.

suppose, towards the old Established Church and its now banished Book of Common Prayer and rites of public worship, yet since, as he has told us, he had at this time no real convictions, the forms of religion being no more to him than empty air, he probably took the oaths and performed the religious exercises exacted of him by Puritan authority without the slightest feeling that any principles were at stake.

When Traherne was admitted to the living at Credenhill in 1657 he carried up to London testimonials from several leading Puritan ministers, and was clearly not in any disfavor or under any suspicion of being a "malignant." Most men in those days believed that the Established Church of England was gone forever. No one could foresee the Restoration. If one were not a Puritan by sincere conviction one had to choose between going over to Roman Catholicism, as his friend Mrs. Hopton did; going abroad into exile; conforming outwardly, but secretly making use of the Book of Common Prayer and secretly attending services; or simply making the best of things and conforming. I am inclined to think on the evidence of Traherne's testimonials and on the evidence of his own confessed indifference at the time, that Traherne followed the last course. Those who foregathered with Royalists for worship (or for less exalted purposes) were more or less marked men; and at the time Traherne lacked the conviction, either religious or political, of which martyrs are made.

Of the outer history of those years between his admission in 1653 and his first degree of Bachelor of Arts, October 13, 1656, we know nothing. From the diary of Anthony à Wood who was reading for his master's degree during this period,[27] from Christopher Wordsworth's *Scholae Academicae*, and from numerous contemporary and eighteenth-century tracts,[28] one can recon-

[27] Andrew Clark, *Life and Times of Anthony Wood . . . from His Diaries* (Oxford, 1891).

[28] e.g. *Well-Wishers to the University of Oxford, and the Answers* (London, 1750-1752).

struct without difficulty the general course of an undergraduate's life and see what Traherne's must have been. One can even learn the more exciting events occurring in Oxford itself at this time, and know what people were talking about, from the hanging of two ex-Royalist officers turned highwaymen, to the first public imbibing in coffee, regarded as a highly undesirable innovation by the more conventional. We know from one reference that Traherne kept a diary; had it survived, and had it covered this period, it might well have rivaled Wood's; but as it is we unfortunately have no knowledge of the more particular outward events of Traherne's undergraduate life.

But of its far more important inner history in this period we have a fairly clear outline, from the statements and suggestions he has given us in the *Centuries* and *Poems*.

Traherne began this time at Oxford chiefly conscious, as we have seen, that life as he had lived it did not satisfy him, and would never satisfy him, together with an instinctive conviction that though most men failed to find it, another plane of living did exist and could be won if the will were strong enough to endure the pains of search. Mentally and spiritually he was still in the dark, not even sure of the object of his groping. The most hopeful factor was his own awareness of his state, his discontent and determination to find at any cost the lighted highway.

As yet I did not see the wisdom and depths of knowledge, the clear principles, and certain evidences whereby the wise and holy, the ancients and the learned that were abroad in the world knew these things, but was led to them only by the fame which they had vulgarly received. Howbeit I believed that there were unspeakable mysteries contained in them, and tho' they were generally talked of, their value was unknown. These therefore I resolved to study, and no other. But to my unspeakable wonder, they brought me to all the things in Heaven and in Earth, in Time and Eternity.[29]

Of the two hungers, for knowledge and for a religious phi-

[29] *Centuries* III, 54.

losophy, the former proved the easier to satisfy. Oxford herself guided and determined his studies, and gave him the fullest opportunities for intellectual attainment and development; and Traherne surrendered himself to Oxford with a joy and a depth of satisfaction that recalls the Renaissance. The glow of his enthusiastic welcome to learning, of his eager reception of the facts of science and the figures of history, those "glorious secrets" and "glorious persons" as he terms them, still quickens his account of these days.

> Having been at the University, and received there the taste and tincture of another education, I saw that there were things in this world of which I never dreamed; glorious secrets, and glorious persons past imagination. There I saw that Logic, Ethics, Physics, Metaphysics, Geometry, Astronomy, Poesy, Medicine, Grammar, Music, Rhetoric, all kinds of Arts, Trades and Mechanisms that adorned the world pertained to Felicity: at least there I saw those things, which afterwards I knew to pertain unto it: and was delighted in it. There I saw into the nature of the Sea, the Heavens, the Sun, the Moon and Stars, the Elements, Minerals, and Vegetables. All which appeared like the King's Daughter, all glorious within.[30]

He has told us something of his work in his major studies, of the new avenues of thought opened up to him by his reading in "Humanity" and divinity and ethics and "Natural Philosophy," and even names for us some of the standard authorities whose wisdom he imbibed—"the secrets of nature with Albertus Magnus, or the motions of the Heavens with Galileo, or the cosmography of the moon with Hevelius, or the body of man with Galen, or the nature of diseases with Hippocrates . . . or of poesy with Homer, or of Grammar with Lilly."[31]

Traherne has only one fault to find with the intellectual fare provided by Oxford, but that a serious one. It is that all these facts and theories and philosophies were presented to the students in detachment, sundered from the greater whole of life. The criticism is made from the viewpoint of maturity, and one

[30] *Ibid.*, III, 36.   [31] *Ibid.*, III, 41.

does not imagine that Traherne as an undergraduate hard at work acquiring the raw material of information had the penetration to see that "he is nothing, if he knows them merely for talk or idle speculation, or transient and external use"; that only "he that knows them for value, and knows them his own, shall profit infinitely."[31] There are several passages where this prevalent fashion of studying things in isolation, and under their temporal aspect only, is censured by Traherne as he looks back on these undergraduate days.

"Nevertheless some things were defective too. There was never a tutor that did professly teach Felicity, though that be the mistress of all other sciences. Nor did any of us study these things but as *aliena*, which we ought to have studied as our own enjoyments. We studied to inform our knowledge, but knew not for what end we so studied. And for lack of aiming at a certain end we erred in the manner."[32] "He Knoweth nothing as he ought to Know, Who thinks he Knoweth anything without seeing its Place, and the Manner how it relateth to God, Angels and Men, and to all the Creatures in Earth, Heaven, and Hell, Time and Eternity."[33] "Howbeit there we received all those seeds of knowledge that were afterwards improved; and our souls were awakened to a discerning of their faculties, and exercise of their powers."[32]

The satisfaction of his spiritual needs proved a slower and more difficult process. It was a stupendous thing he was unconsciously demanding, a conception of God and the Universe which should satisfy the needs of a spirit at once critical and beauty-loving, and that should compel by its splendor the full allegiance of his nature. He has told us explicitly that after that time of painful awakening he knew that for him the rites of Christian worship were meaningless and that he had no God. For to him, to have no adequate conception of God was to have no God. There is here that same element of ruthlessness, of refusal to compromise, which is so marked a characteristic of Traherne's thinking and doing. "To be satisfied in God is the highest difficulty in the whole world. . . . For we naturally expect infinite things of God;

[32] *Ibid.*, III, 37.   [33] *Christian Ethicks*, p. 124.

and can be satisfied only with the highest reason."[34] The Deity is a reality to a man only when his conception of Him compels adoration, and to Traherne the "mere lazy dream" with which most men content themselves is a form of atheism. "For so glorious is the face of God and true religion, that it is impossible to see it, but in transcendent splendour. Nor can we know that God is, till we see Him infinite in goodness. Nothing therefore will make us certain of His Being but His Glory."[35]

It was this rational conviction of His Being that Traherne lacked at the commencement of this period. Intuitively, or as he prefers to explain it, because of the spiritual experiences of infancy, he knew of both the absolute existence of a Deity and of a relation of harmony that might be established between the soul and that Deity. It was his present task to make that relationship a fact of his adult life.

A true God, he had said in the passage just quoted, must satisfy a man's "highest reason"; and herein at first lay for Traherne the crux of the difficulty. Rational theology was still in its infancy. Such a demand as this was not only new but bitterly censured as impious. For tradition then had a binding power almost impossible to conceive today; and men in general, and certain sects in particular, postulated the nature of God and indeed His very existence on the traditional testimony of the Scriptures. And the Scriptures and the dogmas of the Church derived their validity from external authority, an authority above reason and exempt from the investigation of reason. But the Reformation had established for Protestantism the right of private judgment in matters of conscience; and slowly but surely the field of rational investigation in matters of religion grew wider, till by Traherne's day it was possible for the claim just quoted to be made, that highest reason is the touchstone of the Divine. But Traherne made this claim in maturity. He had first, before attaining that serene conviction of the harmony of faith and reason, to follow the guidance of reason; and reason, it is plain, led him for a period to question the very basis of orthodox belief.

The period of scepticism began, as we have seen, before Traherne went up to Oxford; it lasted for most of that period. "This thirst hung upon me for a long time" is his own phrase. It takes time to build a new world when the old one has been shattered by the impact of scientific discovery and cold reason. The seventeenth century, still medieval in many ways—as witness Milton's theology—and yet ushering in modern science, imposed on most of its thinkers this painful experience of collapse. Traherne with his strong native propensity to question and explore was predestined to that experience.

A close and critical study of the Bible ensued; a study to which perhaps we owe the wide familiarity with its words and phrasing that later enriched his writing. Side by side with this study of the Scriptures went a study of philosophy. It is noteworthy that in the poem "Dissatisfaction" the turning to ancient philosophies is made to precede his final acceptance of the Christian creed:

> *Philosophy!* canst thou descry
>   My Bliss?
> Will Books or Sages it to me disclose?
>   I miss
> Of this in all: They tell me Pleasure,
> Or earthly Honor, or a fading Treasure,
>   Will never with it furnish me.
> But then, Where is? What is, Felicity?
>   Here Men begin to doat,
>   Stand unresolv'd, they cannot speak,
> What 'tis; . . .
>
>   Weary of all that since the Fall
>   Mine Eys on Earth can find,
> I for a Book from Heven look,
>   Since here
> No Tidings will salute or eas my Mind:
>   Mine Ear,

My Ey, my Hand, my Soul, doth long
For som fair book fill'd with Eternal Song.
O *that!* my soul: for *that* I burn:
That is the Thing for which my Heart did yern."

In the end Traherne reached a point from which he gained his first rational conception of the purpose of human life, the purpose of his own life, and the nature of God and of religion; and he reached it by way of his studies in science and in ethics. It was characteristic of the best thought of his age that this should be so; and it was peculiarly characteristic of Traherne. From earliest childhood he had been aware of the wonder and delight of "corporeal things"; in his closer study of them at the university, the wonder returned in another form, and he began to see behind their marvels as revealed by science the hand and mind of some divine designer.

Natural Philosophy . . . taking it as it is usually bounded in its terms, it treateth only of corporeal things, as Heaven, Earth, Air, Water, Fire, the Sun and Stars, Trees, Herbs, Flowers, Influences, Winds, Fowls, Beasts, Fishes, Minerals and Precious Stones, with all other beings of that kind. And as thus it is taken it is nobly subservient to the highest ends: for it openeth the riches of God's Kingdom and the natures of His territories, works and creatures in a wonderful manner, clearing and preparing the eye of the enjoyer.[36]

Ethics opened up to him "the mysteries of morality, the nature of affections, virtues and manners"—the mysterious inner operations of the minds and souls of men; and the quest as well of so many great men to find a way of life that would bring happiness. "I was very much animated by the desires of philosophers which I saw in heathen books aspiring after it [Felicity]. But the misery is *It was unknown.*"[37] Here, too, in human minds and souls and characters he began dimly, and then with increasing clarity, to perceive design. To perceive that the design, however and wherever perceptible, is a unity; to see that there is an eternal revelation of the Divine, that the revelation contained in Scripture

[36] *Ibid.*, III, 44.   [37] *Ibid.*, III, 56.

is but partial, and yet that it is also authentic because of its perfect accordance with the larger design—these are the further and remarkable steps Traherne advanced to make in these and the ensuing years.

> All these put together discover the materials of religion to be so great, that it plainly manifesteth the Revelation of God to be deep and infinite. For it is impossible for language, miracles, or apparitions to teach us the infallibility of God's word, or to shew us the certainty of true religion, without a clear sight into truth itself, that is into the truth of things. Which will themselves when truly seen, by the very beauty and glory of them, best discover and prove religion.[38]

How remarkable a statement this is for a seventeenth-century Christian will appear still more plainly when we discuss Traherne's place as a "Platonist" of his day. It is clear that it amounts to a definite rejection of the authority of the Bible merely as traditional authority. "It is impossible for language, miracles, or apparitions . . . to shew us the certainty of true religion." It claims that there is an authentic revelation of God in all scientific truth, in all truth of fact; and that only when the things proclaimed by tradition in religion or elsewhere make good their claims before the common judge of all truth, the human reason, is their truth valid. The truth of revealed religion for Traherne is discovered by the beauty and glory of the greater pattern into which it and all truths fit.

We have also in these sentences a light on Traherne's own processes of reconciling religion and reason. He clearly accepted Christianity, the teaching of St. John and St. Paul, because for him it most perfectly embodied a vast and rational philosophy of God and man, a philosophy that would include the glory and wonder and goodness of all material things, and the glory and potential divinity of man. For the greater part of his life he was thinking out and living out that philosophy, and for a few years putting it on paper. In its completeness it belongs to another period of his life. But what does belong to the close of this first

---

[38] *Ibid.*, III, 45.

period at the university was the dawning of a greater and vaster conception of God and of religion, and of human nature, a first glimpse of that "transcendent splendour" in which God must be conceived before adoration becomes possible.

The natural corollary of this was a great peace, with clear vision of a new path of spiritual endeavor. That, however, by the chronology of the *Third Century*, came fully only after the second spiritual crisis. What particularly belongs to this first university period is the twofold quest I have endeavored to outline—the quest for knowledge and the quest for an honest faith; and the gradual merging of the two in what was to be for ever after the master passion of his life.

CHAP. VI.

The Second Crisis.

TRaherne, again to quote Wood's brief summary, "took one degree in Arts, left the House for a time, and entered into the sacred function." On graduating he must have subscribed to the Engagement, the terms of which were, "I do declare and promise that I will be true and faithful to the Commonwealth of England as the same is now established without a King or House of Lords." This bitterly hated Engagement was ordered in October 1649 by the Committee for Regulating the Universities, and was strictly enforced by the Visitors.

When Traherne "left the House," that is, Brasenose College, he probably returned to Hereford; over a year elapsed between his graduation in October 1656 and his appointment to the living of Credenhill in December 1657. For some of that time we must naturally suppose him to have been in Hereford, collecting testimonials from Hereford ministers; and it seems most likely that he was there all that period, as this was his home. His own phrase, "being seated among silent trees . . . had all my time in mine hands," implies a lengthened stay.

It was in this interval, according to the chronology of the *Third Century*, that he faced his second spiritual crisis. This, too, like the first, happened to him "in the country," but unlike that other it was neither sudden nor dramatic.

On the contrary, it is suggested that it was but the culminating point of a long, slow process of change—a process perhaps involving the greater part of this year and the preceding year or two; yet it was in itself clear-cut and definite, involving a deliberate, far-reaching choice between sharply opposed alternatives. He had finished his university course; he had taken his first degree; he had now to choose what was to be his future way of life. He had the opportunity (how we can only surmise) of entering on a career that would entail great "care and labour," but which promised considerable financial rewards—"many thousands per annum" in his own words. It may well have been that it was the law that was attracting him. As the *Roman Forgeries* proves, Traherne had in him the makings of a lawyer; and ambition, backed by that definite offer of patronage implied in his words, might well have urged him in this direction.

On the other hand there was that perception he had gained of a radiant inner happiness more alluring than any temporal felicity; but the price of it was no less than the surrender of all worldly ambitions and the complete dedication of one's life to the quest of it.

Traherne did not drift into holiness, or into mysticism; no one can. His words imply a definite choice, the rejection of a definite career of prosperity. The careers of such men as Orlando Bridgeman and Heneage Finch show what rewards the profession of law had then to offer men of ability. Yet ever since the terrible hour in the fields under that lowering evening sky Traherne's face had been set in another direction; those veils of delusion which bestow their glory on the kingdoms of this world had been torn away forever from his mental vision; and so the second memorable decision was made as it was—a decision best related in his own words.

> When I came unto the country, and being seated among silent trees, and meads and hills, had all my time in mine own hands, I resolved to spend it all, whatever it cost me, in search of happiness, and to satiate that burning thirst which Nature had enkindled in me from my youth. In which I was so resolute, that I chose rather to live upon ten pounds a year, and to go in leather clothes, and feed upon bread and water, so that I might have all my time clearly to myself, than to keep many thousands per annum in an estate of life where my time would be devoured in care and labour. And God was so pleased to accept of that desire, that from that time to this, I have had all things plentifully provided for me, without any care at all, my very study of Felicity making me more to prosper than all the care in the whole world.[39]

This was definite consecration of himself to mysticism, to the attainment by discipline of firsthand experience of union and communion with God, a decision requiring courage in the making and the utmost endurance in the execution. Yet the decision itself, and the consequences of it, show afresh Traherne's fixity of purpose and strength of will.

The decision of itself could not bring peace or certainty, and though it marked the beginning of a climb to still higher levels of spiritual attainment, it was followed, rather like the first, by a period of restless bewilderment.

> When I came into the country and saw that I had all time in my own hands, having devoted it wholly to the study of Felicity, I knew not where to begin or end; nor what objects to choose, upon which most profitably I might fix my contemplation. I saw myself like some traveller, that had destined his life to journeys, and was resolved to spend his days in visiting strange places: who might wander in vain, unless his undertakings were guided by some certain rule; and that innumerable millions of objects were presented before me, unto any of which I might take my journey. Fain would I have visited them all, but that was impossible. What then should I do? Even imitate a traveller, who because he cannot visit all coasts, wildernesses, sandy deserts, seas, hills, springs and mountains, chooseth the most populous and flourishing cities, where he might see the fairest prospects, wonders and rarities, and be entertained

[39] *Ibid.,* III, 46.

with greatest courtesy: and where indeed he might most benefit himself with knowledge, profit and delight: leaving the rest, even the naked and empty places, unseen. For which cause I made it my prayer to God Almighty that He, whose eyes are open upon all things, would guide me to the fairest and divinest.[40]

The way out of his uncertainty came by the clearer and clearer comprehension of that design he had dimly seen before; by the perception of the divine more and more unmistakably in the history of mankind, in the teaching of Christianity and in all the things of earth; and also by the perception of an underlying unity in all things, so that "everything in its place is admirable, deep, and glorious: out of its place like a wandering bird, is desolate and good for nothing."[41]

There is nothing in the *Third Century* to indicate how long it took to acquire this new power of vision, or how many years are covered—it is reasonable to suppose it took some years—by the extraordinarily interesting spiritual history related in *Méditations* 52 to 60. What is abundantly clear is that it began "When I came into the country"—between the October of 1656 and the December of 1657—and ended only in the finding of an understanding of life and of God completely satisfying, and bringing with it a deep abiding peace of heart and mind.

"I perceived that we were to live the life of God when we lived the true life of nature according to knowledge. . . . I was infinitely satisfied in God and knew there was a Deity because I was satisfied."

"I no sooner discerned this but I was seated in a throne of repose and perfect rest." The sense of liberation and of peace, or as Traherne puts it, the power and joy of coronation, is clearly perceptible in the meditation that closes this series. I quote it almost in full:

This spectacle once seen, will never be forgotten. It is a great part of the beatific vision. A sight of Happiness is Happiness. It transforms the Soul and makes it Heavenly, it powerfully calls us to communion with God, and weans us from the customs of this world. It puts a lustre upon

---

[40] *Ibid.*, III, 52.   [41] *Ibid.*, III, 55.

God and all His creatures and makes us to see them in a Divine and Eternal Light. I no sooner discerned this but I was (as Plato saith, *In summa Rationis arce quies habitat*) seated in a throne of repose and perfect rest. All things were well in their proper places, . . . and I was to be restored to God's Image. Whereupon you will not believe, how I was withdrawn from all endeavours of altering and mending outward things. They lay so well, methought, they could not be mended: but I must be mended to enjoy them.[42]

That mending, that purification of the will, constitutes the spiritual history of the next ten years.

The record of Traherne's appointment to Credenhill can be seen in the Lambeth Palace Library.[48] It reads:

Thomas Traherne, cl ["Clerk" implies ordination] Admitted the 30th Day of December 1657 to the R. of Crednell als. Creddenhill in the County of Hereford Upon a pres: exhibited the 23 Day of December 1657 from Amabella Countesse Dowager of Kent, the patronesse thereof. And certificates from Wm. Voyle, Wm. Lowe, Samuel Smith, George Primrose, Robert Breton, Benjamin Baxter of Upton upon Seaverne, John Chomley.

I have not been able to find out anything interesting about Traherne's patroness, Amabella.[13a] Voyle, Lowe, and Primrose were the leading Puritan clergy of Hereford city, appointed by Parliament after the ejection of the clergy of the Established Church. Samuel Smith was a famous preacher, who was appointed to Hereford in 1654, and who is described in the language of the times as "Godly, orthodox, and painful." He was also a writer, as was Baxter. All of these men were Puritans from sincere conviction; all of them suffered ejection and poverty at the Restoration; and that these men should furnish Traherne with testimonials proves that he was at this time under no suspicion of secret use of the Book of Common Prayer, or of con-

---

[42] *Ibid.*, III, 60.   [48] Lambeth Palace Library MS. 999, f. 161.
[43a] I am indebted to the Rev. F. E. Hutchinson for the following information: "Daughter of Sir Anthony Benn, Recorder of London, she married first, Anthony, younger son of the Earl of Westmoreland; secondly, she married Henry Grey, 9th Earl of Kent. She was called 'the good Countess' and died at the age of 92 on 20 Aug., 1698."

sorting with the "malignant." It seems in fact fairly plain that at this period Traherne must be regarded as a Puritan, and that he was ordained by the Puritan regulations, and appointed to Credenhill as showing promise of also being "godly, orthodox, and painful."

Traherne's ordination and presentation to the living of the little parish of Credenhill, near Hereford, followed fourteen months after his graduation as bachelor of arts; and at the end of an absence from Oxford which covered this period in the country which we have been considering. We can hardly fail to see in his entry into the service of the Church a further consequence of his new dedication of himself to the spiritual life.

Traherne's ordination and presentation to a benefice is difficult to understand if we suppose that he immediately went to live at Credenhill and took up his duties as rector. For he was not legally of age to do so. He was only in his twentieth year in 1657; and the legal age was twenty-four.

But this I think is what happened: Traherne was ordained and presented to the living in 1657; but left the care of the parish and the income of the living with the man who had previously held it —the Reverend George Primrose—while he himself returned to Brasenose. Wood said he left his college "for a time," which implies a return. In 1661 Traherne received his degree of master of arts, a fact which implied a further residence at Oxford. And by 1661 Traherne would be legally of age to act as rector. There is also the research work that went into the making of his book *Roman Forgeries* to be accounted for; and this I think occupied the years 1658 to 1661 at Oxford. No other explanation fits all the facts.

This brings us now to that second, postgraduate period at Oxford.

Thus, the second spiritual crisis, like the first, was followed by a period of intense intellectual effort; an effort apparently independent of the major purpose of "mending" himself to fit the real universe as he now understood it. The new study was not like the old, wide-ranging and explorative, but confined to one field; yet there is an intimate connection between the old and the new, and also between the new study and newly wrought religious philosophy. In his spiritual progress Traherne had reached the point of believing that there was such a thing as felicity, a state of being which Plato, Plotinus, St. John, and St. Paul had described and claimed to have experienced; and further, of dedicating himself to personal attainment of it. In his gradual synthesis of the worlds of the mind and the spirit he had reached a point of believing that true religion and the truths of science and history could not be in opposition. Remembering his old scepticism of the literal truth of the Biblical statements and teaching, and of the teachings and practice of the Church, it is not fanciful to see that he would be impelled to study for himself the earliest records of the Christian Church, to judge and weigh their authenticity and the position of that Church which he felt, but did not yet know by reason, to be the purest vehicle of a heritage of Truth. As a child he had wrestled with problems till he found for himself the solution; the same pride and independence characterizes his maturity.

Traherne seems never to have shrunk from paying the price of firsthand knowledge in any field he chose to explore; and how intense the study of these years was, how immense the range of reading, how dry and how difficult, the chapter on *Roman Forgeries* will make plain; for in that book he garnered the harvest of these years. But at the end of it Traherne emerged absolutely sure of the honesty and rightness of his position as a priest of the Anglican Church, aflame with zeal for her cause, and fully armed to do battle in her name. These years of study completed the transformation from scepticism through an indifferent Puritanism to the ardent Anglo-Catholicism that was Traherne's final theological position.

It has been said of Traherne that he was a Christian but not a sectarian. This is only broadly true. Like all the Platonists of his day he emerges as a convinced adherent of the Church of England. In the *Roman Forgeries*, as it finally appeared in print, and in the *Meditations* and very markedly in *The Book of Private Devotions*, Traherne appears constantly as an enthusiastic High Churchman, conscious of the continuity of the Anglican Church in doctrine and ritual with the early apostolic Church, and proud to be an heir of its traditions. It is true, as we have seen, that he was ordained by Puritans, obtained his first benefice from a Puritan patroness, and was armed with a sheaf of testimonials from the leading Puritan divines in Herefordshire. Since he continued to hold his benefice after the Restoration, it is equally true that he complied with the requirements of the Act of Uniformity; that is, that he must have given his formal assent to the Book of Common Prayer, and been episcopally ordained before St. Bartholomew's Day, 1662. After the Restoration, Puritan preachers in possession of livings were suffered to remain, unless the old incumbents were alive, provided they complied with these conditions. Some sixteen hundred ministers could not reconcile it with their consciences to do so, and therefore surrendered or were expelled from their livings. Among these were the ministers who had signed Traherne's certificates—Voyle and Primrose and Smith and Lowe. But not Traherne himself. Yet one feels, I think, not the slightest doubt of the sincerity of Traherne's later High Church principles. The way for the change was made by his studies in ecclesiastical history; and one need not feel any uncomfortable doubt whether now, as perhaps in 1657, expediency had anything to do with his professed principles. Appearances are certainly against a man who is a Puritan under the Commonwealth and a High Church Anglican under Charles II. Yet what Johnson, with his sound common sense, said of Dryden in a similar case may well be equally applicable to Traherne:

That conversion will always be suspected that apparently concurs with interest. He that never finds his error till it hinders his progress towards wealth or honour, will not be thought to love truth only for herself. Yet it may easily happen that information may come at a commodious time; and as truth and interest are not by any fatal necessity at variance, that one may by accident introduce the other. When opinions are struggling into popularity, the arguments by which they are opposed or defended become more known; and he that changes his profession would perhaps have changed it before with the like opportunities of instruction.

His investigation into the early records of the Church necessarily brought under his study and review all the points at issue between the Roman Catholic Church and the Reformed Churches, and also between the old Anglican Reformed Church and the new non-episcopal sects; with the consequences we have seen. His judgment may be questioned, but not I think the more important matter of his intellectual integrity.

It is probable that it is of this period that the friend of Traherne's who wrote the Bibliographical Preface to the *Serious and Pathetical Contemplation* said:

Tho he had the misfortune to come abroad into the world in the late disordered Times when the Foundations were cast down, and this excellent Church laid in the dust, and dissolved into *Confusion* and *Enthusiasme*; yet his Soul was of a more refin'd allay, and his Judgment in discerning of things more solid and considerate then to be infected with that Leaven, and therefore became much in love with the beautiful order and *Primitive* Devotions of this our excellent Church. In so much that I believe he never failed any one day either publickly or in his private closet to make use of her publick Offices, as one part of his devotion.

These words have in their context a pre-Restoration reference, and seem peculiarly applicable to this period now under review.

We have at present no more record of Traherne's outward life for his second period at Oxford than for his first. He speaks in the preface to the *Roman Forgeries* of the man who met him at the door of the Bodleian and who induced him to have a discussion with his cousin, as being "an intimate friend of mine"; and in spite of all his concentration on his studies one feels that such a mind and such a personality could not have failed both to need friends and to attract the friendship of those around him. Yet the one name that he mentions is that of the head librarian of the

Bodleian, Dr. Barlow, who lent him from his private library a rare book he had been unable to obtain. This is the same Dr. Barlow of whom Anthony à Wood speaks as being interested in him because he was an eager student; and one may suppose that it was for the same reason that Dr. Barlow was attracted to Traherne, and willing to oblige him with the loan of a valuable book. It is at least possible that Traherne may have known Anthony à Wood himself; and also Theophilus Gale, in whose writings and theories he was certainly deeply interested; so interested in fact that he spent many hours laboriously copying into his commonplace book long extracts from Gale's *Court of the Gentiles*. It has been suggested by one student of Traherne, Mr. J. W. Proud, that the poems prefixed to the earlier volumes of this work of Gale's are of Traherne's composition. It is possible; but the evidence is slight. It is also possible that a certain allusion in Gale's *Theophilie* (1671, pp. 393-4) is to Traherne; it certainly fits him well:

O what *rich* and *delicious* lives might the friends of Christ lead, would they but *eye* and injoy Christ in al their *Creature-Comforts*. I have known one, and indeed a great friend of Christ, who I verily believe injoyed more of Christ and his *Gracious Presence* in his *Civil Employments* and *Creature Injoyments* than many (yea, may I not say than most) Christians do, in their most *spiritual duties* and *Ordinances*. O, what might we injoy of Christ, in the *Visible Book of Nature*, and *Creature-Comforts*, had we but spiritual hearts!

Gale and Traherne were at Oxford at the same time; and the description is so apt as to be striking. But the fact remains that nothing has yet been discovered to throw any real light on Traherne's social activities in either of his periods of residence in the University.

While he was thus mainly absorbed in his study of the Councils and the early Fathers, events in the nation were rapidly approaching the climax of the Restoration. When it was finally known that the Parliament had acknowledged Charles II as king,

Never was a scene so altered as the face of the City, which but two moneths before being at the very Brink of Destruction, was now overflowed with a full tide of Gladness: for during the two dayes in which the letters aforesaid were delivered, and Printed to publick View, there was a perfect Vacation from all Business, every man indulging himself his share in the general satisfaction, in such a measure that *London* seemed rather a Theatre of Pleasure than a Seat of Traffique.

The official proclamation quickly followed, carried out with all imaginable pomp and ceremony.

After this they went to Cheapside where his Majesty was Proclaimed a fourth time, where the shouts of the people were so great that though all the Bells in the City rung, Bow Bells could not be heard there. . . . The numberless Bonfires, the Ringing of Bells, and shooting off the Guns, and the joyful Expressions of the People did declare them beyond the art of the Pen.

For a detailed and enthusiastic account of all the ceremonies of the King's arrival, the processions and the liveries and the feastings and the pageants, James Heath's *The Glories and Magnificent Triumphs of the Blessed Restitution*, from which the foregoing are taken, gives one a most vivid contemporary picture; and since James Heath was a student, too, it gives us the reaction of the youth of the universities to that frenzy of national excitement. It is possible that Traherne, like Heath, went up to London at this time, drawn by the strong tide of national feeling; references to "coronations" are frequent in his writings. The image rose in Traherne's mind whenever he thought of some great and gorgeous spectacle; and the spontaneity suggests a firsthand impression.

In November 1661, Traherne received his degree of master of arts, probably as a result of those attainments in scholarship and those researches into the history of the early councils which had already won him a measure of respect among his contemporaries. All the rest of his life he was to be honored as "learned."

And about this time he left Oxford and at last took up his residence and his duties at Credenhill.

Credenhill.

TRaherne said that in the light of the new understanding which followed the spiritual crisis, he was "withdrawn from all endeavour of altering or mending outward things. They lay so well, me-thought, they could not be mended; but I must be mended to enjoy them."

In another passage, he has told us that this period of "mending" lasted ten years. Exactly ten years elapsed between his ordination in 1657 and his departure from Credenhill for London in 1667.

These years, the four at Oxford of hard thinking and the six at Credenhill of hard living, are clearly the ten years of "mending"; the ten in which, by deliberate effort of will and sheer tenacity of purpose, he actually remade himself into another person.

And of these, the six years at Credenhill are perhaps the more important.

Up to that time, ever since that evening of utter desolation in the lonely field, his energies had been engaged in achieving a philosophy and a creed. Not that he could do this in a vacuum devoid of daily life. The renunciation that preceded his ordination, and the intense study of the second period at Oxford, were direct consequences of ideas he had come to hold. Still, the main task of these years had been intellectual, the formulating and coordinating of his conceptions of God and of life and of religion. He ended the period possessed of an ardent Christian philosophy to which his keen brain and his strong emotions alike could give allegiance. That was no mean achievement; and I do not in the least wish to belittle it when I suggest that what he went on to do in the years at Credenhill was still more remarkable. For there he set out to translate that Christian philosophy into practical daily living.

When Traherne tells us the story of this in the fourth of the *Centuries*—modestly avoiding now the first person—he makes it all seem so logical and simple that we can miss how extraordinary was not only the achievement but even the attempt. How many professing Christians seriously try to achieve complete sinlessness? How many even think it desirable, let alone possible? But to Traherne it seemed merely logical. He looked on sin as infection; and he looked on infection of mind and spirit as a modern physician looks on infection of the body. I know of no other parallel that conveys Traherne's attitude so exactly. Just as the physician says that infection is something to be dealt with promptly and persistently, since ill health is neither a desirable nor necessary state of body, so it seems just as plain to Traherne that infection of the spirit must be dealt with, since ill health of the spirit, "sin," is neither desirable nor necessary. Like the physician, he believed that health, or holiness, is a positive, joyous well-being, a natural harmony. Like the physician, he knew there were rules of health, and remedial measures to overcome bad habits. It seemed to Traherne, as to a wise patient seeking bodily restoration, only plain common sense to put these remedies faithfully into practice.

Traherne was not seeking to cure himself merely of evil actions; he recognized these but as symptoms. What had to be cured was evil existent in thoughts, ideas, motives. He had to reorient his whole thinking and feeling—a much more difficult task.

So difficult a task that all but the most ardent have shrunk from it; that none but the ardent are even willing to believe possible.

Some of Traherne's "techniques" for regaining holiness we can learn from his writings.

His major faults he faced frankly and set about uprooting; chiefly by compelling himself consistently to practise the opposite virtue. Some faults he has specifically named, and we recognize them as very likely in one of his temperament: a hot tongue, impatience with stupidity, resentfulness of contradiction, covetousness of money, a tendency to compromise in order to win popularity, vacillations of moods, waverings on this hard path of self-imposed discipline.

Thus one essential remedial technique was constant watchfulness for symptoms, and ruthless "uprooting" of recurrent growths. "A little grit in the eye destroyeth the sight of the very heavens, and a little malice or envy a world of joys. One wry principle in the mind is of infinite consequence."

Another health measure was the regular absorption of the spiritual food necessary for growth and energy. He "lived by rule" and obliged himself to set aside each day regular times for prayer and reading and meditation, as well as for attendance at the services of the Church. He would begin the day—probably at four in the morning—with one such period; he would end the day with another; there would probably be seven other set times. We should not think such care in nourishment unnecessary or unusual for a patient on a special diet; to Traherne it seemed just as logical to take over a discipline that had been practised and proved good from earliest Christian times for providing for the needs of the spirit; for the spirit, like the body, must draw its food from sources external to itself.

Another remedial measure was a constant exercise of the faculty of wonder, the use of the inner eye to see the mystery and beauty and intense significance of the ordinary things of life, and thereby to see the glory and greatness of the Creator. Traherne strangely anticipates Blake, who had the power to see "A world in a grain of sand, and a Heaven in a wild flower"; Traherne says, "You never enjoy the world aright, till you see how a sand exhibiteth the wisdom and power of God."

The dynamic providing for Traherne the necessary "will to live" was as usual seated in the emotions. Traherne shared with all the great Christian saints and mystics a passionate personal devotion to Jesus of Nazareth.

Such then was something of Traherne's practice during the years at Credenhill; the aim of it—spiritual health and happiness, or friendship with God here on earth. (Traherne had no patience with those who would postpone felicity to beyond the grave.) He did not achieve his aim in completeness. As he confessed. "His practices are so short of these glorious principles that to relate them would be to his shame."

Nevertheless he did achieve an astounding measure of the strange beauty of holiness. And therein lies the secret of his greatness, and all his unusual quality as a man and as a writer.

Traherne however was a human being, living in a world of human beings. He had to achieve whatever he did of practical Christlikeness while playing a part in the general drama of life; and for the most exacting part of it the stage happened to be the little village of Credenhill, the little world of a poor parson.

Credenhill's Church of St. Mary stands today very much as it was when Traherne lived in the adjoining rectory and "never failed any one day publickly to make use of the publick offices of this our excellent Church unless some very unavoidable business interrupted him."[44] Behind it rises steeply the thickly wooded hill, the ancient Roman encampment from which the village takes its name. The gray stone church, with its treasures of precious glass, stands square-towered on the crown of a lesser rise; and from its porch one may look southward across one of the fairest prospects in all fair Herefordshire.

> The Sun, that gilded all the bordering Woods,
> Shone from the Sky
> To beautify
> My Earthly and my Hevenly Goods;
> Exalted in his Throne on high,

[44] Preface to the *Contemplation*. Free quotation. Cf. p. 66.

He shed his Beams
In Golden Streams
That did illustrat all the Sky;
Those Floods of Light, his nimble Rays,
Did fill the glittr'ing Ways,
While that unsufferable piercing Ey
The Ground did glorify.

The choicest Colors, Yellow, Green, and Blew
Did all this Court
In comly sort
With mixt varieties bestrew;
Like Gold with Emeralds between;
As if my God
·From his Abode
By these intended to be seen.
And so He was:[45]

So might Traherne have thought as, emerging from the cool dimness of his church some fine morning, he paused in the ancient porch to enjoy the scene spread out before his gaze.

At the foot of the hill on which the church stood ran the high-road; Hereford lay to the southwest, four miles away, and Kington fifteen miles to the northwest. Straggling along either side of the road lay the few cottages of Credenhill village, whence Traherne's parishioners would have come, or from the more distant farmhouses, tree-sheltered among those cultivated fields that checkered and colored the wide landscape. The scars of the Civil Wars would all be healed by 1661, and the ancient beauty of the land be restored. Traherne's loveliest nature poetry probably owes its inspiration to the beauty he enjoyed at Credenhill.

The spiritual history of these years is made quite plain to us in the *Fourth Century*; I have already indicated it in the opening paragraphs of this chapter, and as the *Centuries* is readily accessible, there is no need for extended quotation. In discussing that

---

[45] *The World.*

spiritual history, however, Traherne also gives us in passing some pictures of his daily life; and these are interesting.

For the first and the last time in his life, he was head of a household. His income was only £50 a year; but that would be sufficient to keep a servant. He would also have to farm the glebe-lands of his rectory. He found this rather a trial. "He saw that in Paradise a great help to this kind of life was the cheapness of commodities and the natural fertility of the then innocent and blessed ground." But Credenhill was not Paradise; the poorest saint must have a certain amount of money, and the ground of this world yields its produce only to those who till or pay for its tillage. "Now the earth being cursed and barren, there was danger of want, a necessity of toil and labour and care, and maintenance of servants." Surely it is of this household of his he is thinking in one of the Thanksgivings in his *Contemplation*:

> Were I alone
> Briars and thorns would devour me;
> Wild beasts annoy me; . . .
> The Earth a Wilderness
> And I in solitude,
> Naked and hungry,
> Blind and brutish,
> Without house or harbour;
> Subject unto storms;
> Lying upon the ground:
> Feeding upon roots;
> Therefore thou providest for me, and for me they
> build, and get and provide for me
> My Bread, Drink,
> Clothes, Bed,
>
> My Houshold stuff { Books
> Utensils
> Furniture
>
> The Use of Meats, Fire, Fuel,
> They teach unto me, provide for me.

"My Household Stuff—Books, Utensils, Furniture. . . ." How very characteristic is that order of mention!

His relations with his parishioners Traherne gives us from several points of view. He realized his own greater spiritual development and insight. He knew that he had gifts of healing to bestow on them if they would but accept his teaching. As priest, he saw himself as physician, and the erring and evil among his people as the sick and the blind—an attitude towards sin extremely rare in the seventeenth century. I think one can imagine the loving patience and the gentle persistence with which such a man would essay his ministry of healing. "Did they see the beauty of Holiness or the face of Happiness, they would not do so," he cries, moved by the tragedy of their blindness and its consequences. "Blind wretches that wound themselves offend me. I need therefore the oil of pity and the balm of love to remedy and heal them. . . . To think the world therefore a general Bedlam, or place of madmen, and oneself a physician, is a most necessary point of present wisdom." His task as a priest he saw to be "like a God, to bring Light out of Darkness, and order out of confusion."[46]

He lost in these years the old tinge of arrogance. He perceived quite clearly "that Christians are of two sorts, perfect or imperfect, intelligent and mature, or weak and inexperienced"; yet that every true Christian, whatever his intellectual attainments, is a true student of wisdom. "Every man therefore according to his degree so far forth as he is a Christian, is a philosopher." What he still attacked was the "conceit that a little knowledge is sufficient, which is a mere lazy dream to cover our sloth or enmity." The weak Christian, he says, may have implicit faith, and be obedient in some measure; but only the one who knows and understands will ever possess "the riches of the full assurance."

Neither spiritual nor worldly arrogance can exist in one who thought that he was to treat every man in the person of Christ. That is both as if himself were Christ in the greatness of his Love, and also as if the man were Christ. . . . For . . . he was well acquainted with this

[46] *Centuries* IV, 21.

mystery—That every man being the object of our Saviour's Love, was to be treated as our Saviour, Who hath said "In as much as ye have done it to the least of these my brethren, ye have done it unto me." And thus he is to live upon Earth among sinners . . . conversing with the poor and seeing the value of their souls through their bodies.[47]

It was thus that he envisaged himself as the servant of his parish; but he also realized that the service was reciprocal, and there were ways in which his parishioners rendered essential service to his own spiritual needs. These people were they

> towards whom, before whom, among whom he might do the work of fidelity and wisdom, exercise his courage and prudence, show his temperance, and bring forth the fruits of faith and repentance. For all those are the objects of our joy that are the objects of our care. They are our true treasures about whom we are wisely employed.[48]

For this reason his parish, his place of service, was inexpressibly precious to him.

If he might have had but one request of God Almighty, it should have been above all other, that he might be a blessing to mankind. That was his daily prayer above all his petitions. . . . He could not help it. But he so desired to love them, . . . that he protested often that he never could enjoy himself but as he was enjoyed of others, and that above all delight in all worlds, he desired to be a joy and blessing to others.[49]

When I consider, O Lord, how they come into thy Temples, fill thy Courts, and sing thy Praises.

> O how wonderful they then appear!
> What stars,
> Enflaming Suns,
> Enlarging Seas
> Of Divine Affection,
> Confirming Patterns,
> Infusing Influences
> Do I feel in them!
> Who are the shining Light
> Of all the Land (to my very Soul):
> Wings and Streams,
> Carrying me unto thee,

---

[47] *Ibid.*, IV, 28-29.   [48] *Ibid.*, IV, 39.   [49] *Centuries* IV, 32.

The Sea of Goodness, from whence they came. . . .
Destroy not my people, for how then shall I
   walk in the light of thy Countenance?
Should I not rust, O Lord, and grow dull and heavy?

Though I believe in Jesus,
   Being taught it by their means,
Though I see him on the Cross,
   Adore him in the Heavens,
And shall always remember my Friend in thy Throne,
   Need I not Spurs, Wings, Enflamers? . . .
   Give me wide and publick Affections;
So strong to each as if loved him alone.
   Make me a Blessing to all the Kingdom
A peculiar Treasure (after thy similitude) to every Soul,
   Especially to those whom thou hast given me by love,
    make a shining light, a Golden Candlestick,
A Temple of thy presence in the midst of them.[50]

We thus know fairly well what Traherne thought of his parishioners. One cannot help wondering what his parishioners thought of him! It might not always be comfortable to have a practising saint for a rector; we lesser mortals value comfort ~ ¹ are apt to resent those who disturb it. A friend of these days, possibly a parishioner, has given us a glimpse of this other side of the picture. "He was so wonderfully transported with the Love of God . . . and with those inexpressible Felicities to which we are entitled . . . and was so full of them when abroad, that those who would converse with him, were forced to endure some discourse upon these subjects, whether they had any sense of Religion or not." No tactful, tea-party rector, this, but one uncomfortably ardent and uncompromising. "And therefore to such he might be sometimes thought troublesome."[51] We can understand that. Their resentment must have found expression, too; Traherne speaks of being "surrounded with reproaches . . . besieged with offences, receiving evil for good, being disturbed by fools and invaded with malice." Things apparently were not

[50] *Contemplation.*

always smooth in the parish—as one would expect with a crusading rector.

But there were others who liked him; so that this same biographer goes on to say, "He was a man of a cheerful and sprightly Temper, free from anything of the sourness or formality by which some great pretenders to Piety rather disparage and misrepresent true Religion than recommend it; and therefore was very affable and pleasant in his conversation, ready to do all good offices to his Friends, and Charitable to the Poor almost beyond his ability."[51] This has a ring of truth in it, and it was written twenty-five years after Traherne's death, when flattery could have no point. One feels that to those among Traherne's parishioners and friends at Credenhill who were hungry for spiritual food—and are not such to be found in every group?—the few years of his active ministry must have been an experience as quickening as it is rare.

Two other important features of Traherne's life at this time are now known to us. One is, that it now became his habit to "digest his notions of these things into writing," devoting to that practice "most of his time at home."[51] All through his life he had kept commonplace books, into which he carefully and laboriously entered extracts and summaries of his reading. Two of these books have survived—a notebook of his university days, and one in use in his last years. At what period he began to give literary expression to his religious experiences and to compose his own books of devotions we do not know; probably it was while he was at Oxford. But before he came to Credenhill it is unlikely he would have either the desire or the leisure to devote much time to writing. Here, however, he would have ample time; and the requirements of the religious "Society." to which he belonged would supply an additional incentive. It was at Credenhill, I believe, that he wrote the little book of Thanksgivings that I refer to as the *Contemplation*, its full title being too unwieldy

---

[51] Preface to the *Contemplation*.

for everyday use; and here he wrote the *Meditations on the Six Days of the Creation*, *Meditations and Devotions on the Life of Christ*, and the lost poem on "Moderation" that in 1673 he spoke of as "made long ago" (cf. p. 147). When he left Credenhill, he left behind these manuscripts with his closest friend.

And that brings us to the second important fact of these days of Traherne's, his friendship with Mrs. Susanna Hopton.

But that lady deserves a chapter all to herself.

CHAP. VIII.

Susanna Hopton.

IT has always been known, ever since Bertram Dobell published the romantically recovered manuscript in 1908, that Thomas Traherne had written his exquisite *Centuries of Meditations* for a woman friend. Therein, indeed, lay no small measure of their charm; for, intended in the first place for no eyes but hers, there was a total absence of self-consciousness, an ease of the flow of thought, an intimacy and a tenderness that made this work, half devotions, half autobiography, unlike anything in our literature. But the identity of the lady whom Traherne loved in the exalted Platonic mode which men and women apparently achieved in the seventeenth century has hitherto been a mystery.

We knew from allusions in the *Centuries* that Traherne and she were sundered by "a hundred miles," which is almost the exact distance of London from Hereford; that this book was begun to console her, and him no less, for the pain of absence; that she was wealthy and charitable; and that she was extremely devout. More than this we could not guess; any more than the identity of the friend who cherished for twenty-five years after Traherne's death the manuscript of his ardent *Contemplation upon the Mercies of God*, and then preserved it for all time by

having it printed by Dr. Hickes; or the identity of the lady for
whom were written the original devotions which Philip Traherne, the poet's brother, revised and published in 1685 as *The
Soul's Communion*. But now it is an established fact that the unknown person in the two latter instances was Mrs. Susanna Hopton; and there is a mass of evidence to show that she was also
the lady of the *Centuries*.

Thus as Traherne's patron and personal friend, one who
shared his religious enthusiasms, one who was distantly connected with him by marriage (Philip Traherne having married
her only niece), Mrs. Susanna Hopton catches the reflex of our
interest in Traherne. But indeed, she is a woman of strong and
vital personality who is well worth knowing for her own sake.

She was born in 1627, in Staffordshire, in one of the numerous
families of Harveys that all through this period were steadily
rising in wealth, importance, and rank. The Harvey men were in
the iron trade, and "Turkey merchants." They were adventurous
and persistent and pugnacious; and worldly success came to them
in many fields. Someone in want of a plot for novel or film
should look up the history of the Harvey Lord Mayor of London whose only daughter, the child of his old age and then
barely fourteen, was coveted by King James I as a wealthy bride
for his worthless favorite Villiers, and should retell the tale of
the old man's dangerous battle of wits against King and court,
and the victory of obstinate love over greed. That was the stock
Susanna Harvey came of; and she inherited her full share of the
family pugnacity and shrewdness. Born of middle-class parentage, she was not highly educated; but she could read and write;
she had a tenacious memory and a most acute intelligence; and
so, though she herself regretted it, the fact that she was "never
bred in Scholastick education" proved no serious handicap.

In the stormy times of Charles I she was a militant Episco-
palian and a militant Royalist. When the Puritan party defeated
both Church and Charles, and abolished the one and beheaded
the other, Miss Harvey, with a spice of defiance, and wholly in

her own forthright fashion, marked her extreme aversion for the Puritan sects by going over to Roman Catholicism; and her aversion to the Parliamentarians by acting as a secret agent for the defeated Royalists. Her husband-to-be had been a prominent Parliamentary officer in Herefordshire; but like many others he had little dreamed when he took up arms against the King to what lengths the struggle would go; and after Charles's execution he was henceforth to be counted a Royalist. He was a very gallant soldier of great dash and recklessness, much loved by his men; and he turned these talents to secret-service work, collaborating with Mistress Susanna Harvey. Sometime in the period just before the Restoration these two were married, well matched in courage and loyalty; and to the end of their long life together Richard Hopton and his "ould Sue," as he sometimes called her, seem to have been a perfectly happy pair.

On the Restoration, Mrs. Hopton returned to the Church of England, and Richard reaped the reward of his services to the crown in lands and leases in Herefordshire, and an appointment to a chief-justiceship on the Welsh circuit. The Hoptons were henceforth people of very considerable wealth and great importance in the affairs of Herefordshire. They had several establishments, but lived chiefly at Kington, which is only fifteen miles from Credenhill.

Mrs. Hopton had always taken religion seriously, if somewhat austerely, and on her return to the Church of England she apparently determined that in her personal religious life she would use no half measures. Nothing is in stronger contrast with our own day than the fairly general attitude of the seventeenth century that a lukewarm religion is worse than none. Traherne and Mrs. Hopton are typical of the many who took a religious life as seriously and as wholeheartedly as a modern scientist takes his researches, and with the same conviction of its rationality. In time, with Mrs. Hopton's thoroughgoing spirit, her house became the center of a "family," or religious society—a feature of seventeenth-century Protestantism as yet unexplored. Members

of a "family," while in the world and of the world, lived by
rules of conduct as strict as those of the cloister, binding themselves to such observance by vows, and leading a life of the utmost piety and selflessness. The community of Nicholas Ferrar
at Little Gidding is well known; but there were countless others,
and one certainly in Herefordshire, of which Mrs. Hopton, and
in all probability both Thomas and Philip Traherne, were moving spirits. Spinckes, a friend of hers, has left on record an account
of her way of life; and whatever else we think of it, we cannot
but admire its wholehearted thoroughness.

> For she was well known to keep up a constant Course of Devotion, not
> only in herself, but in her Family, and not only on the Lord's Day, but
> throughout the whole Week, setting apart five times every Day for
> religious Worship; from which she would not suffer herself to be diverted
> by any Business that was not very extraordinary. Even in her old Age,
> and the cold winter Season, she would be up, and in the Closet at her
> Mattins, by four of the Clock in the Morning. From which Customs she
> was for a long time not to be discouraged, either by the Effects of her
> declining Age or by the Extremity of Weather. . . . Tho' some time
> before she died she was prevailed with to forbear till five or six. [She was
> eighty-two when she died.] She neither indulged herself in Diet nor
> sleep, but contented herself with less in both respects than those about her
> judged convenient for her, so much was she above gratifying the Flesh.
> . . . She was a constant Observer of not only the Feasts, but Fasts, of the
> Church, and was much scandalised at the generality of those who profess
> themselves Members of the Church of England for showing no more
> regard to such Days. . . . As her Prayers, so did her Alms likewise ascend
> up to Heaven. . . . For she was not sparing in these; but as she had a
> Fortune to do it, so she took care to dispense them bountifully . . . and
> was liberally munificent when she died.[52]

One wonders what Richard Hopton thought of all this. As a
busy judge, as administrator of his brothers' as well as his own
scattered properties, and as one involved in considerable litiga-
tion, he could hardly have followed so exacting a régime, even if
he had the desire to do so, which one doubts. Richard Hopton
had too keen an eye for the main chance to have in him the mak-

[52] Preface to *A Collection of Meditations and Devotions in Three Parts* (1717).

ings of a mystic. One revealing little prayer of Mrs. Hopton's, which escaped into print shows the gulf between them in spiritual ideals and outlook. It was to someone such as Thomas Traherne that she must look for understanding and help in the deepest interest of her life.

But Mrs. Hopton's time was by no means wholly given over to the performance of religious duties. She had a very wide circle of friends, and in particular of clergy of the more militant stamp She read with great gusto all the chief controversial books on the questions then in hot debate between the Roman Catholic and Protestant Churches; she read both sides, though an ardent partisan, and enjoyed keenly the verbal swordplay. She also debated these matters with her clerical friends, and became herself an authority on all these controversial questions "not much inferior to the best Divines," as the learned Dr. Hickes once remarked. Toward the end of her life she was an equally militant Nonjuror; and she showed her displeasure with Philip Traherne, who took the oath to William and Mary, by pointedly omitting him from any legacy at her death.

Mrs. Hopton found time not only for reading and discussion but also for a certain amount of writing. Nothing we have of hers is original work; her literary efforts were confined to compiling devotional anthologies (*Daily Devotions*, 1673) or adapting the devotional works of others (*Devotions in the Ancient Way of Offices Reformed by a Person of Quality*, Second edition, 1701). She must also have spent a considerable amount of time in laboriously making her own copies of works circulating, as they frequently did at that time, in manuscript. These literary interests of Mrs. Hopton have proved of the greatest value to us; for we owe to them the preservation of at least three of Traherne's manuscripts which came into her hands.

Most of these activities of Mrs. Hopton—devotional, polemical, literary—were direct expressions of her religious energy; but she was also too practical, too well balanced, and too shrewd to neglect her home or her worldly interests. Her will, which may be seen in the Probate Office at Llandaff, is a very human record of a house-proud mistress of a well appointed home, one who knew her linen press and dairy and kitchen no less well than her drawing room. Listen to her here: "I give to my faithful servant Hester White £100 . . . my great Still, and all my linen except my diaper, six pair of holland sheets and four pair of Pillowbeers, two pairs of ordinary sheets and all my silver spoons, the jack in the Kitching, the Spittle . . . all my Brass except my great Dairy Kettle. . . ." Or here, where she is thinking of a humble little "cookmaid," who is to receive, among other things, "all the tin and wooden ware in the Kitching, one ordinary bed and bed-cloaths, the dish-water kettle, piggins, and household spoons. . . ." It is a long will, as may be imagined, generous and warm-hearted, with friends in every walk of life suitably remembered.

Ballard included a brief biography of Mrs. Susanna Hopton in his *Memoirs of Several Ladies of Great Britain*, which, though defective in many ways, supplies this interesting contemporary note:

Papists, dissenters, and all enemies to the Church of England she would encounter and confute; for she was an excellent casuist and divine. She had a sound judgment, tenacious memory and a ready wit. Her discourse and style upon serious matters was strong, eloquent, and nervous; upon pleasant subjects, witty and facetious; and when it required an edge, was as sharp as a rasor. For she knew exactly well what was proper to be said upon any occasion, or in any company. She was a rare manager and economist, and set down every day what she received in, and paid out: and by such care was enabled to be charitable to the poor in the highest degree, and hospitable to her friends in a generous manner.

I shall also give in Ballard's words the closing chapter of her life:

Not long before her death she removed from Kington to Hereford, to the inexpressible affliction of the neighbourhood. . . . When she had lived to a good old age, she at last fell sick of a very sharp fever, about the latter end of June, which she bore with uncommon courage, patience, and resignation, and died of it in the faith and communion of the Church of England, and constant to her principles, at Hereford, in the eighty-second year of her age, on the twelfth of July following, about two of the clock in the afternoon, A.D. 1709.

By her express wish, her body was laid to rest beside her husband's within the altar rails of the little parish church at Bishop's Frome, where their memorials are still decipherable.

She reminds one of Mrs. Battle, with a passion for religion instead of whist. She has the same generosity, the same pugnacity, the same hot intolerance for lukewarmness. Whatever Susanna Hopton did, she did with all her energy, whether it was being a Royalist agent, or an efficient housewife, or a churchwoman, a friend or foe. There are still Hoptons at her Richard's family home at Canon Frome; and still a Hopton at the little church where she and her husband lie buried.

Susanna Hopton outlived Traherne by a quarter of a century. And Traherne, as I have mentioned, left behind with her when he went to London in 1667 a few of his devotional works in manuscript. In 1699 Mrs. Hopton had one of these printed; this is the little book with the long name not of its author's bestowing. This little book had a commendatory letter by Mrs. Hopton's friend, Dr. Hickes; and a biographical preface of its unnamed author from which I have freely quoted and which, as I have related earlier, furnished Dobell with an important clue in his search for the identity of Traherne by telling us that the author had been private chaplain to Sir Orlando Bridgeman.

On her death, several more of Traherne's manuscripts that had been in her possession came into Dr. Hickes's hands. He recognized their worth, and decided to publish some of them; but by a curious error of judgment he believed they were of her own composition. Then Dr. Hickes died, and his intention was carried out by a common friend, Spinckes. Thus through Dr. Hickes's error was perpetrated a mistake in authorship that was nearly repeated in our own century with Traherne's works by Dr. Grosart.

However, in spite of the mistake, a good deed was done; for

the writings were saved from destruction. Not all, however. There was a book of poetry that has not yet been recovered, and may never be. And there were probably other works in prose of which we know nothing. Nevertheless, we owe it to Mrs. Hopton's loving care and her preservation of these manuscripts for twenty-five years that so much that is fine and beautiful of Traherne has been saved for us.

Still more we owe to her the exquisite *Centuries of Meditations* written expressly for her, in the handsomely bound little notebook she had presented to him; written with a delicate and beautiful penmanship that perfectly matches the delicate beauty of the work. We owe the very conception of this book to Mrs. Hopton, for it was born of the urgency of Traherne's desire to share with his beloved but less fortunate friend the riches of his own spiritual possessions.

Outstanding as are the services Mrs. Hopton has rendered to the memory and literary fame of her friend, her practical services to him during his short life were also noteworthy.

Traherne and Mrs. Hopton probably met for the first time during Traherne's second period at Oxford. Richard Hopton desired that his wife-to-be should renounce Roman Catholicism; but Susanna, being Susanna, would not lightly do so. She had to be convinced of the rightness of the step. So Richard sought out "the best Divines that these parts afford"; and by conversation and by correspondence, we are told,[53] Susanna was finally brought to the point of formally returning to the Protestant faith. Philip Traherne explicitly tells us one factor in this was her "just and rational conviction of these gross errors and forgeries on and by which the Church (or rather the Court) of Rome hath founded and upheld her greatness."[54] Traherne, we know, was hard at work at this time on the researches that he afterwards published as *Roman Forgeries*; he was certainly one

[53] *A Second Collection of Controversial Letters* (Hickes and Ballard, 1710), *op. cit.*

[54] Philip Traherne's Preface to *The Soul's Communion with her Saviour* (1685).

of the most eminent of the local Herefordshire clergy; and the allusion to "correspondence" exactly fits in with his periods of absence at the university.

So Mrs. Hopton returned to the Church of England; and Thomas Traherne had his merits brought to the notice of Amabella, Countess of Kent, who had the benefice of Credenhill in her gift. Are the two facts unrelated? I hardly think so; though I have no proof.

In similar fashion, I think, when the time was ripe, was Thomas Traherne brought through Mrs. Hopton's good offices to the notice of Sir Orlando Bridgeman. The Harveys had great influence. One of them was the wife of Sir Heneage Finch, who was solicitor-general under Charles II. To Finch, I think, Richard Hopton owed his substantial preferments in the law after the Restoration—and the blind eye on his earlier Puritan activities. We know for a fact that Philip Traherne owed his various appointments to Finch whom he named his "patron and friend." Sir Orlando Bridgeman was also an eminent lawyer and the personal friend of Finch as well. This I believe solves the mystery of how so important a person as Sir Orlando came to hear of an obscure Herefordshire rector and offer him so highly coveted a post as his own private chaplaincy.

But the relation between Susanna Hopton and Traherne was never that of Lady Bountiful and humble recipient of favors. The whole tone of the *Centuries* shows this beyond all doubt. Traherne was the leader, the dominant one of the two. His love for her may have been strengthened by many deeds of kindness, many good offices on her part; but he knows that he has still richer gifts to bestow on her than any of these. The extraordinary blending of great tenderness and austere purity in their relations can be felt in this the very first of the *Centuries*: "An empty book is like an infant's soul, in which anything may be written. It is capable of all things, but containeth nothing. I have a mind to fill this with profitable wonders. And since Love made you put it into my hands, I will fill it with those truths you love without knowing them; and with those things which, if it be possible shall show my love; to you, in communicating most enriching truths; to Truth, in exalting her beauties in such a soul."

An extraordinary relationship, truly, for a man and woman, each ardent by temperament, each profoundly attracted to the other—possible only because each had accepted all the implications of a religious life. Each was a member of a "family"—of the same "family" in all likelihood; each "lived by rule"—the same Rule, I suggest, for that tiny corner of Hereford would hardly have numbers for two such groups. Over and over again each must have strengthened and inspired and encouraged the other. "Thou, Lord, hast made Thy Servant a sociable Creature, a lover of company. . . . Need I not Spurs, Wings, Enflamers? O my God, how often should I die were it not for these?" Traherne once wrote in his *Prayer for the Nation* during those difficult years of discipline at Credenhill. I think we can understand something of what the friendship, the like-mindedness, the kindred zeal and the affection of Mrs. Hopton meant to him in those lonely years. And I think we now have the clue to one strange little thanksgiving that crept into Mrs. Hopton's anthology of prayers:

"I praise Thee, for the super-exalted love of a Redeemed person."

CHAP. IX.

London.

IN 1667 Traherne left his rectory at Credenhill to become private chaplain to Sir Orlando Bridgeman, Lord Keeper of the Seal, and, it seems probable, never saw Herefordshire or his Herefordshire friends again. A hundred miles of difficult traveling now effectively separated him henceforth from those familiar scenes, a journey not lightly to be undertaken in days of foot-pads and highwaymen and of execrable roads.

Traherne's motives in making this complete break with a way of life that in its simplicity and its opportunities for living the inner life must have well suited one part of his nature, are not difficult to understand. From a worldly point of view such an appointment as this was an honor, and such posts as these were eagerly sought after, not only for themselves, but as steppingstones to higher ecclesiastical preferment. Traherne's appointment to this chaplaincy, as well as Philip Traherne's appointment at Smyrna and his subsequent benefices in England, hitherto have seemed inexplicable freaks of fortune. But their connection with Mrs. Hopton has furnished the clue for both.

Yet it would be unfair to assume that Philip Traherne's appointments, or that of Thomas Traherne as private chaplain to the Lord Keeper of the Seal—an appointment far more important both in its powers for influence and as a stepping-stone for ambition than one might at first realize—were entirely the result of backstairs influence. It is true that there was never an age when patronage was more powerful, or nepotism exer-cised its privileges in more unquestioned fashion. But the hon-orably great, besieged though they were with importunate clients for favor, did not exercise their powers lightly. There are records to show with what meticulous care Sir Heneage examined the claims of rival candidates, particularly clergy. It was to him a solemn matter of conscience that the best should be chosen; and it is in the highest degree improbable that a man of Sir Orlando's rigid integrity would choose—and he would have unlimited choice—anyone for the post of his own private chaplain who was not of outstanding merit. Traherne's life, short as it was, was thus not entirely uncrowned with worldly success. The gifts of mind and spirit revealed in his books did not pass unnoticed in his own day. It would have been strange indeed if they had; and we see the proof of that recog-nition in the fact that in those days of a plethora of clergy, many

of whom were doomed by sheer numbers never to receive all
their lives even the humblest of livings, this young man of
obscure parentage, living in the depths of the country, should
have won the favor of the Lord Keeper of the Seal.

It is natural to suppose that Traherne actively desired this
change. He was not one to despise worldly success or honor. "If
not in Heaven, yet certainly on Earth, the Goods of fortune
concur to the Compleating of *Temporal Felicity*, and therefore
where they are freely given, are not to be despised," he wrote
in *Christian Ethicks*; and that idea is all of a piece with his
philosophy. He probably also fully realized that the natural
consequence of his accepting this chaplaincy would be in time the
offer of some considerable preferment.

By 1667, too, we can imagine that Traherne was needing
fresh contact with the world of books and scholarly intercourse.
He had been for six years in the remote, tiny, narrow world
of Credenhill. In six years he must have well-nigh exhausted
the rich harvest of the days at Oxford. Knowing the quality
of Traherne's intellectual powers, one is astonished not that he
should wish to leave Credenhill, but that he should have remained there so long. Before Traherne's last books could be
written, before he himself could attain full development, there
had to be a richer, more varied contact with life; and this chance
that came to him to be a member of a great and influential household in London may well have seemed to Traherne a way of
fulfillment opened for him by God himself. "From that time
to this, I have had all things plentifully provided for me, without any care at all, my very study of Felicity making me more
to prosper, than all the care in the whole world. So that through
His blessing I live a free and a kingly life."[55] Those words were
written in Sir Orlando's house, and include in their retrospect
what life there had given him. They make it clear that whatever

[55] *Centuries* III, 46.

the motives that made Traherne decide to leave Credenhill for London, he had no regrets.

One thing of which we can acquit him: he did not accept this position with any idea of enjoying his ease. It is true, as I have discovered, that he continued to hold the living at Credenhill; no new appointment was made there till December 1674, when the cause of vacancy is stated as the death of Thomas Traherne.[56] At first sight this looks as though Traherne's moral standards were no higher than those of the many clerical pluralists and absentees of his time. Against this must be balanced two facts; he might easily have reverted to the arrangements I have suggested as being in force from 1657 to 1661, when he was at Oxford; and in the second place, he himself, whenever the family was in residence at Teddington, acted as curate there, though others—Bryan (1668) and Graves (1673)—nominally held the living. Lyson, writing of Teddington in his *Environs of London*, names Traherne as "curate" of the parish; Anthony à Wood confirms this; and the entry in the Teddington Registers of Traherne's burial describes him as "Minnester." This is conclusive.[57] Thus he performed the duties of a parish priest as well as those lighter duties of a domestic chaplain; and his undertaking of the more onerous work is but what one would have expected in a man of Traherne's character. Knowing that he did this, it seems the more unlikely that he should leave the spiritual needs of Credenhill quite unprovided for. His was never a temperament to rust out in ease.

Whenever we see Traherne, at Oxford or at Credenhill and again here at London and Teddington, he is engaged in intensest activity. The literary activity alone of these last seven years of his life is prodigious, and might well have occupied most of the twenty-four hours. Yet writing occupied but a portion of

---

[56] *Institutions of the Diocese of Hereford* (A.D. 1539-1900).

[57] During these years all the entries in the Registers are made by semi-illiterate parish clerks. Traherne's writing does not appear. The entry of Traherne's burial on the tenth of October is by the same person who recorded Sir Orlando's with the following spelling: "The rite onnered Lord Bridgman was burred the 3 of July."

his time. His public offices as a priest, his private offices as a chaplain, his own lengthy personal devotions as imposed by the Rule to which he was vowed, all went on concurrently with his literary labors. He also continued to be, as always, "a Sociable creature, a lover of company," and some interesting reflections of his social interests at this time are to be found in his books.

The center of this new world of Traherne's was of course his patron; and the more one knows of Sir Orlando, the more one realizes how much the friendship between these two redounds to the credit of both. Nothing could show more clearly the footing of that friendship than the wording of Traherne's dedication to Sir Orlando of his *Roman Forgeries*. In that age of servile adulation, Traherne's simple dignity is no less to the honor of him who wrote it than of him it was designed to please: "To the Right Honorable Sir Orlando Bridgeman, Knight and Baronet, One of His Majesties Most Honorable Privy Council; The Author Devoteth his best Services and dedicateth the Use and Benefit of his Ensuing Labors."

Traherne may well have drawn from Sir Orlando his picture in *Christian Ethicks* of the ideal head of a family, who has "little need of Force and compulsion" in maintaining his authority, because of a "religious example which instilles a Reverence, a strict prohibition of all Debauchery, a sweet and affable Behaviour, a plentiful Provision for their comfortable Subsistence, a prudent connivance at smaller faults, a Distribution of Rewards as well as punishments . . . a meek and Gentle reproof of their Faults, a kind acknowledgment of their Good deserts; cordially beloved of all."

Sir Orlando during the years that Traherne was with him lived either at his town house in London, "Essex House Court" in the Strand; or at his villa in the High Street at Teddington. This latter was his favorite, and he escaped to it whenever his duties allowed. The family—Lady Bridgeman and their daughter Charlotte, a girl in her early teens—and his household would accompany Sir Orlando in his longer residences at the one or the other; and of course, the chaplain. But during the first five years of this period, they all lived chiefly in London. The Bridgeman household is a pleasant one to contemplate; especially against the background of Restoration court life and license. Sir Orlando, grown gray in the service of his two royal masters, dignified, self-respecting, just and honorable; fond of books, deeply religious, attracted to the spiritual Platonism of the day; as learned as he was charitable. Such a man would honor the integrity of life and the spiritual fervor of his chaplain no less than his intellectual gifts. Such a man would beyond a doubt encourage in every way the writing to which Traherne was devoting more and more of his thought and energies. Intellectual keenness and spiritual grace; the ease and comfort and formal stateliness of life in a great man's house; the dignified presence of its mistress, whose name was unsullied even in that scandal-breeding age; the light and brightness of the youthful girlhood of Charlotte and her young cousins who were frequent guests—all these are the setting and background of Traherne's life in those closing, happy, fruitful years.

This small world of the Bridgeman household in which he held a position of no small importance had its larger setting in the corrupt social and political life of Restoration London; surely the most cynical, the most flagrantly corrupt, in her history.

I do not need to dwell here on that larger background; it is amply documented. It is necessary only that we remember that Traherne's London was the London of the Great Plague and the Great Fire, just over when he arrived; of Milton, "blind, old, and lonely" yet honored of the few; of Nell Gwynne and the sinister Louise de Kéroualle; of John Evelyn and of Pepys, who have fixed it for us in their diaries.

Through the portals of My Lord Keeper's town house, and through its anterooms, would pass all the typical figures of that social and political world; the talk at My Lord Keeper's hospitable table would range over all the topics of current interest.

Trah'erne watched this procession with kindly yet penetrating eyes; listened attentively yet critically to all the talk; and unconsciously to themselves these varied personages furnished the matter of many a reflection, many an apt illustration, for the books on which he was engaged.

He watched the young gallants, lordly lavish to the poor and needy but nevertheless defrauding poor tradespeople; he observed how the carriage of the body reveals breeding or the lack of it ("a Clown and a Courtier are known by their Postures"); and how the truest physical beauty and charm is a composite thing, a harmony "in the Gesture of the Body, the Air of the Face, the carriage of the Eye, the Smile, the Motion of the Feet and Hands"; that laughter can be loose and impertinent; and how much is betrayed by such things as "excessive Cost in Apparel, a Lascivious wandering of the Eyes, and ungoverned Boldness which turns into Impudence, an extremity of Fear which degenerates into Baseness, . . . immodest and violent strivings after Things we too eagerly desire, inordinate Love, too keen and bitter Resentments, a fierce and raging Anger."

How true a picture of the typical Restoration courtier and of the series of Royal courtesans!

He observed the invincible strength of patronage in this world "where a Nod or a Word is able to prevail more than the strength of Oxen and Horses among the dregs of the People." He reflected on the fact that generations of gentle breeding in conditions of social refinement develop a more highly sensitized type of human being; and on the effect of wealth and of town life on those who enjoy them in contrast with poverty and the toil of the farm. His years at Credenhill, and the memories of childhood, made him realize to the full the numbing and stupefying effects of overwork and poverty, with the result that he admired and approved wealth and birth in a way that may shock our conventionally accepted democratic sentiments.

The actions of Love and Honour belong in a peculiar manner to a plentiful estate: Wants and Necessities when they pinch and grind us in a low condition, disturb all those easie and delicate Resentments [feelings] which find their element in the midst of Pleasures and Superfluities. Hence it is that high-born Souls in Courts and Palaces are addicted more to sweet and honourable excesses, than Clowns and Peasants. . . . Soft and tender Affections are more in the *Court* than in the *Shop* or *Barn*. There is some difference in this respect even between the City and Country.

He watched the men and women of this fashionable world in their courtships, their marriages, and their less honorable love affairs. He saw how the most potent factors of attraction are "Colours and Features, a little red and white, a sparkling eye, a brisk Conversation, a delectable Humour"; that most marriages are founded on temporal causes, such as this physical beauty or considerations of power and wealth; and as for vicious love, "it so bewitches the Senses, that the Soul being captivated by the Force of present Delight is violently carried in an irresistible appetite to those Things which Reason condemns and advises him to shun as Evil." This "Medea's faction," those who see and approve the better but follow the worse, Traherne confesses a little sorrowfully, "most prevail in the World."

He saw or heard of another social disgrace of the time, the bands of drunken roisterers and bullies, often nobly born, who infested the dark streets of the city at night and rendered them unsafe for peaceable folk. "This accursed *'The Black Guard'*," Traherne designates them[58]; and he satirizes in his chapter "Of Courage" in *Christian Ethicks* the insolent parade of personal physical courage of these "Rodomontadoes," these "foolish Hectors doting on their Dice and Duels."

The latest crime, then as now, would furnish the matter of table talk; and there are two interesting topical allusions of this kind to be found in Traherne's *Roman Forgeries*. One refers to

[58] Traherne's use of the word "Black Guard" is earlier than any instance recorded in the *New English Dictionary*.

the notorious highwayman who used to disguise himself as a bishop; the other to that interesting person known as "the German Princess," an imposter who claimed to be German Royalty, and whose matrimonial adventures and audacities as a thief, combined with a gift for acting and a very witty tongue, made one of the most talked-of figures of the time. She was hanged at Tyburn in January of 1673.

What a collection of odd characters march through the pages of Traherne's religious writings! Those already mentioned by no means exhaust the list. We meet the man of "Kind and Bountiful Disposition who is loose and intemperate," who ruins his estate and dies a beggar and "vainglorious fool"; the "Complimental Courtier" aping humility for his own advantage; the "stout couragious man" who for want of discretion is little better than a "Swaggering Hector"; the man who can be "as holy and as temperate and as wise as an angel" without giving offense, because "he giveth many gifts." (The spectacle of fashionable life sometimes lent an ironic note to Traherne's remarks.) He met the scholar who had been soured, not mellowed, by his friendship with the Muses; the professing Christian who is "Splenetick and Revengeful," thus bringing "Disgrace upon his whole Profession"; he suffered at the hands of elderly bores, the type that inflicts on their hearers "discourses of the beginning of their lives," and whose "delight in telling their old stories is as great to themselves as wearisom to others"; he suffered also from the more youthful but equally wearisome species who insist on recounting their amorous adventures, and to whom "the memory of their first Amour is more pleasant than the possession of their last." He watched ambition aspiring and intriguing to be "alwaies near the King's Person"; and the epicure whose life is centered on "his Wine, or Women, or Feasts." When and on what occasions, one wonders, did he stand by, looking on at a royal personage playing with a baby?— "I have oftentimes admired at the mean offices to which Parents stoop, and the familiar boldness they permit to their little ones, to play with their Scepters, and Crowns, and Eyes, and Lips, with their Breasts and Jewels, and sometimes to pinch and hurt, nay and to defile them too, being unmindful of their State, and far from all Anger and Indignation."

Traherne was interested not only in the people but in the trappings of this new world of his. He examined splendid jewels, and noted with pleasure the fine distinctions in cutting, the "very true Engravings that make the jewel glorious," and lend it its sparkle and its luster. Indeed, if some lines in "The World" are to be taken literally, Traherne himself wore a jeweled ring. Rare enamels charmed him with their "curious" art, and exquisite pieces of needlework, that had the reverse side almost as perfect as the right side—a phrase suggesting oriental embroideries; he viewed with pleasure specimens of those inlaid cabinets, that were so fashionable an ornament of great men's houses in this Restoration period. Traherne, it would seem, was responsive to beauty in every form of art. He stood in contemplation before paintings and drawings, noting those "little invisible motions of the Pen or Pencil" which went to the making of the final "delicious Harmony"; and the balance of shade and of light, with the positive beauty of shadow; he reflected how one preliminary prosaic decision of the artist, made before he ever put brush to canvas, silently determined the scope and scale of the finished work of art, and exacted of the painter a given amount of labor—the simple but far-reaching decision on the length and breadth of canvas he should use. He would not have approved of "modern" art: "A Painter may daub his Table [canvas] all over in an instant; but a Picture is made by a regulated Hand."

He read romances in this period, and he visited the theater. In the one he enjoyed the escape to worlds of fair imagination: "Love and Beauty even in Romances are delightful: the very Dreams and *Ideas* of the Perfections of Bliss have a Pleasure, as well as their Reallity." In literature, as in life, Traherne was an interested observer of sexual attraction and conflict, as of those other conflicting "loves" from which all tragedies arise. "It is evidently impossible for any Fancy or Play or Romance or Fable to be composed well, and made Delightful, without a Mixture of Love in the Composture. In all Theatres . . . and Triumphs . . . Love is the Soul and Perfection of all."

He was not only aware of his delight in escaping by means of books or plays into another world of romantic love, but also reflected on the strange pleasure derived from the representation on the stage of tragic love. He does not stay to discuss the point, but gives his conclusion, that however much one identifies oneself with the tragic protagonists, the emotions engendered remain different in quality from those one would feel if enduring these experiences in actual life; and in this difference lies the esthetic pleasure derived from an acted tragedy, and also the power and the purifying effect of emotions aroused by dramatic representation.

The very Representations of Love upon the stage, in its Conflicts and Agonies, produces another kind of sence in the Spectator, than that of Embraces. It is more tender and endearing, touches the Soul in a more Vigorous and lively manner, it makes all fruitions (afterward) more precious; by Fidelity, Courage, and Immoveable Perfection it maketh the Lover more Honourable and Effects far more Serious Alterations in the Soul, solid Joys and tender Compassions, moving and Bleeding Resentments.

Metaphors from the theater freely besprinkle these later writings of Traherne's. For Adam and Eve, the whole universe is "but the Theatre of their Mutual Love"; Eve was intended as but "a fair Prologue to a more magnificent scene"; felicity itself is described as "a Scene above all Interludes." Traherne, like all true playgoers, enjoyed the actual theater, its space, its gildings, its engravings, its effect of transporting one into an environment more magnificent than the normal one. However, the play was still the thing: "Be the Theatre never so Magnificent, the Actions and the Actors are more Delightful to the Spectators."

But more than any other form of art, if one may judge from the frequency and fervor of the references, Traherne loved music. That love goes back to his earliest years, and probably both in Herefordshire and at Oxford and again at Credenhill he had heard and loved good music. It is possible that he was a musician himself—a singer or perhaps a lutanist; for the people of Herefordshire, with their large admixture of Celtic stock, have traditionally been lovers of music, and skilled musicians.

With that analyzing part of his nature, Traherne reflects on the mechanical ways in which music is produced: the "Melodious Song" that comes of "Ductures scarce perceivable in the throat"; and the strange physical effects of the vibration set up by strings of instruments; and how "Melody is the effect of Judgment and Order: it springs from a variety of Notes to which Skill giveth Time and Place in their Union." But it is the whole of Traherne, not merely the busy brain, that pours out to God so often his Thanksgiving for the "Harmonies of Earth," the "Melody of Sounds," for "Songs and Musick wherewith the World is beautified and adorned," for the "Sons of Harmony that fill thy Quires." The interest in music is apparent in all his writings[59]; nor could one who did not love and understand it turn to it so naturally to express the deepest thoughts of his heart. The cultivation and the hearing of good music was an integral part of the social life of the time; and in the Bridgeman household Traherne would certainly enjoy it with greater frequency and higher perfection than would ever have been possible to him before.

Life in London had indeed a great deal to offer to the man who had come up to it from the quiet deeps of Herefordshire to be the chaplain and the friend of a great personage and good

[59] On March 27, 1928, Dr. E. W. Naylor addressed the Musical Association on "Three Seventeenth-Century Poet-Parsons and Their Music." Traherne was one of these, and Dr. Naylor illustrated from his poems Traherne's appreciative treatment of music. See *Proceedings of the Musical Association*, No. 54.

man. Enough I think has been written in this chapter to show with what eagerness he went out to meet all these experiences, how truly he exemplified his own precept:

> Life! Life is all! in its most full extent
> Stretcht out to all things, and with all Content!

Traherne, after the years at Credenhill was too securely poised to be unbalanced by these new experiences, too spiritually awake to be imposed on by externals however fair and brilliant. He had gained in the long years of discipline the constant twofold vision of all things, and an unfailing power of enjoying all things "both in a natural and transcendent way," untroubled by desire. All that was good and all that was beautiful in life and in art in London went to his immediate enriching: and from all that was evil he had learned to extract the medicinal, to turn "poisons into cordials." Traherne's books and the attractive power of the philosophy he both preached and practised gained immeasurably by this vital contact of his with the good and the evil of life, a vitality and a vigor and a width of understanding they could never have had had he remained at Credenhill. Having added these London experiences to the stored wisdom of the earlier years, he can truly say of himself that he has seen and has known "the influences of the stars, the splendours of the sun, the verdure of trees, the value of gold, the lustre of precious stones, the sense of beasts and the life of Angels: the fatness of feasts, the magnificence of palaces, the melody of music, the sweetness of wine, the beauty of the excellent, the excellency of virtue, and the glory of the cherubins."[60] For all his worldly poverty he has lived most richly; and the wisdom of that rich living is harvested in his latest books, and in that philosophy of life we may extract from them.

[60] *Centuries* IV, 82.

Teddington.

IN November 1672 a bitter blow fell on the Bridgeman household.

Sir Orlando had been finding the holding of office under such a king as Charles II increasingly difficult and the conflict of loyalties increasingly painful. For if, like Sir Orlando and many another good Royalist and churchman, you believed with all your mind that the King was a divinely appointed instrument of God; and if moreover you have shed your blood and spent your fortune to maintain that belief, it sets up a pretty problem when your monarch turns out to be a worthless profligate, careless of the national honor and welfare. Will you obey or disobey his edicts? Either is a sin.

Yet Sir Orlando believed himself secure in office. He had done too much for the Royalist cause and for the Restoration to think otherwise.

The time came when Sir Orlando had to refuse obedience. What the King asked of him imperiled, he believed, not only the welfare of the nation but the welfare of the Established Church. And he found himself deprived by the King of office, not only without thanks, but with every humiliating circumstance possible. Shaftesbury, the completely unprincipled Shaftesbury, was to succeed him.

It broke Sir Orlando. He left London at once, and retired to his villa at Teddington; within two years he was dead.

The fall of Sir Orlando from place and power meant also the fall—at least for the present—of any hopes of preferment and wider service that Traherne might naturally have entertained. But there seems to have been no thought in his mind of "letting go the great wheel when it runs downhill." Traherne accompanied the family to Teddington; and with characteristic ardor flung himself into battle as Sir Orlando's champion. Sir

Orlando was dismissed in November 1672. By November 1673, Traherne's book *Roman Forgeries* was on sale in London; and *Roman Forgeries*, boldly dedicated to Sir Orlando, was a telling bit of propaganda in support of Bridgeman's anti-Roman Catholic principles.

This was the first of Traherne's writings to appear in print. It was anonymous; its author is described merely as "a Faithful Son of the Church of England."

The writing of part of this book, and the whole preparation of it for immediate publication, must have been done by Traherne at Teddington.

During all the years in the Bridgeman household Traherne was reading hard and writing steadily. We know from the copious extracts in the back of the Dobell folio some of the books he was reading carefully—for example, Gale's big folio, *The Court of the Gentiles*. The Bridgeman library would give him access to expensive books of this type. We know, too, that he was reading afresh along his old path of early Church history; for while much of the material of *Roman Forgeries* was gathered in the second period at Oxford from books and manuscripts in the Bodleian, much too is of later date; and the great *Collections of the Councils* that he studied in the Bridgeman home were weighty and numerous volumes. It is interesting to note in passing that when he had been a little over two years in London he went back for a visit to Oxford, and was awarded his degree of bachelor of divinity, on December 11, 1669.

He had also been working over a period of time on the lovely *Centuries of Meditations*. Apart from the composition, the minute and perfect penmanship must have occupied many hours. He had written a considerable amount of poetry, with increasing facility and power; and had one collection of it well on the way to preparation for publication—the collection Philip afterwards copied and emended, but still did not publish.

And during these years, and particularly during the last two at Teddington, he was at work on his larger book, *Christian*

Ethicks. He was writing this when Sir Orlando died; and continued to work on it in the short remaining interval of his own life. He did not live to see the press proofs.

Sir Orlando Bridgeman's will may be seen at Somerset House. It is a strictly businesslike document, with no legacies to anyone outside the family. There are two codicils and a memorandum; the second codicil was added in May 1674, "in this my present sickness"; and the memorandum was written at eleven o'clock at night on June 4, when the old man thought he was dying, and was worried, it would seem, about the manner of his legacies to his daughter Charlotte. It is of interest to us because it was penned with "Mr. Traherne, the Lady M. Bridgeman and Mistress Elizabeth being in the room." (Elizabeth and Magdalen were Charlotte's cousins.) It is of more interest to us that Traherne signed it as a witness, as he also signed the will itself and one of the codicils. And thus we have preserved three autograph signatures of Traherne.

Sir Orlando rallied a little after that final codicil, rallied and lingered another three weeks.

An ornate monument to his memory stands in the neglected little church at Teddington—neglected because a larger modern building is now the parish church. There is no memorial to his chaplain. Yet today we are interested only in Sir Orlando because at one time there dwelt in his household a very rare human being named Thomas Traherne.

Sir Orlando died June 25, 1674. After his death, Traherne remained on with the family; a proof that they valued and needed him, that they relied on him in their grief and bereavement.

By September of that year Traherne was also seriously ill; so ill that he thought it time to make a will of his own. His brother Philip was away in the Levant; but Philip's wife Susan, Mrs. Hopton's goddaughter and niece, was near; and so was another personal friend, one John Berdo. He sent for them. They both arrived at Lady Bridgeman's house on September 27. When they had come into his bedroom where he was lying ill, he said, "I have sent for you to make my Will for me." John Berdo asked, "Will you have it made in writing?" and Traherne answered—I think we can see the twinkle—"No. I have not so much but that I can dispose of it by word of mouth!"

So they set about the business of making his will. Mrs. Cockson (probably the housekeeper) and Mary Linum, the laundry maid, were brought in to witness it; and heard what I think is a very odd and very characteristic disposal of his goods:

"I desire my Lady Bridgman and her daughter the Lady Charlott should haue each of them a Ring And to you [speaking to the said Mr. Berdo] I give Tenn Pounds and to Mrs Cockson Ten shillings And to Phillipp Landman ffyve shillings and to John Rowland the Gardiner ffyve shillings and to Mary the Laundry maid ffyve shillings and to all the rest of the servants half a crown apeece. My best Hatt I give it to my brother Phillipp And sister [speaking to Mrs Susan Traherne the wife of his brother Phillipp which Susan was then present] I desire you would keepe it for him And all the rest of my Clothes that is worth your acceptance I give to you And for those that are not worth your accepting I would have you to giue them to Phillipp Landman or to whome you please with my old Hatt All my Books I give to my brother Phillipp And [still speaking to the said Mrs Susan then present] I make you and my brother Phillipp my whole Executors."[61]

He remembered every servant in the Bridgeman household. He remembered his old hat and his new one—hats were rather expensive articles—but he quite forgot that he owned five cottages in Hereford City! I think that can be accounted for if we assume that they had long been in fact what Philip at once made them legally on his return—almshouses at the free disposal of poor Christian folk of All Souls parish.

"All my Books I give to my brother Philip." A very precious legacy. We shall have to see a little more of Philip in the next section, when we are considering how he carried out that trust. Into his care and keeping were soon to pass everything Traherne

[61] For a transcription of the document, see *Poetical Works*, p. 304.

had written except the two books in print and the manuscripts he had left behind with Mrs. Hopton in Herefordshire.

That will was made on September 27. Traherne never rallied from that sickness. The exact date of his death we do not know; but we know from *Athenae Oxonienses* (iii. 106) that he was buried on October 10 beneath the reading desk in Teddington Church.

"He died young, and got early to those blissful mansions to which he at all times aspired." He was at the most thirty-seven years of age. Possibly the strain of those last two years, and particularly of the last two months, had weakened his physique. The autumn in England is a treacherous season for those whose stamina is undermined. But maybe the spirit had merely burned away the walls of its clay prison; maybe it was fully fledged for its next flight. John Buchan in his book *Memory Hold-the-Door* records the prophetic words spoken of Lawrence by his wife three weeks before his death: "He is looking at the world as God must look: and a man cannot do that and live." Perhaps this was also true of Traherne.

For whatever the measure of sadness, bereavement, ill-health, disappointment of these last years, whatever the revulsion from the spectacle of human baseness in Restoration London, Traherne in his innermost being was living on a high mountain peak of existence with a new perspective of all earth's sorrows and joys. He had traveled far on the strangest, loftiest journey possible to the spirit clad in human flesh; he was very close to God; he was radiantly, securely, profoundly happy and at peace.

If you doubt it, read his *Christian Ethicks*, written in the latest years, and the richest repository of his wisdom and his joy. Read his *Centuries of Meditations*, interrupted by the adventure of death. Have contact with the man himself, and you cannot but feel the force of the fire that glowed within him, or fail to be warmed and illuminated. Dobell was an agnostic; and Dobell came from his study of Traherne to write:

An exemplary preacher and teacher, who gave in his own person an example of the virtues which he inculcated, one with whom religion was not a garment to be put on, but the life of his life and the spring of all his actions—such was Thomas Traherne. Much as I dissent from his opinions, and much as my point of view as regards the meaning and purpose of life differs from his, I have yet found it easy to appreciate the fineness of his character and the charm of his writings. It is not necessary that we should believe as Traherne believed in order to derive benefit from his works. Men of all faiths may study them with profit, and derive from them a new impulse towards that plain living and high thinking by which alone happiness can be reached and peace of mind assured.

Again, four years later, Dobell wrote:

I am almost tempted to assert that he was the truest Christian that ever lived—by which I mean that he was the one who believed most entirely in the faith, and ruled his conduct most strictly in accordance with its precepts . . . a more perfect Christian than Traherne could not be. Nor has the Church, I firmly believe, ever had an advocate whose life and whose works could plead more eloquently in its favour than the life and the works of the author of the *Centuries of Meditations*.

Truly, his life and his works plead eloquently. In days as troubled and perplexed as our own, as dark and as full of suffering his path of life took him to country and to city, to university and to court, to the rich world of books and to the bustling world of political affairs; yet as he traveled his spirit found and traveled the mysterious path of complete fulfillment. So that his plea is always "Follow where I have trod! Come, see what I have seen and know what I have known. For here and here alone is Felicity." Or in his own inimitable prose:

I will open my mouth in parables, I will utter things that have been kept secret from the foundation of the world. Things strange, yet common; incredible, yet known; most high, yet plain; infinitely profitable, but not esteemed. Is it not a great thing that you should be Heir of the World? Is it not a great enriching verity? In which the fellowship of the Mystery which from the beginning of the World hath been hid in God lies concealed! The thing hath been from the Creation of the World, but hath not so been explained as that the interior Beauty should be understood. It is my design therefore in such plain manner to unfold it that my friendship may appear in making you possessor of the whole world. .... I after His similitude will lead you into paths plain and familiar, where all envy, rapine, bloodshed, complaint, and malice shall be far removed; and nothing appear but Contentment and Thanksgiving. Yet shall the end be so glorious that angels durst not hope for so great a one till they had seen it. (*First Centuries*, 3-4.)

The earthly life closed in that autumn of the year 1674. Friends mourned their loss; and a few recorded their grief. Sir Edward Harley wrote in his diary on October 21, "My worthy friend Thomas Traherne, and my cousin . . . both dead on the same day." Thomas Good, Master of Balliol and prebendary of Hereford, wrote to the Dean of Worcester: "I believe it is not news to you that Thomas Traherne is dead; one of the most pious ingenious men that ever I was acquainted with. It has pleased Divine Providence to take him out of this uneasy troublesome world to a better place. *Fiat voluntas Dei.*"

But slowly the tides of the years washed away all memory of the man; and silenced even the enduring message hidden in anonymous books and unprinted manuscripts.

To our generation have returned in mysterious fashion both the man and his message. And again I quote Bertram Dobell:

"It is not by any words of another that Traherne will be finally judged. If his own words still have the fire of life in them—as I firmly believe they have—they will carry their message to the ears of those fitted to receive it during many coming generations: may I not say indeed, even as long as the language of Shakespeare and Milton endures."

PART THREE.

Thomas Traherne the Writer.

"Praises are the breathings of interior love, the marks and symptoms of a happy life."—CENTURIES III, 82.

Traherne's Writings.

I N Thomas Traherne we have the unique spectacle of an author whose first book was published less than a year before his death; and whose books have been "appearing" at wide intervals over the course of two and a half centuries, with the process still incomplete! Among lost manuscripts of Traherne that time may bring to light we know there were the original of *Poems of Felicity* that Philip Traherne used; a book of poems, conjecturally Traherne's, that Mrs. Hopton's executor found among her papers and showed to Ballard, who was much impressed by them; and the diary to which there is a reference in the Dobell commonplace book. There were probably more. But any one of these would be a very precious "find."

In the ensuing chapters I shall endeavor to give some account of each of Traherne's known writings, treating them in the order of publication. (A complete list is given in the Appendix.)

However, before I can set off on the plain highway of literary criticism, there are two brief but not irrelevant detours to be made.

One concerns Philip Traherne.

The early life of Philip Traherne is completely obscure. We know nothing of him from his infancy at Lugwardine till he came up to London in 1664, some years ahead of Thomas, and was appointed to a minor London curacy. We know that Thomas regarded him with tender affection; and that they corresponded during Philip's absence in Smyrna, where he was appointed a chaplain, talking in their letters of such intimate things as dreams and emotional moods (see Traherne's poem "On Leaping over the Moon").

Of Philip's later life there is ample knowledge. We see him clearly as an excellent Greek and Arabic scholar; but a sick and self-pitying person, rigidly honest, worldly, greatly desiring the favor of the great and servile in seeking it; greatly valuing security—a snob. Shoemaker's son, he took to himself a coat of arms; he changed his name—and posthumously that of Thomas—to the more aristocratic form of "Traheron." After he returned from the Levant, he received a pretty good appointment to Hinton Martel, in Dorset; and if you want Philip in a nutshell, I think you have it in the first entry in the register there:

David the son of John Williams and Agnes his wife was baptised on Munday the 14th of February 1675/6 by Philip Traheron, B.D. Then newly instituted and inducted to the Rectory of Hinton Martel in his Majesty's Right by a Presentation granted him under the Broad Seal of England by the voluntary (tho undeserved) kindness of his Most Noble Friend and Patron Heneage, Lord Finch, Baron of Daventry and Lord High Chancellor of England, bearing Date the 22nd of December 1675.

It was little David Williams's baptism; but there is no doubt who Philip thought was the most important person there!

So Thomas Traherne, in leaving "all my Books . . . to my brother Philip" could hardly have selected a more unsatisfactory literary executor. For Philip did nothing to give the real Thomas to the world. While he took meticulous care to preserve the manuscripts, he did little else. True, he published one as *The Soul's Communion with her Saviour* in 1685; and he prepared for publication, but did not publish, a volume of Thomas's poems. But whatever he published or prepared for publication, he "corrected" with a heavy hand. In my notes to the collected *Poetical Works* I have given in full detail all such "corrections" as can be detected; all I need say now is that as Philip and Thomas were poles apart in outlook, as one would expect from their totally different personalities, Philip either did not understand or did not appreciate the profound truth and beauty embodied in his brother's words. Whatever the reason, too often he destroyed it. Sufficient proof is the instance I used in my

reface to the *Poetical Works*: this is what Thomas wrote in his
poem *The Estate*:

> We plough the very Skies, as well
> As Earth, the Spacious Seas
> Are ours; the Stars all Gems excell.
> The Air was made to pleas
> The Souls of Men: Devouring fire
> Doth feed and Quicken Mans Desire.

And this is what it became with Philip's revision:

> For this the Hev'ns were made as well
> As earth, the spacious Seas
> Are ours: the Stars that Gems excell,
> And Air, design'd to pleas
> Our Earthly part; the very Fire
> For Uses which our Needs require.

The unfortunate thing is that for a great deal of Thomas
Traherne's poetry and that some of his latest and best, only
Philip's version has survived. Of this something more will be
said in the chapter on Traherne's poetry.

My other detour is more personal. In the list of Traherne's
works (see Appendix). I have included the *Meditations on
the Six Days of the Creation*, and also the *Meditations and
Devotions on the Life of Christ*; whereas they were published as
by an anonymous lady, easily recognizable as Mrs. Susanna
Hopton. With the second there is little difficulty. It is merely
a question of whether it is Philip's or Thomas's. My reasons
for reversing the original ascription of authorship for both these
works and claiming them as Thomas's rest on what I believe is
unassailable evidence; an opinion other critics have endorsed.[62]

[62] Helen C. White, in her *Metaphysical Poets*, is an exception. She suggests that
they may be translations of Continental books of devotion. In reply I would say
that Dr. Hickes and Nathaniel Spinckes hailed them as *original* works of great
value; and both these gentlemen were scholars in this field. They were right, I
believe, in all they say of these books, except that they were written by Mrs.
Hopton.

But to set out that evidence is a tedious business. It involves th
circumlocutions and deviations of several of Dr. Hickes'
prefaces; it necessitates lengthy quotations from these preface
and also of parallel passages. I have already summarized an
presented that evidence in my preface to the *Poetical Works*. So
with I hope the reader's indulgence, for the rest of this boo
I shall regard the authorship as proven; referring anyon
who is particularly interested in this point to the preface an
the originals from which I there quote.

To me it was almost as exciting a moment when I discovere
these hitherto unknown works of Traherne as it was for Bertrar
Dobell when at last he had the proof of the authorship of his tw
Traherne manuscripts. I came to it, as he did, by a winding trach

It began by my trying to find out something about on
Jonathan Edwin, who printed both *Roman Forgeries* an
Christian Ethicks for Traherne. On a certain day in 1673, h
registered two books at once: one, *Roman Forgeries*; the othe
Daily Devotions. This was so unusual that it set me at onc
to having a look at this book, *Daily Devotions*. It was at leas
possible that this was a single commission; in other words, tha
Traherne had given him this to print at the same time as th
Roman Forgeries. But when I had looked up the various editior
of this work I found it was ascribed to a Mrs. Susanna Hoptor
That was the first I had ever heard of that lady. I then set abou
finding out all I could about her. A good deal came to ligh
including her supposed authorship of the *Devotions* publishe
after her death by Nathaniel Spinckes for Dr. Hickes. When
studied these, I was astonished and delighted to discover i
Part II the original of Philip Traherne's *The Soul's Com
munion with her Saviour*.

It was becoming increasingly evident that there was som
connection between Mrs. Hopton of *Daily Devotions* an
Thomas Traherne. But as yet I had no proof that they ha
ever met or heard of each other; there was no evident connec

tion beyond the fact that they had lived for a period in Herefordshire within fifteen miles of each other.

The definite proof of a close connection came into my hands in the Probate Office in Llandaff, South Wales, where a helpful and dust-covered official extracted for me from an extremely dusty collection of seventeenth-century wills the original will of Mrs. Hopton. In this will I read with great satisfaction her first bequest; which was to "my beloved niece and godchild, Susanna, wife of Mr. Philip Traheron, Of Wimborne Minster, Dorset."

So, again like Bertram Dobell, what I had long been sure of on literary grounds found more tangible proof. And this discovery in turn gave the key to much in the history of Thomas Traherne, as the earlier chapters in this book have shown.

The general reader of today who desires acquaintance with Traherne's writings is limited to the modern publications of his poetry and of the *Centuries*. The limitation is however less serious than it might be; for in Part II of the *Poetical Works* and in the *Centuries* we have Traherne at his best.

Apart from those still in manuscript, Traherne's other writings are accessible only in their rare first editions—a state of affairs I hope time will remedy. No critical interpretation of a great book can be otherwise than a poor substitute for the book itself. But in the meantime, until these books become more accessible, the following chapters will, I hope, give the reader some impression of the nature and quality of Traherne as a writer. Mr. Robert Allerton Parker's bibliography of contemporary criticism and comment will also serve as a valuable guide to students who wish to pursue further their study of Traherne.

Roman Forgeries, 1673.

SInce we are to consider Traherne's writings in order of publication, order of composition being too much a matter of guesswork, we meet at the outset the work of Traherne's which many of his admirers try to pass over as quickly as possible. *Roman Forgeries* is sometimes regarded as a piece of folly, a waste of energy. Bertram Dobell expressed that view vigorously: "One can hardly help regretting that the book should have been written, for, well as it is done, it might have been done equally well by a writer of far inferior gifts, while it is impossible not to feel that Traherne was wasting his genius in its composition." Others have regarded it as a regrettable, indeed inexplicable, lapse on the part of an otherwise well-mannered dreamer, and felt that the only thing to do was tactfully to ignore it. And indeed the fiction that Traherne was an amiable simple soul who sentimentalized prettily over green fields and children is shattered by this book. Which, I venture to think, is an exceedingly good thing; and for that alone, to get a new and right perspective of the intellectual quality and austerity of Traherne, the book repays our study.

Roman Forgeries is, frankly, what its name implies—a book of religious controversy, and an attack, undisguised and unpalliated, on the Roman Catholic Church. To this we owe the apologetic tone of modern reference; for we are apt today to dismiss all such matters as bigotry and bad manners. Whether in so doing we really display broadmindedness and Christian courtesy, or something not so amiable, need not detain us now. Certainly it would be foolish to allow a preconceived aversion from its subject to deter us from a firsthand and careful study of this work of Traherne's. We need to remember that Traherne himself valued it, and chose it as his first bid for honor as an author. It is worth-while to find out why.

Roman Forgeries, moreover, is no mere exercise in vitupera-
tion. It is an attempt to discuss, in the spirit of impartial historical criticism, the genuineness of certain historical records. It
recognizes that the Christian Church is, among other things, an
institution; and as such it has a history which is a fit subject
for detached historical survey. As the findings of that survey
have a scientific value for the assessment of the comparative
value of competing forms of Church government, it sought to
offer from the scientific side a solution of pressing church problems, which at the time were also problems of politics. *Roman
Forgeries* is from this point of view an interesting example of
the way in which the new scientific spirit of the seventeenth
century was permeating every avenue of men's thought.

On this survey of Church history a long line of scholars was
engaged right through the seventeenth century. Indeed the
work had begun in the previous century. It cannot of course be
pretended that they were, any of them, as detached and impersonal as a modern historian discussing, say, the rise of democ-
racy. They believed too ardently in the value of their researches;
their researches had too intimate a bearing on their personal
and national religion and on current political issues, for that
to be possible. But it remains true that they were actuated by
the scientific spirit, and sought the establishment of fact rather
than the support of faction.

Traherne has his place as one of the succession of scholars
engaged on this work. He made an original contribution that
was valued well into the next century, and gave the next in-
vestigator, Dean Comber, his starting point as well as his title.[63]
In order to appreciate what Traherne achieved, some survey of
the state of religious controversy at that time is necessary. I shall
endeavor to be as brief as possible.

In the long dispute between the "reformed" Catholics of

[63] Dean Comber, *Roman Forgeries in the Councils* (1689). There is a reference
to Traherne in the Introduction.

England and the Roman Catholics, both parties claimed the early records of the Church, the doctors, Fathers, Councils, and canonical scriptures, as their heritage; and broadly speaking, during the latter half of the sixteenth century, battle was joined to show that such and such an ancient authority was for or against some point at issue. Neither impugned the genuineness of the records and authorities to which both appealed. Here and there passages were suspected by writers on both sides. Anachronisms or contradictions were noted. But there was not, for a long time, anything approaching an impartial critical examination of these records themselves. Too much of the medieval spirit survived, even in the seventeenth century, for that to be easily possible. The new discoveries in science, changing men's whole conception of the physical, were unwelcome even to men as mentally adventurous as Donne. And when it came to dealing with matters of church history and the very foundations of practice and belief, most men found the old attitude of uncritical acceptance the only one of which they were capable.

The first great contribution to the cause of critical investigation was the compilation of the *Magdeburg Centuries*. The thirteen folio volumes of this colossal work appeared at intervals from 1559 to 1574, a work inspired by the genius and enthusiasm of Matthias Flacius, and carried out by the united, well organized labor of many hands, at the cost of much travel in search of manuscripts and much incredibly laborious toil. The great achievement of this work was that it put the records into the hands of scholars.

In the history of controversy, the first two pairs of opposed champions, Jewel and Harding, Rainolds and Hart, were almost solely concerned with points of doctrine. The first to begin real criticism of the sources was, by his own claim, William Crashaw, the father of the poet.

My accusation against the Romish Church [he wrote in one of his prefaces] is that they have razed the records, and falsified the monuments of men's writings, altering the bookes of learned men after they were dead . . . taking out such words, sentences, and whole discourses as make against them, and adding the contrarie. . . . So that the crime is no lesse than corruption and forgerie in the highest degree. . . . This wickednesse and treason to the Truth lying thus open to be seene, and yet unseene of the most, it was thought good by my Superiors to have it discovered to the view of the world. . . . To this end I have here begun and broke the ice.

He appealed to his readers to oppose such falsification in the name not only of religion but of scholarship. "If there be in you the worthy qualities and ingenious nature of scholars, you cannot be patient at this injurie done to the reverend Writers who are dead, to yourselves that live, and to learning it self that shall live forever." His love of learning, a love above all partisanship, is one of the finest traits in Crashaw, whose reputation both as a man and as a controversialist has been sacrificed to point a contrast with his more famous son.

After Crashaw, the attack on the Anglican side was made at two points, one group of scholars continuing the arguments on doctrine, the other busying themselves with the question of "Roman Forgeries." With the former we are not concerned. Of the latter the most important was the learned Dr. James. His book was published in 1611, with the title *A Treatise of the Corruption of Scripture, Councels, and Fathers by the Prelates, Pastors, and Pillars of the Church of Rome for Maintaining of Popery and Irreligion*. It is usually alluded to as Dr. James's *Corruption of the Fathers*, and does in fact chiefly concern itself with them, though, as his title shows, he carries the warfare back to the "Councels and Scripture." But his main energies were given to preparing critical texts of Gregory and Cyprian and general exploration of "the Fathers," that "huge Ocean, wilderness, or world of matter, never yet largely treated of, onely pointed out or discovered by others."

With reference to Traherne's book, it is interesting to note that Dr. James looks forward to the day when some student will undertake the special investigation of the Councils that he and his generation were making of the fathers. Traherne was thoroughly familiar with Dr. James's books, as his frequent quotations prove; and it is possible that the following passage determined his own research, especially as this field continued to be neglected. Dr. James had written:

What a pitty is it, since the *Councels* have been so many times published by our *Aduersaries*, to our great disadvantage (as by *Zerlin*, *Crabbe*, *Nicolinus*, *Binius*, and now lately at Rome by *Paul* the fift), that no *Protestant* hath, as yet, taken any paines, if not to restore the bodie of the *Councels* unto its former health and integritie, yet to keepe it from decaying and growing worse and worse. If each Father apart and by himself considered, bee much to be regarded; how much more respect, honour, and reuerence, is due vnto so venerable and graue a *Senate*, and *Synode* of so many hundreths of learned *Bishops, Doctors, and Fathers* of the Church?[64]

If any man shall doubt of the truth heereof, let him compare the last Edition of the *Councells* at Rome with *Binius, Binius* with *Nicolinus, Nicolinus* with *Surius, Zerlin,* or *Crabbe*; and he shall find the latest prints the worst, and the worst accounted best by the *Romanists.*[65]

Traherne's *Roman Forgeries* so exactly carries out this suggestion of Dr. James that one feels sure he had it well in mind when undertaking his work.

Dr. James's *Corruption of the Fathers* and Traherne's *Roman Forgeries*, which is in some measure its direct sequel, are nevertheless separated by a long interval of time. Traherne's book marks the resumption of scholarly interest in this research after a long interruption. For between Dr. James and Traherne lies the long, increasingly bitter and complex strife between the High Anglicans and the sects of Puritanism, and between sect and sect; a strife that culminated in the Civil Wars. In the heat of the quarrel of Protestant with Protestant, the old quarrel of Protestant with Roman Catholic lapsed, or sank into relative unimportance. On the Restoration, with the return to power and

---

[64] *A Treatise of the Corruptions*, Part II, p. 102.

[65] *Ibid.*, Part V, p. 5. ("Zerlin" is a variant of "Merlin.") Cf. also *Centuries* III, 55.

prestige of the "True Reformed Church of England," controversy with Dissent was for the time being ended, and that Church became once more conscious of a great task unfulfilled. The Church of England had from the beginning desired a healing of the breach made at the Reformation. Its leaders were firmly convinced that whereas at a determinable point in history the whole Christian Church had diverged in some particulars from the teaching and practice of the primitive Apostolic Church, they, by the grace of God, had seen the error of their ways and returned to the right path. A certain section of Christianity still wandered astray; but the Reformers believed, with an ardor of conviction difficult even to conceive today, that sufficient energy of argument, sufficient proclamation of what they regarded as invincible truth, would bring about a reunited Christendom. That the breach between the Roman Catholics and themselves should prove permanent would have seemed as incredible as disastrous. Behind seventeenth-century controversy on the Protestant side there is to be heard constantly the note of a not ignoble pity for the "poor seduced Papists."

With the Restoration came again to national consciousness the realization that the victory had not yet been won; and with it the call for volunteers for a new crusade. But the faith and hope of the days of Elizabeth and James I were never again to be recaptured. The apparent fruitlessness of a controversy, now over a hundred years old; the dissension within the Church of England itself and among the Protestants generally; the growing influence of a materialistic spirit; the tone of the Restoration period and its postwar reaction against religion as the chief cause of the late national upheaval—all these combined to dampen the old intense ardor and quench its eager hope of glorious achievement. But the leaders of the Church, though well aware of the difficulties, still called on its members to do battle for the great ideal of a Christendom united in truth.

I know not how it comes to pass [said Stillingfleet in one of his sermons] but so it often happens, that they who are most secure of truth on their side, are most apt to be remiss and careless; and to comfort themselves with some good old sayings, as *God will provide*, and *Truth will prevail*, though they lie still and do nothing towards it; but certainly such negligence is inexcusable, where the matter is of so great importance, the Adversaries so many, and an account must be given shortly in another world of what men have done or suffered for their Religion in this.

Certainly, with the Duke of York a professed Roman Catholic, and Charles II suspected of secret adherence to that faith, it behooved the worldly-wise to "lie still and do nothing." At this juncture Traherne chose to publish his uncompromising *Roman Forgeries* in support of Sir Orlando's defiance of the King.

Roman Forgeries is a small octavo volume. With its "Premonition," "Advertisement to the Reader," "Appendix," and twenty-four chapters of text, all in large print, its pages total no more than 342. Its very appearance is in striking contrast with the bulk and weight of its forerunners; and deliberately so. "It is intended to be little," Traherne wrote, "for the use and benefit of all." It was planned for a different public; not for scholars, as controversial works usually were, but for the average layman, for the less learned clergy and the rank and file of the Church of England. Traherne apparently felt that there was need of a book that in a clear, readable, yet logical and forceful manner would present to such people as these a view of ecclesiastical history which would strengthen their loyalty to the Church of England.

This purpose affected in various ways the method of his writing. Since his book had to be "little," that it might be cheaply purchased, easily read, and conveniently carried in the pocket, he was obliged strictly to limit his subject matter. He wisely chose to exclude the "Fathers at large." He said: "I will not meddle with their *Amphilochius, Abdias, S. Denis*, etc., but keep close to *Records* . . . such as *Apostles Canons, Decretal Epistles*, and *Ancient Councils*; which they have either depraved by altering the Text, or falsified, as it were, by Whole-Sale, in the intire lump: and I shall concern myself in the latter, more

than the former. .'. . I shall not descend into the latter
Ages, but keep within the compass of the first 420 years." By
thus choosing a limited period of time, and that the most primitive and important, and discussing not debatable passages in
genuine records of those times but records wholly spurious,
Traherne secured at once emphasis, clearness, and effectiveness
of attack. Setting aside all minutiæ, all the fine subtleties beloved
of scholars, he painted his picture of deliberate forgery in broad
effective strokes—the only sort of picture likely to be retained
in the memory of the average reader.

For the benefit of the same reader Traherne also adopted a
form of continuous narrative, and in so doing broke new ground.
The older controversialists were chiefly concerned to marshal
facts in incontrovertible argument; their Euclidean demonstra-
tions left no room for the topical allusions, the metaphors from
natural history, the allegorical use of classical myths which
Traherne uses effectively to drive home a point or mask the erudition of his work.

For these reasons, Traherne's *Roman Forgeries*, in comparison with the works of Rainolds and James, is light and easy to
read. Nevertheless, it is a scholarly work; it was recognized as
such in its own day; and the modern reader, driven to consult
encyclopedias and theological dictionaries at every other page,
will find it harder to believe that this was once a popular work
with a considerable sale than that it is erudite. Yet it is true that
the deliberately imposed mask conceals the real depth of its
scholarship, and that in its own day it represented a fresh contribution to the critical study of ecclesiastical records.

The old charge of corruption and forgery made against the
Church of Rome reaches in Traherne's book the fountainhead,
the records of the early Councils. In the history of the controversy we can trace the gradual development of that charge. We
can see it made vaguely and generally, as in Jewel, against certain Fathers; then more definitely, then specifically of certain
passages; next against certain decretal epistles and other docu-

ments; then against the later Councils; and finally, Rome is accused of tampering with the most primitive and precious of all records (Scripture excepted), the canons of the early Councils. Traherne was not the first actually to frame this charge, for Dr. James had included it in his general indictment; but Traherne was in fact the first to marshal evidence to prove it. So serious was the accusation, and so unfamiliar to his readers, that he realized they might well be shocked into incredulity, and into anger with him for making it. ". . . Because it does not easily enter into the heart of man to conceive that men, especially Christians, should *voluntarily* commit so transcendental a crime, the greatness of it makes it incredible to inexperienced people, and renders them prone to excuse the malefactor while they *condemn* the accuser." Sixteen years later, Dean Comber carried Traherne's work some stages further; and in the preface to his book, which is called *Roman Forgeries in the Councils during the First Four Centuries*, he paid a tribute to the value and originality of Traherne's work, and acknowledged his own indebtedness.

Traherne was thus a specialist in a difficult field of scholarship, and sufficiently master of his material to offer an original contribution to knowledge. How much labor, how much reading that entailed, we can only guess. Certainly a bibliography of the books and authors named and quoted from in *Roman Forgeries* would be formidable. Yet it must neglect many whom he would have read—Casaubon for instance—but does not chance to name; and all the Fathers whom it was his purpose then to "meddle with"; all the material ruthlessly rejected that the small amount selected might stand unencumbered; all the wider studies "As may perhaps in another volume be more fully discovered, when we descend from these *first* to succeeding Ages." Reference to books and authors, of course, did not necessarily imply firsthand knowledge in the seventeenth century any more than in our own. The seventeenth century had its own substitutes for the modern digest. But with Traherne, the ease with which he handles his material, the ability to produce the telling fact as he needs it, and the aptness of the quotations are convincing proof of his real familiarity with those "Books of vast Bulk and Price as well of great Majesty and Magnificence" to which he refers. In particular he had made a special study of the great collections of the Councils. He had a detailed knowledge of five of these—Merlin, Crabbe, Carranza, Surius, and Nicolinus—and a good general knowledge of four more. Each collection would involve several volumes folio; and we have his own assurance that "I do not trust other men's information, but mine own eyes; having myself seen the collections of the Councils, and searched into all their compilers for the purpose."

In the light of all this it is no longer remarkable that even in that age of scholastic giants, Traherne's contemporaries— Aubrey, Anthony a Wood, Dr. Hickes, the Master of Balliol— judged him "learned."

The table of contents of *Roman Forgeries* reveals at a glance its chief weakness, a lack of structural unity. Traherne to the end of his short life had never learned to subordinate the parts to the whole, though no other book is so chaotic in arrangement as this first. The first twelve chapters are a compact unit, and it is these that may have been the original nucleus of the work. Here he describes the early Councils, points out the rise of the Papacy in the tenth century, demonstrates that all the forged documents support the papal claims, and argues a deliberate purpose in their manufacture and distribution. He describes the effect of the Reformation in putting libraries of manuscripts and rare books into antipapal hands; and has something to say of the work of the Inquisition and its censorship of books. Then he follows exactly the line laid down by Dr. James, and reviews one by one the great collections of the Councils, showing how their compilers still made use of documents long proved to be forgeries. In each review he notes how far the author adopts the forgeries accepted by his predecessors, how far he differs from them in rejecting certain of these, what he adds to the material, and the genuineness or fraudulence of these additions. Because of the scope of his work, he "passes over many instances," as Dean Comber remarked; but nevertheless he frames along broad lines a telling indictment of the compilers as being "the Pope's sworn Adjutants" rather than impartial historians.

The chapters on the Councils contain all that would be of interest in this book to scholars. What he has to say of the forged Decretal Epistles, and the stories of notorious frauds, would already be well known to them. Traherne is merely repeating these statements for his different audience. But he has selected his material with considerable skill; and with his energy, and his power of pursuing fallacy through twists and turns of argument, and his humorous ironic commentary, there is no doubt it is an effective piece of work.

The main structural link of Chapters 12-24 is the relation of their material to Binius's *Concilia Generalia et Provincialia.*[66] It would almost appear that Traherne made a more detailed study of this Collection subsequently to writing the first section; these last chapters are by way of a commentary on Binius, showing that he either admits certain documents to be forgeries, or makes use of certain other admitted forgeries. The weakness of the two concluding chapters, made up of fragments and by the pettiness of their charges detracting from the grave indictment of the opening section on the Councils, is in part redeemed by the very effective appendix, giving from Baronius the great cardinal's admission of the amount of spurious material unworthily used by his Church, and his warning of the danger of such a course.

Whatever unity there is in the book as a whole is provided by the common topic, forged documents purporting to be authentic, and still more by the personality of the author, whose eagerness to convince and subdue, unflagging energy and intense personal conviction give wings to his logic.

[66] Second edition, nine volumes folio (1638).

As a controversialist, Traherne does not fall short of that high standard of courtesy set by his predecessors. One of them had finely said, "All who agree in the love of the same truth may seek that Truth in love"; and they had striven for a reunited Christendom in that spirit far more often than is generally believed. Traherne completely avoids irrelevant personalities. For the most part he is content to let what he believed were facts speak for themselves. Sometimes we have a dry comment, as when he remarks, "Melchiades was dead before the Donation was made by Sylvester. It is therefore very unlikely that Melchiades should make mention of that Donation"; sometimes he waxes indignant and characterizes some particularly brazen deception as "impertinence"; sometimes he betrays a satisfaction not untinged with malice when he has succeeded in exposing a clever piece of trickery; sometimes he is depressed by the evil of which man is capable for temporal gain. Yet underneath the varying moods an ideal burns steadily, an ideal of a unity of truth to which all lesser truths must accord, truth of scholarship, truth of history, truth of religion.

We can feel the force of this ideal in many a passage, in such as this, for instance, from his conclusion:

The *Councils*, and true Records, we Reverence with all the Honour due to Antiquity. And for that very cause, we so much the more abhor that admixture of Dross and Clay, wherewith their Beauty is corrupted. Had we received the Councils sincerely from them, we should have blest the Tradition of the Church of *Rome* for her assistance therein: but now she loveth her self more than her Children, and the Pope (which is the Church Virtual) is so hard a Father that he soweth Tares instead of Wheat, and giveth Stones instead of Bread. . . . We abhor her practices, and think it needful warily to examine and consider her Traditions.

There is in fact nothing in Traherne's manner of conducting the controversy that need make us regret his entry into it; and nothing that will contradict or render suspect his pleading elsewhere for love as the power which alone can remove the thorns and briars of the world.

When Traherne published his *Roman Forgeries* it was, as we have said, an act of championship for a man as well as a cause. Sir Orlando Bridgeman interpreted ecclesiastical history in the same way as Traherne, and therefore could not honestly do otherwise than oppose any attempt at the reestablishment of Papal supremacy in England.

It was a crucial time in the history of the national Church. No man could foresee the future, with the Revolution of 1688. For the moment, King and court and politicians, leaders of litera- ture such as Dryden, all seemed riding on a wave of pro- papalism which threatened to engulf every obstacle. Traherne, passionately convinced that the Roman Catholic Church was not founded on truth, could not do otherwise than take up arms against it. It is possible that Traherne was mistaken in his judgment; but it is not possible to believe that Traherne wrote *Roman Forgeries* in a mere fit of bigoted spleen. There can be no doubt that he was wholeheartedly convinced of great issues at stake. If we can understand Traherne's sincere amazement that any man could conceive truth of religion in contradiction to truth of history, we can understand why he wrote *Roman Forgeries*.

For the student of Traherne the main interest of *Roman Forgeries* is not its subject matter, nor its polemical power, nor the way it shows the new spirit of rational investigation at work in the forbidden fields of religion, but the revelation it affords of the power and quality of Traherne's intellect. Here alone do we meet Traherne as prosecuting counsel, and a formidable one. By it alone we know the width and scope of his reading, the profundity of his scholarship, his powers of weighing and sifting evidence, of detecting fallacy in argument, of pursuing truth through mazes of bewildering subtleties. Without it, we could never have known on what a solid bedrock of shrewdness, experience, culture, and highly trained judgment he built his philosophy of life, his soaring mysticism. What he has to tell us of his discoveries and experiences in religion are not to be so easily discounted as the delusions of an excitable Celtic brain, when once we have become aware of the power of intellect, the relentless logic so cold, yet so impassioned in pursuit, that went to the making of *Roman Forgeries*.

CHAP. XIII.

Traherne's Share in *Daily Devotions*, 1673.

THe volume entitled *Daily Devotions, consisting of Thanksgivings, Confessions and Prayers. By an Humble Penitent,* which appeared in 1673, proved so popular that by 1689 it was in its third edition, by 1703 in its fifth; in 1717 it was again reprinted as Part III of Spinckes's *Collection* of Mrs. Hopton's works. It has a somewhat curious history, which is of interest not only because Mrs. Hopton was Traherne's friend, but because it seems certain that Traherne received the posthumous fame of its success.

In order to trace its story we have to explore the devious windings of Dr. Hickes's prefaces.

In the preface to *A Second Collection of Controversial Letters*, written in 1710, the year after Mrs. Hopton's death, when Dr. Hickes felt at last free to disclose her identity, he wrote:

I have already spoken of her Diligence in reading Books relating to the *Popish Controversie*, and her making Collections out of them. And I beg leave of the Reader farther to acquaint him, that she was not less studious in reading Books of Devotion and gathering the choicest Flowers out of them. That excellent Book of Devotion without her Name, Entituled *Daily Devotions consisting of Thanksgivings etc. By an humble Penitent* was her collection and Composition, of which she communicated some few Copies in MS., by which means, as I suppose, it came to be printed at *London* for *Jonathan Edwin*, 1673. In the beginning of the Preface it is said "The following Meditations, Praises, Prayers and Confessions were the Devotions of a *learned*, and pious Christian humbly offered up in due Order." This Edition I conceive might be occasioned by a MS. Copy out of a deceased Clergy-Man's Study, who was taken to be the Author thereof.

The italics are intended by Dr. Hickes to suggest that "learned" was a deliberately misleading word as applied to Mrs. Hopton. That Traherne is the "deceased Clergy-Man" who was "taken to be the Author thereof," and to whom Mrs. Hopton communicated a copy in manuscript, is made somewhat plainer by what follows. Still in the same preface, Dr. Hickes is discussing the fifth edition of *Daily Devotions* which appeared in 1703, in Mrs. Hopton's lifetime, and which, with its additions, was evidently the subject of a conversation between Mrs. Hopton and himself. These are Dr. Hickes's words:

For it was afterwards set forth with this Title Page *The Humble Penitent, or Daily Devotions, consisting of Thanksgivings etc. With a preparative Exercise to a good Death.* To which is added *The Sacrifice of a Devout Christian*, or *Preparations to the worthy Receiving of the Blessed Sacrament. By a late Reverend* Divine *of the Church of* England. *The Fifth Edition. London. Printed for Matthew Gilliflower,* 1703. In the beginning of the Preface of this Edition, the words in the former are thus altered: "The following Meditations etc. were the Devotions of a most learned and pious *Divine* of the Church of England . . ." and as to the additional part *The Sacrifice of a Devout Christian*: The true Author of the Book told me it was not of her making, nor did she know by what Hand it was done. Yet there is an Hymn at the end of it which is taken out of the *Lauds for Our Saviour's Office* in the *Devotions in the Ancient Way of Offices* of which I may now tell the world she was the *Reformer*; which confirms me in my conjecture that the *Daily Devotions consisting of Thanksgivings* tho' hers was printed from a MS. of a venerable deceased Clergyman of Herefordshire, with whom she had intimate Correspondence, and who esteemed the admirable *Devotions in the Antient Way of Offices*, as much as she did.

Mrs. Hopton had several clerical friends; but to none of them do the words "of Herefordshire," "deceased," "venerable" (of course in its older meaning), and "with whom she had intimate correspondence" apply, with one exception—

Thomas Traherne. Because of the nature of the friendship between them, there is also no one more likely than he to be in possession of a manuscript copy of her collection of devotions.

Several interesting facts emerge from Dr. Hickes's statements. It is clear that Mrs. Hopton did not authorize the printing of this book in 1673—Dr. Hickes's "conjectures" are obviously derived from Mrs. Hopton's statements. (It is also clear that Traherne was regarded by the writer of the 1703 preface as a "most learned and pious Divine of the Church of England," and that Traherne therefore enjoyed some measure of posthumous fame.) As for the particular additions to that fifth edition, which are reprinted by Spinckes, they are of no importance. They are certainly not Traherne's; and as for the appearance of a hymn from John Austin's *Devotions*, that does not imply, as Mrs. Hopton's remark suggests, that it was pirated from her "reformed" *Devotions*. Mrs. Hopton's "reformed" *Devotions* merely reprint the versions of the hymns that had appeared in the earlier "unreformed" versions. All this additional matter might easily have been added by the bookseller.

The important points for us are that these *Daily Devotions* in their first edition were claimed by Mrs. Hopton to be of her "collection and Composition"; and that they were printed without her authorization and, as she believed, from a manuscript copy she had given to Traherne.

The *Transcripts of the Stationers' Registers* throws a curious light on that conjecture. Under the same date of September 25, 1673, appear the following entries:

Jonathan Edwin. Entred for his copie under the hand of Master Warden Mearne a coppy or booke entituled *Dayly devotions consisting of thanksgivings, confessions and prayers*, in two parts.

Jonathan Edwin: Entred for his copie under the hand of Master Warden Mearne a coppy or booke entituled *Roman forgeries or a true account of false records detecting the counterfeit antiquities of the church of Roome*, by Tho: Traherne, S.T.B.

So the interesting fact stands revealed that *Daily Devotions* and *Roman Forgeries* were registered by the same bookseller on the same day; and that bookseller an obscure one in a humble way of business, who from 1671 to 1679 printed only thirty-eight books, including reprints, and many of these in conjunction with others; who was also the printer of *Christian Ethicks,* and whom Traherne chose rather than someone better known to print and distribute both his books, suggesting that he had some personal motive for the choice. Jonathan Edwin rarely printed two books in one term; and all this, together with Mrs. Hopton's words, makes it pretty plain that the Herefordshire clergyman from whom he acquired *Roman Forgeries* and *Daily Devotions* at the same time were the same person.

Daily Devotions was thus printed from a manuscript in Traherne's possession, but not (as Mrs. Hopton conjectured) from one pirated from his study, but by his own arrangement with Jonathan Edwin.

That Traherne should thus cause to be printed someone else's book without consulting her or ever telling her is at first sight a very unexpected proceeding on his part.

As for his keeping her in ignorance—for it is plain that Mrs. Hopton never knew what the Stationers' Registers reveal to us—that can be accounted for without difficulty. The arrangement with Jonathan Edwin was made in the autumn of 1673. For the ensuing winter, communications would be almost at a standstill; and the following spring and summer were troubled by the illness and death of Sir Orlando Bridgeman, followed quickly by Traherne's own illness and death. A year seems a long time to us; but in the seventeenth century one spoke of a "recent death" that had happened nine years before, or of a "new" book that was twenty years old. It is not at all remarkable that a year—especially so troubled a year—should have thus elapsed without word of the publication having reached Mrs. Hopton.

Since Jonathan Edwin, however, knew of Traherne's part in

procuring this publication, the rumor that this book, though anonymous, was the work of a "learned Divine," and the explicit statement to this effect in the preface to the fifth edition, and the indirect statement in the original preface, are not so puzzling to us as they were to Dr. Hickes.

But the real problem remains; and that is, what justification Traherne could have had for thus publishing without Mrs. Hopton's knowledge or consent what she claims to have been her "collection and composition." Mrs. Hopton's veracity is above question; and so, I believe, is Traherne's moral honesty.

The answer lies in the contents of *Daily Devotions*. By far the greater part consists of extracts from well-known books of devotions. Some of these are acknowledged in their titles, i.e. *A Prayer to the Holy Ghost out of St. Augustine; Confession of Sin out of Bishop Andrews; Deprecations out of Bishop Andrews*. A great deal more is also directly based on other devotions, particularly on Bishop Andrewes's *Schemes of Prayer* (VI, par. 5) and on his *Intercessions for Sunday and for Monday*. The *Thanksgivings for all Persons and Times* in *Daily Devotions* follows very closely Bishop Andrewes's *Thanksgiving* in *A Second Form of Morning Prayer*.

On the other hand, there are paraphrases and selections, and personal additions such as the prayer for her husband and the thanksgiving for the "super-exalted love" of the friend referred to earlier, which are probably all Mrs. Hopton's. But it is beyond doubt, I think, that some of her selections were taken from the prayers and meditations written for their "Society" by Traherne himself.

I am inclined to think on grounds of style and content that parts of the *Thanksgiving for all Persons and Times*; the *Prayer upon the Third Hour*, with its quoted couplet; the *Prayer for the Sixth Hour*, which also has a couplet, and the *Prayers for the Ninth Hour*, are Traherne's, with a good deal of material borrowed from Andrewes. So vast is the field of devotional literature that it is not possible always to be certain of originality; yet many passages in these do echo Traherne's phrases and have his characteristic ring about them, in addition to that mannerism of quoting fragments of verse. Indeed it is practically certain that all the Meditations on the Passion in *Daily Devotions* are based on the similar group in the *Meditations on the Life of Christ:* but whether the recasting is Traherne's or Mrs. Hopton's is not so clear. I am inclined to think, however, that they are Traherne's own. The *Prayers for the Ninth Hour*, the *Additional Devotions for the Evening*, and the *Compline*, are full of phrases which occur in the longer consecutive Meditations. They are condensed on the whole, but there are here and there occasional expansions of some idea which do not correspond with anything in the others, and which seem to indicate that these also are Traherne's.

The hand of Traherne in composing much that is original in *Daily Devotions* is definitely proved by comparing a passage from the *Paraphrase of the Objective Hymn of Praise* with a passage from the *Contemplation*, and with a further passage from the *Centuries of Meditations:*

Daily Devotions: *Paraphrase of the Objective* *Hymn of Praise.*	*Serious and Pathetical* *Contemplation:* *Thanksgiving for the Glory of* *God's Works.*
For the glory of the Sun, which comes forth as a Bridegroom out of his Chamber, rejoycing as a Giant to run his course.	The Sun is as a Bridegroom coming forth of his Chamber, and rejoyceth as a strong man to run his Race,
I praise thee for its Beams, whose light and splendor revives mine eye,	His Beams
	Which enter and revive mine eyes,
beautifies and quickens	Which beautify and quicken
all the Earth,	all the earth,
	. . . .

digesteth Minerals,	They digest Gold,
	Cherish Minerals,
Animates the Air,	Animate the Air,
enlivens Trees	Quicken Trees,
perfects Flowers,	
excites the influences of	Excite the Influences of the very
the Heavens, raiseth	Heavens,
Exhalations, dissolveth	Melt the Waters,
Ice,	Inspire living Creatures,
	Ripen Fruits,
	Perfect Flowers,
	Raise Exhalations,
Causeth the Rivers	Cause the Rivers,
to flow, begetting	Begetting,
propagating and cherishing	Propagating,
all the Creatures, which	Enlivening, ⎫ all those
are the life and beauty	Cherishing ⎬ Creatures
of this habitable World.	Preserving ⎭
	That are the life and beauty of
	my Habitation.

Compare this also with Meditation 8 of the *Second Century:*

It raiseth corn . . . it melteth waters . . . it infuseth sense into all your members, it illuminates the world to entertain you with prospects, it surroundeth you with the beauty of hills and valleys . . . it sprinkleth flowers . . . it concocteth minerals, raiseth exhalations, begetteth clouds, sendeth down the dew and rain and snow, that refresheth and repaireth all the Earth.

This passage from the *Centuries* proves that this association of ideas was natural with Traherne; the exact parallels in phrasing in the other two that he was beyond doubt their common author. It is also clear that the *Contemplation* is based on the *Paraphrase,* and not vice-versa; for the passage is integral in the one and more or less a digression in the other.

If then we may be confident of Traherne's authorship of the *Paraphrase,* particularly on account of that parallel passage, but also on account of a general resemblance to his other writings in thought and style, there is the more likelihood that a certain amount of other work of his occurs in this book. I have mentioned those prayers which seem to me to bear evident marks of his authorship; and there is also one poem that is almost certainly his. We have no reason at all for thinking that Mrs. Hopton wrote verse; it would be somewhat surprising if she did. Dr. Hickes, who says so much of her, never mentions any such talent on her part. Mrs. Hopton's "printed works" were but three; her "reformed" devotions of John Austin, *Devotions in the Ancient Way of Offices,* contained forty hymns, but these were all taken bodily from the Roman Catholic editions of this work. This one poem in *Daily Devotions* (omitting the six in the *Hexameron* which are here ascribed to Traherne) is all we have to show for this supposed talent of hers; and, since Traherne wrote some of the prose of the *Daily Devotions,* it is highly probable that he (who certainly was a poet and writing verse early in life) wrote this poem, poor as it is.

If Mrs. Hopton, who as Dr. Hickes tells us, was "studious in reading Books of Devotion and gathering the choicest Flowers out of them," gathered and arranged and at times expanded all these selections from printed books and from the manuscripts of Traherne, she was perfectly justified in considering that these *Daily Devotions* were "of her collection and composition." On the other hand, if all that is new and original in this book was of his own authorship, Traherne was surely perfectly justified in having the collection printed. Traherne's share in *Daily Devotions* may in fact be considerably larger than one can now be certain of. But of the *Paraphrase* one can feel confident; and to have restored this beautiful prose-poem to its rightful author is not unimportant.

The preface to the first edition with its statement that these were the devotions of a "learned and pious Christian" and that they are "very Rational, Comprehensive, and Emphatical," I take to be the work of the bookseller, and by way of advertisement. He adds the interesting statement that "several learned and holy men have seen and approved" this devotional work. If that be fact and not flourish, it suggests that Traherne may have made use of these devotions in the Bridgeman household, and had perhaps been urged by Sir Orlando to publish them for the use, or as the preface puts it, the "assistance and delight," of a wider circle.

The *Paraphrase*, with whatever else in *Daily Devotions* is Traherne's, belongs in date of composition to his Credenhill period. The connection with Mrs. Hopton proves that; and also the *Paraphrase*, though quieter in mood, has marked affinities both in phrasing and thought with the *Serious and Pathetical Contemplation*. Mrs. Hopton, one imagines, made the collection between 1661 and 1667, and early in this period. The phrase on the title-page, "By an humble Penitent" has possibly a backward reference to her recent return to the Church of England. For she uses the same phrase about herself in her *Letter to a Romish Priest* with particular reference to that event. The date of composition of the *Paraphrase* is thus probably about 1661, and earlier than the *Contemplation*.

CHAP. XIV.

Christian Ethicks, 1675.

ROman Forgeries is the only book of his that Traherne had the satisfaction of seeing in print. With *Christian Ethicks* begins the still-unfinished series of posthumous publications. Traherne died in October 1674, "immediately after this Copy came to the Presses," as its first publisher tells us. The text, lacking his proof corrections, is in consequence full of errata, and the pagination badly confused.

Like the *Centuries of Meditations*, which was probably being written at the same time, *Christian Ethicks* belongs to Traherne's last, most fully developed period; and was written primarily because, in his own phrase, he was "in danger of bursting" with the joy of his discoveries about life.

Till we are satisfied we are so clamorous and greedy, as if there were no pleasure but in receiving all: When we have it, we are so full, that we know not what to do with it: we are in danger of bursting, till we can communicate all to some fit and amiable recipient, and more delight in Communication than we did in the Reception. . . . It is a Principle so strong, that Fire does not burn with a more certain Violence.

The strange vividness of Traherne's writing, its power to move the reader, comes, as all his critics have seen, from this bursting forth of a violent inner energy.

In *Christian Ethicks* Traherne set out, as the title implies, to provide a treatise on human conduct; which seems at first sight a strange vehicle for the expression of ecstatic happiness. In form he followed a well-established tradition, for ever since men have pondered on the meaning of life, they have pondered on the cognate problem of right behavior. Stoic, Epicurean, Platonist, each had offered his solution; and these solutions were but some of the many inherited by Christianity from paganism. But Christianity gave to ethics one important new idea, derived from Judaism, the idea of an external Lawgiver and an external, immutable Law. With this Palestinian tradition, Christian ethics tended to become merely the interpretation of the Law for particular cases. The Law itself was assumed to be contained in the Scriptures and the canons of the Church; its sanctions, divine rewards and punishments and the discipline of the Church.

This quasi-legal view of ethics was current in Traherne's day, though men were seeking a way of escape from its rigidity. Philosophically Traherne rejected it; verbally, though somewhat reluctantly, he accepted it as valid. He failed more conspicuously here, I believe, than anywhere else to rise above the accepted ideas of his day.

In setting out to write a new book on Christian ethics, Traherne was hampered not only by settled tradition but also by contemporary conviction and practice. The seventeenth-century English writers on ethics were all casuists. Jeremy Taylor's *Ductor Dubitantium* (1660), a ponderous eight hundred-page folio, is entirely devoted to applying the Law to particular cases of conscience; so is a great percentage of his other work. So is that still more famous bestseller of the time, *The Whole Duty of Man* (1659). The popularity of such books shows clearly what Traherne's contemporaries understood by "Christian ethics." Traherne's book, written to express his mysticism and to inspire others to follow that way of life, has nothing to do with isolated cases of conscience. His task was "to light the Soul to the Sight of its Perfection." Anyone who bought *Christian Ethicks* expecting the usual exhortations to virtue and the usual and much more entertaining castigations of vice must have been woefully disappointed. Traherne is not even interested in vice. He is Beauty's lover, he has "gone in unto Felicity, and enjoyed her beauties, and come forth her perfect lover and Champion." And so, as he says, "I do not speak much of Vice, because I am entirely taken up with the Worth and Beauty of Virtue." But such abstention did not make for popularity in a seventeenth-century book on ethics much more than it does in a modern novel.

Aristotle, though waning in repute, was still diligently studied in the universities. Traherne was familiar with his works, quotes from him on occasion, and differs from him respectfully when differ he must. It was from Aristotle he took that definition of felicity which he made the keystone of his own ethic: "Felicity is the Perfect Fruition of a Perfect Soul, acting in Perfect Life by Perfect Virtue." Aristotle, he says, "never heard . . . of sitting down in the Throne of God, yet by a lucky Hit (if I may so say) fell in point blank upon the Nature of Blessedness."

But "the Heathens, who invented the name of Ethicks, were

very short in the Knowledge of Man's End"; and for Traherne that wavering or mistaken idea of the purpose of life invalidates all pre-Christian philosophy. It is the Christianized Aristotelianism of Aquinas, and the Christianized Platonism of St. John that Traherne found acceptable.

In *Christian Ethicks* Traherne is particularly indebted to Aquinas. This is interesting, as in England (though not on the Continent) the Reformation had seen a strong reaction against both the teaching and the scholastic methods of that great medieval thinker, whose *Summa Theologica* had long dominated theology and ethics; and by Traherne's day he had ceased to influence the thought of Englishmen. Yet Traherne turned to him, and not only read but inwardly digested the scholastic subtleties of argument of all those ponderous Latin folios, as his use of the material in *Christian Ethicks* amply proves. Incidentally this affords another instance of Traherne's intellectual capacity and wide scholarship.

Traherne's indebtedness to Aquinas is very great; yet it is equally true that *Christian Ethicks* is no mere epitome of *Summa Theologica*. The scientific framework is largely borrowed, but even here there are some significant differences. Virtue is for Traherne not only "a right and well ordered Habit of Soul" but "a right and well ordered Habit of Soul by force of which we attain our Felicity." He will not consider the virtues in isolation; he sees the part always in relation to the whole, the whole being for him mysticism as a way of life. He links each virtue with all the virtues—"Love without Discretion is a mischievous Thing; Love without Prudence an Helpless Thing; Love without Courage a feeble and cowardly Thing."

Judged as a scientific textbook *Christian Ethicks* is hopelessly bad, full of digressions, incomplete, confused; but as a demonstration of the splendor of holiness it is another thing. It is one of the finest books of its kind in English literature.

In the more important matter of ideas, Traherne's divergence from Aquinas is still more marked. On the freedom of the human will, and on whether intellect or love is the more potent for the attainment of happiness, Traherne and Aquinas hold opposite views; with the result that philosophically their difference outweighs their resemblance.

Traherne's Christian Platonism is so essential a part of his thinking at all times that it finds no more marked expression in *Christian Ethicks* than in the *Centuries* or poems or anything else he wrote (*Roman Forgeries* alone excepted); and any discussion of the features of that Platonism is better postponed till it can include the whole field of his work. There are several long quotations in *Christian Ethicks* from Hermes Trismegistus, and considerable use of the imagery of Plato and Plotinus. Traherne's general classical reading also provides him with a store of illustrations, always used aptly and with some of their Elizabethan liveliness.

In his preface Traherne refers to two books on ethics then enjoying great popularity, the anonymous *Whole Duty of Man*, and Pierre Charron's *De la Sagesse*. The latter is too completely alien in tone and temper to be regarded as contributing anything to *Christian Ethicks* except insofar as its intellectual scepticism was a challenge to intellectual faith to proclaim itself. The *Whole Duty of Man* might also be regarded as a challenge; for though it is very different in its sound orthodoxy from Charron's book, which is materialism wearing a cloak of religion in conscious mockery, yet Traherne knew there was much more in the adventure of holy living than its unknown author had discovered. There is in the *Whole Duty* not a spark of Traherne's passion to lift either thought or language into beauty; and this very factor made for its popularity. The nation had had its fill of religious passion. Obedience, not individual experimenting, suited the mood of the burnt child. It is characteristic of Traherne that he was consciously stirred by its deadness to write such a book as *Christian Ethicks*, a book explicitly based on personal experience—"from the knowledge I gained in the nature of *Felicity* by many years earnest and diligent study"; a book which makes felicity the goal of life, and felicity to be no less than the union in love of the individual soul and God; a book set on fire with a flame of devotion the other never knew.[67]

Of the books that influenced Traherne in writing *Christian Ethicks* two more must be mentioned—Barrow's *On the Duty and Reward of Bounty to the Poor* (1671) and Hobbes's *Leviathan*. In Barrow, Traherne found a fellow-enthusiast; he copied long extracts from him into his commonplace book, and the prose style and the tone are so like Traherne's own that they have misled one critic[68] and the extracts have been published as Traherne's. The mistake is a natural one, for the resemblance is striking. Traherne's debt to Barrow's sermon is clear in *Christian Ethicks* whenever he is discussing liberality and charity as almsgiving.

Traherne's direct references to Hobbes are interesting. They show us that *Christian Ethicks* was also intended as a refutation of Hobbes's teaching, and they show us Traherne in a rare mood of wrath. From 1651, when the publication of the materialistic *Leviathan* caused such a storm that Hobbes believed his very life was in danger, every new Christian book on ethics dealt in some fashion with Hobbes's central ideas; and so does Traherne's *Christian Ethicks*. With Hobbes, man is a strong and selfish animal; self-love is his only principle, and material welfare his goal. His natural desire is not peace and brotherhood, but domination. To Traherne, a thinker who proclaimed so base a view of human nature, and who was so sceptical of morality, was an enemy of the whole human race. In attacking

---

[67] Traherne must have had the *Whole Duty* at hand when writing *Christian Ethicks*; for he took pages 287-292 bodily from the other book (I, 29, 33, 36-38). As the book appeared, there is no acknowledgment of the borrowing. But as in *Roman Forgeries* Traherne is careful to indicate authorities, the omission here is probably a printer's error. In spite of this lengthy quotation, Traherne owes little to *The Whole Duty* except the stimulus of irritation!

[68] An article by J. W. Proud, "Thomas Traherne," *Friends' Quarterly Examiner*, January 1917.

Hobbes, he carries the war into his territory. He agrees that self-love is the mainspring of human action; but denies that Hobbes understands what self-love is. In a fiery passage of shrewd analysis and vigorous attack Traherne lays bare the poverty of Hobbes's narrow materialistic definition; then, taking wing, shows us height upon height of the soul's self-love till we reach the final peak where self-love and selflessness are one—and "my Love to my self, being thoroughly satisfied, turns into the Love of God, and dies like a grain of Corn in the Earth to spring up in a new and better form, more glorious and honourable, more great and verdant, more fair and delightful. . . ." Traherne was fighting for a cause in *Christian Ethicks* quite as definitely as in *Roman Forgeries*.

Christian Ethicks owes something of its richness and solidity to the fact that it sprang from a mind deeply stored with the learning of books. It owes still more to the fact that Traherne was an original thinker whose borrowings are no dead mosaic of literary reminiscences but are transmuted in the crucible of his mind to something new and alive. Traherne is almost miraculously free from the shackles of his age—from Puritanism, from medievalism, from scepticism. To Traherne's astonishing originality of thought and power of intellect we have as yet paid scant critical tribute. These qualities in Traherne make for the vigor and charm of *Christian Ethicks*, as of everything else he writes.

And finally, *Christian Ethicks* owes not a little to the fact that its writer had been for some six years a member of a great political household in London.

That circumstance is of more importance than might first appear. But *Christian Ethicks* and the *Centuries of Meditations* owe so much to it that one might almost say that if Traherne had remained in Credenhill he could never have written them. He had poise and a breadth of outlook when he came to write these books that he owed in no small degree to the richness of his contact with life. He had had some eight years of intense study in the sheltered peace of Oxford; years of mental and spiritual emancipation but nevertheless of contact with books rather than with men and movements. This had been followed by some six years of life as the rector of a tiny village in remote Herefordshire; again years of fruitful growth, of communion with nature and of intense spiritual discipline; but again, years of isolation. Then he came to London, to live in the household of the great Lord Keeper of the Seal; and *Christian Ethicks* shows on every other page by some allusion or apt illustration that Traherne's eager spirit went out to the world of men and art with as vivid an enjoyment as it had done to the natural beauty of Herefordshire.

Traherne's philosophy, though he himself gave us no formal exposition of it, was completely thought out. The type of intellect that wrote *Roman Forgeries* would permit no amorphousness or loose ends. Traherne's personal life was also his philosophy translated into practice, and by the time he wrote *Christian Ethicks* conflicts had ceased. Thus when everything he thought and everything he felt was in accord with a larger, clearly perceived design, everything he wrote, since he wrote sincerely, must share that unity; and so strong is the force of this, that the lack of coordination between the chapters in *Christian Ethicks* and the weakness of structure are hardly perceptible.

Christian Ethicks is therefore a many-sided book. It is a scientific discussion of morality and an analysis of the major "good habits," with a demonstration of their importance in a rational scheme of life. It is an attack on a materialistic philosophy, and an eloquent counterproclamation of the reality and value of the spiritual. It is an attractive exposition of what Traherne himself half humorously called "Christian Epicureanism," a plea that man was meant to enjoy all the good material things of life; that felicity, if it transcends, yet also includes the joys of the senses. It is further (since Traherne says that you cannot see even a grain of sand truly until you have first seen God, nor perform the simplest act of ordinary life wisely till

you know what life means) one of the most brilliant and per-
suasive pleas we possess for mysticism as the rational way of
living.

Principally, it is autobiography of the truest kind; it is the
intimate record of one who in the things of the spirit had reached
"Journey's End"—the phrase is his own—and who wrote this
book for others "to encourage them to Travel, to comfort them
in the Journey."

CHAP. XV.

A Serious and Pathetical Contemplation, 1699, and *Hexameron,* 1717.

THe attractive little book of devotions, *A Contemplation of
the Mercies of God,* or, to give it once again its whole unwieldy title, *A Serious and Pathetical Contemplation of the
Mercies of God in several most Devout and Sublime Thanksgivings for the Same,*[69] appeared anonymously in 1699, under the
aegis of the famous and learned Dr. Hickes, Mrs. Hopton's
friend. It is a slender duodecimo, expensively produced, well
bound, well printed on thick paper, and embellished with an
engraved frontispiece. The two groups of Thanksgivings, which
probably represent work done at different times, are preceded by
two prefaces. The second is a brief character sketch of the author
with a minimum of biographical facts, written, it would seem,
by some Credenhill parishioner—possibly by Mrs. Hopton herself; and for all its meagerness it proved of inestimable value
for the identification of Traherne as the author of the Dobell
manuscripts. The first preface is in the form of a letter from

[69] Someone other than the author must have been responsible for this eulogistic
title. Traherne had the habit of leaving titles to be added last, as the spaces in the
manuscripts of the *Centuries* and the *Book of Devotions* show. Probably the same
thing happened with the manuscript from which this book was printed.

Dr. Hickes to the bookseller who was printing these thanksgivings. In this letter, Dr. Hickes alludes to Mrs. Hopton as the one who had recommended the publication of this *Contemplation*, and pays on his own behalf a generous and practical tribute to its devotional quality. "Send me twenty copies of the Book well-Bound," he wrote. "I believe I shall have occasion for a greater number, for the Book in everything answers to its title; and as I have received great delight and benefit in reading it, so I shall recommend it to persons of parts and pious inclinations.'

The first group of thanksgivings consists of a complementary set of seven—*Thanksgiving for the Body, for the Soul, for the Glory of God's Works, for the Blessedness of God's Ways, for the Blessedness of His Laws, for the Beauty of His Providence, for the Wisdom of His Word.* Then comes a short *Appendix to the Former Thanksgiving*, obviously by its title a later addition. The eighth, *Thanksgiving for God's Attributes*, differs considerably in form from the earlier ones, being much more regular; and the final *Thanksgiving and Prayer for the Nation* shows a marked change of subject. The impression given is that the first seven were conceived and written as a whole; and that the last three are miscellaneous additions.

Many circumstances point to the conclusion that the *Contemplation of the Mercies of God* is early work of Traherne's, written before he went up to London. The type of heroic couplet occurring in two of the poems in this book offers strong evidence of this. In later work, for instance in "Thoughts" of the Dobell manuscript, there will be found a considerable proportion of run-on lines and couplets, with remarkable dexterity in the use of this meter, but here we have almost exclusive use of end-stopped lines and couplets.

We can the more safely date the poems of the *Contemplation* since exactly the same rigid handling of the couplet occurs in the poem "Moderation," of which two fragments are preserved, and which Traherne speaks of as "made long ago."[70] Indeed, it is possible from their subject matter that the two sets of couplets in the *Contemplation* are further extracts from that early poem. Again, the unrestrained use of parallel phrases and the piling up of synonyms in the *Contemplation* indicates that this is early work. Here this is no defect, the rapid pouring forth of words perfectly suiting the pouring forth of feeling. But as Traherne grew older his critical judgment led him to curb what was always a natural tendency. How deliberately the prose of the *Centuries* has been pruned the deletions in the manuscript prove.

There is the further circumstance that the manuscript of the *Contemplation* was in Mrs. Hopton's possession, and not in Philip Traherne's, to whom passed all those books and papers Traherne had with him at the time of his death. Lastly, the final thanksgiving of this collection is dated by its contents as post-Restoration and evoked by serious national disasters, by, one would say, the Great Plague and the Great Fire of London of 1665 and 1666. If we may accept that the last by position was the last written, then we may date the whole series as composed before 1666, presumably between 1661 and that date. For the student of Traherne it is part of the value of this book that it shows us Traherne at another stage of his development than does *Christian Ethicks* or the *Centuries*.

The form of these devotions is unusual. The printer, fortunately for us, has been careful to reproduce the pattern of words as it occurred in the manuscript, and there can be no doubt that Traherne took considerable trouble with the actual design of his writing, that is, the pattern presented to the eye by the arrangement of words and lines. A study of his manuscripts shows that very clearly. There is an easily accessible instance of it in the facsimile of the two stanzas from the poem "Wonder" reproduced in the *Poetical Works* (Dobell, 1932). Endings as well

[70] See *Centuries* III, 18-21; and the same poem in *Christian Ethicks*, introduced by the phrase, "Take it in verse made long ago upon this occasion."

as beginnings of lines are designed to conform to an intricate pattern of varying lengths; once in copying, Traherne made a mistake, made the sixth line of the stanza pair with the fourth instead of the second. He noticed it when he had written two words; so he carefully erased them and began his line again at the right place. In the seventeenth century, poet and reader alike derived pleasure from this patterning; hence Herbert's *Easter Wings*, and hence the popularity of the long irregular stanza. And in these thanksgivings Traherne indulges that pleasure to the full. Nor is it merely an extrinsic charm; the groupings of words, and the length of lines, do determine emphasis, and thereby rhythm, with at times undeniable beauty of effect. The following might be taken as an example:

> For inflaming my Soul with the Thirst of Happiness;
> For shewing me its Objects, and the manner of Enjoying them;
> For causing me to prefer Wisdom above hidden Treasure and
> to search for her as for Gold and Silver.
> I Bless and Praise thy Holy Name.
> The Desire satisfied, is a Tree of Life.
> Had I never thirsted, I should never have valued, nor enjoyd,
> WISDOM.
> I know by experience, that she is better than Rubies,
> And all the things I can desire, are not to be compared with her.
> She maketh me a possessor of all thy Joys;
> Bringeth me to the Store-house of thine everlasting Riches;
> Seateth me in Paradice,
> Surroundeth me with Flowers,
> Yea with all the Delights in the Garden of God.[71]

In these thanksgivings Traherne uses sometimes prose, sometimes verse, but chiefly what Dr. Hickes described as "numerous periods . . . of the *freer* sort," that Bertram Dobell aptly compared with Walt Whitman's verse. With its flexibility, and its effect of rhythmic chanting, it is a well-nigh perfect medium for the expression of triumphant exultation, the dominant mood of these thanksgivings.

[71] *Christian Ethicks*, p. 33.

There are also three poems, two, already referred to, in heroic couplets, and one in stanzaic verse.

The subject matter of these thanksgivings is indicated by the titles I have quoted; though Traherne is no respecter of titles, and swoops off on wide circles of his own at times. It is noteworthy that certain ideas which will rarely be found in other writings of the day, and which were to be characteristic of Traherne to the end, already find their expression here. What other devotional writer, for instance, would do as Traherne does in the first of these, and write a special *Thanksgiving for the Body?* It is difficult for us to realize how powerful the old medieval spirit still was in the second half of his century, and how strongly many pious men condemned the growing interest in the physical world which gave birth to modern science. Traherne's attitude clearly reveals him as one of the more enlightened thinkers of the day. He was enthralled by the wonder of the body as a piece of marvelously organized machinery. The newly born sciences of anatomy and physiology were bursting the bonds of dead tradition; and Traherne was caught by the excitement of that release. One fine passage from these devotions which illustrates this enthusiasm has been printed by Bertram Dobell in the *Poems of Thomas Traherne.*

But Traherne's exaltation of the body does not end with the thought of it as an "organized wonder." To that is linked the still vaster thought that it is the focus and the sole reason for existence for the whole physical universe. Much of Traherne's later thought on its significance already appears in this *Contemplation*—such as the idea that all the economic and social relationships of men depend on the ultimate fact that they possess bodies which must be served; and also the idea which underlies some of his most mystical poetry, that God Himself and all spiritual beings enter into the joys of the material world only by the mediation of the material bodies of men.

When Traherne turns to the soul, in his second thanksgiving, and throughout all the series, one finds the same elaboration of

the theme, the same richness of associated ideas, the same proof
of profound meditation; together with a joy in the exploration
and delineation of these new vast kingdoms of the spirit, a triumphant consciousness of his own power, that he will never again
wholly recapture. "I am able to do more than my Soul durst once
attempt to imagine," he cries on one occasion, exultingly.

These thanksgivings are intensely personal. One cannot
imagine they were intended for the use of anyone but himself,
so intimately are they the fruit of his experience and the cry of
his own needs. Because of that they have much to tell us of
Traherne himself. They tell us of little simple things, of his
liking for his fellows ("Thou, Lord, hast made thy Servant a
sociable Creature, a lover of company") and that he thanked
God for his "Household stuff—Books, Utensils, Furniture";
they also let us share so intimate a thing as his own ideal for
himself as a priest. This I think is one of the most beautiful passages in these devotions:

> O my Lord, make me like thee!
>   O Son of God,
>   In my love to Sinners . . .
> Let my love be Genuine, Divine, and Free.
>   And for the delight I take,
>   To rescue and save them,
>   To exalt and crown them,
>   Let me pour out my self,
>   My spirit, Soul and Blood,
> My Time, Labour, Health, Estate, Life and all.
>   O 'tis Heavenly, Divine, Angelical!
>   The glorious Victory over all the World
> Is love continuing beyond unkindness:
>   Fill my love with the Zeal of thine.
>   Like thine, O Lord, I desire it should be;
>   A flame of thirsting Industry,
>   Out-living hatred . . .

O my God, do not deny me.

Forgive my former ⎰ Flatness
　　　　　　　　⎨ Intermission
　　　　　　　　⎱ Deadness:

Let me love every Person as Jesus Christ . . .
O learn me this, and the whole is learned.
Learn me this, the Divine Art,
And the Life of God.

In one respect these thanksgivings differ markedly from *Christian Ethicks* and the *Centuries*. There is exultant joy in them, but there is not the steady shining radiance, the perfect serenity of the later works. There is a kind of fitfulness, a tendency to drop suddenly into moods of contrition and shame for past misdeeds. That perhaps is because the memory of his unregenerate days was still sharply present when he wrote them; and though the sense of escape heightens the note of exultation, the past still has power to cast its shadows.

If any one theme of thanksgiving predominates throughout this collection as a whole, it is the glory of the universal brotherhood of man in their universal sonship of God; and it is this idea which gives to the last one, *A Thanksgiving and Prayer for the Nation*, its strange quality. This thanksgiving is unlike anything else that Traherne wrote. We often see him gladly conscious that he was born in a civilized country to enjoy the blessings of law and order; but nowhere but here does his love of England as England find expression, or his feeling of oneness with her in times of great suffering break forth into such a cry of pain. The tone of urgency and suffering is fully explained by the disasters that speedily ended the hysterical rejoicings of 1660—the Great Plague, the Fire, the shameful defeats in war, the worthlessness of the King on whom such hopes had been fixed.

Traherne, who had surrendered as completely as any man can the sense of material ownership, yet had an extraordinarily strong sense of spiritual possession; the people of England are *mine*, he cries, and what shall I do if these my spiritual treasures

be taken from me? He pleads with God for the lives of his countrymen in words that sound strangely prophetic of modern war,
and move us no less by the quality than the passion of their love.

> Yet shall I be the sufferer in my people's ruin,
>> Shall nettles grow up in our pleasant Palaces,
>>> Brambles in our Treasuries,
>> Owls and Satyrs dwell in our Temples,
>> Briars and Thorns in the rubbish of our Stones!
> O my Lord, let me rather be blotted out of the book of
the living, than be so bereaved,
>> Robbed of my Children,
>>> Spoiled of my Glory . . .
> O Lord, the children of my people, are thy peculiar Treasures
Make them mine, O God, even while I have them!
>> My lovely companions, like *Eve* in *Eden*!
So much my Treasure, that all other wealth
>> is without them
>>> But Dross and Poverty.
> Do they not adorn and beautify the World,
>> And gratify my Soul which hateth solitude! . . .
> Destroy not my people, for how then
Shall I walk in the light of thy Countenance?
>> Should I not rust, O Lord, and grow dull and heavy! . . .
>> Need I not Spurs, Wings, Enflamers?
>> O my God, how often should I die,
>> Were it not for these, thy Glorious Hosts?

In none of the multitude of English books of devotion will be
found a prayer for the preservation of the nation in the least like
this; for no one, except perhaps Blake, has ever had Traherne's
regal sense of divine sonship, or a love of humanity grounded
quite as his.

If any literary sources are to be sought for this *Contemplation*
of Traherne's, they may chiefly be found in Bishop Andrewes's
Devotions and in the Authorized Version of the Bible. To Andrewes may be traced on occasions the phrasings and more
particularly the method of cataloguing and of exhaustive treatment. As for the Bible, Traherne was so steeped in it, that the

apposite text or illustration was instantly at hand, and its language is blended inextricably with his own. The rhythm of the Psalms largely determined Traherne's prose-rhythm, and their device of varied reiteration his own reiterations. This will be evident even from the few extracts already given in this chapter.

But the greatest quality of these devotions, the quality that caused the critical Dr. Hickes to read them with delight and benefit, and evoked the epithet "sublime" in their present title, is not to be conveyed by the most liberal use of quotation. Nothing but these prose-poems themselves can give us their swift-soaring flight; nothing but themselves can show us what strange love songs are these and how great a lover is this Traherne, whose beloved is not of this earth.

Hexaneron, or, *Meditations on the Six Days of the Creation*, was published by Nathaniel Spinckes in 1717 as Part I of his *Collection of Meditations and Devotions*. Of all Traherne's works it is the most symmetrical, and in many respects the least satisfactory.

In form it consists of a single group of meditations, closely linked in subject, closely paralleled in treatment. There are for once no appendices, no miscellaneous additions. The six meditations, one for each day of the Creation, stand complete, each strictly confined to the events of that day as recorded in Genesis, yet moving in stately progress up and on to the grand culmination of the Sixth Day, the Creation of Man. Each begins with the appropriate verse from Genesis, and develops into a series of detailed eulogies of the wonder and beauty and serviceableness of the thing created, all fields of knowledge being drawn upon to provide the matter; each new aspect displayed is rounded off with a prayer of aspiration; and each ends with a set of verses. Nothing else of Traherne's has such elaborate treatment or such strict observance of a structural plan.

And nothing else of Traherne's has so little power to delight the modern reader. The cause of its failure is implied in what has already been said of its form. The *Contemplation* and the *Centuries* share a quality which has given to the great books of religion their enduring appeal, generation after generation finding afresh in them the satisfaction of its own particular needs. Such books deal with the timeless and the permanent in human nature. But the *Hexameron*, fine as some of the superstructure may be, is built on an intellectual conception no longer tenable. As for all medieval scholars, as for his own age and the next, as for Milton, so for Traherne the record of Creation in Genesis is history, and its statements facts of science. The modern reader is sundered from Traherne's literalness of interpretation by all the scientific discoveries of the centuries between, by the very hypothesis of evolution, by a new conception of the relationship between religion and science; in these meditations he therefore feels himself taken into an unreal world of myth. The unreality unfortunately tends to infect whatever there is of more enduring value there.

Internal evidence points to an early date of composition for these meditations. Like the *Contemplation*, and the *Meditations* to be considered in the next chapter, they belong in all probability to the Credenhill period (1161-1667), as is also suggested by Mrs. Hopton's possession of the manuscript. They were written late enough in Traherne's life for the main features of his philosophy to be clearly defined; Traherne will have little more ever after to add to what he has written in the sixth of these meditations on the divine capacity of human nature. But they are also young enough for their experience to be drawn more largely from books than life; and to share with the *Contemplation* a poignancy of remorse for a not-too-distant period of "Wantonness and Avarice," and to feel not wholly secure in the present.

The erudite bookishness of these meditations links them to *Roman Forgeries*. Only a student who had read widely in many fields could have assembled so effortlessly the wealth of illustration here made use of. All the most apposite Scriptural references to bird and beast, curious scholastic lore of many kinds, all the sciences, that scholastic symbolism which saw most things of nature as premeditated sermons—all these are woven into their texture with a patient elaboration and fertility of resource which bespeaks true devotion as well as wide learning. One might compare the result to some piece of ancient stitchery richly wrought with quaint and charming devices.

These meditations are more plentifully besprinkled with paradox and conceits than any other work of Traherne's. He has always a tendency to paradox and to the inverted phrase even in his most serious moments, and in his latest and maturest work. Traherne is of Donne's century, and could not wholly escape the influence of the fashions he set. So in this *Hexameron* one finds teeth described as a "Port-Cullis of Pearl"; St. Peter's tears of penitence as the rainwater which made him clean; other penitential tears as a sort of celestial fire engine—"Tears are the best Engines and Water-works to quench the Devils Fires." (Tears seem to have an irresistible tendency to provoke these excesses!) But fashionable conceit and a passionate fervor of sincerity are rarely compatible; and so, on the whole, Traherne is free from the worse forms of that than prevalent literary disease. Even in the *Hexameron* the lapses are but occasional; and they cease entirely whenever, as at the close of the sixth meditation, the emotion deepens and the prose takes from it a new note of beauty.

For these *Meditations on the Creation* are not wholly bookish and artificial. There was on Traherne's part too much genuine love of the beauty of the created world, and too personal a feeling of gratitude to the Creator, for that to be possible. One feels the touch of life even in so simple a sentence: "What a delicate Sight is it to behold the Corn in its first springing Verdure, in its encreasing Growth, thick-bearded, strong-headed, and at last full-blown and bending itself in its Fullness to us, and for us!" There is less rapture in the *Hexameron* than in the *Contemplation*, but there is the same energy; the same lofty Platonism and sense of the magnificence of life, and the same orientation of the whole mind to the things of religion. In spite of all the cumber of pseudo science, these vital qualities of Traherne's personality still make their warmth felt.

As has been mentioned, each of these six meditations is followed by a poem. Four of these poems are in heroic couplets, two in stanzas of simple form. The couplets are of the stopped variety as in all Traherne's early work in this meter; and greater complexity of stanza pattern also belongs to his later period. The poems on the whole are poor, and the influence of Sylvester's famous translation of Du Bartas's *Weekes and Workes* makes for an unusual number of classical allusions and conceits.

The two stanzaic poems have a more characteristic ring of Traherne than those in heroic couplets. Each deals with a favorite subject—one, the sun, the other, the glory of man. The first suggests many aspects of the manifold symbolism of the sun which Traherne never wearies of developing; the second has all his reverence for the godlike potentialities of humanity.

What Spinckes, writing of this *Hexameron* in his preface, says of it is interesting in many ways. He gives a brief review of other *Hexamerons* known to history—those of Prudentius and St. Ambrose in the fourth century, of St. Basil and Anastasius in the sixth, and that of Bede as the only other in English literature. In so doing, he probably gives us Traherne's models, if he needed other than Sylvester. He then proceeds to a warm eulogy of this new *Hexameron* by Mrs. Hopton, for so he believed it to be; and this praise from a man of Traherne's own century, and a scholar and a critic, may help us, when approaching these meditations as devotions, to separate the devotional wheat from the scientific chaff. Approaching them as literature, no qualifications are needed; our business is then to understand, not evaluate, the author's mental attitude; and certainly English literature contains no other song of Creation comparable with Traherne's.

Meditations and Devotions on the Life of Christ, 1717.

THough these *Meditations and Devotions on the Life of Christ* were published by Spinckes in 1717 as Mrs. Hopton's, and from a manuscript in her own handwriting, there is no possibility that she was the real author. What we have in Spinckes's edition is the original version of that work written for Mrs. Hopton's use, part of which in a condensed form had already been published by Philip Traherne in 1685, as *The Soul's Communion with her Saviour*. We possess in this work a most important addition to the prose writings of Traherne, important in itself, and particularly important in the light it throws on Traherne's stages of development as a mystic.

These meditations constitute an even larger body of prose than the *Meditations on the Six Days of the Creation* which I have also added to the list of works by Traherne. In Spinckes's edition they occupy 228 pages of print, and number more than eighty thousand words.

They fall into five main groups: the first group consists of meditations on the principal events in the early life of Christ (the Incarnation, Nativity, Circumcision, and the like); the second, meditations on the Sermon on the Mount, and on the Lord's Prayer; the third, a large group on "Christ's Preaching, Works, and Miracles," taking these in order as they are recorded in St. Matthew's Gospel, Chapters VIII to XXV, and then, in the words of a note, "digressing from St. Matthew to take in most of the remarkable things out of the other Evangelists which St. Matthew mentions not." In this digression, Luke VII to XXI and John I to XXI are traversed. There are no meditations based on St. Mark; but from these other three gospels a comprehensive survey is given of the ministry of Christ, together with devotional and personal applications in the manner that will be shown by extracts quoted later. The fourth group has a single theme, the Passion, and is practically one long meditation, the longest in the whole collection; the fifth is a series of shorter meditations on the Burial, Descent into Hell, Resurrection, and Coming of the Holy Ghost. Thus the whole work centers on Christ, and is a most interesting amplification of Traherne's adoration and personal love of Jesus of which a brief but vivid glimpse is given in the *First Century*.

The *Meditations on the Life of Christ*, it must be confessed at once, bear very little general resemblance to the *Centuries of Meditations*; but the latter are hardly meditations in the usually accepted sense of the word. The *Meditations on the Life of Christ* were intended, as Philip Traherne has told us, as "brief aspirations on the Gospel History"; and are strictly bound by that history. Their purpose is to recall some event in the life of Christ and to make a personal application of its teaching; and in consequence, there is a far greater proportion of penitence for sin, and a far greater amount of insistence on discipline, than in any other of Traherne's works. Yet those meditations on the Cross which occur in the *First Century* show that contrition for sin was certainly a part of Traherne's religious life, for all its joy; and since he lived by rule, and kept the fasts of the Church and the hours of prayer, he was no stranger to the life of mortification and must have exercised a most rigorous physical self-control.

It is not an accident that his later works reveal so little of this; they do reveal something of it, enough to prove its existence; but by the time he wrote his greatest books he had proved his own words in *Christian Ethicks*: "All the Difficulty is in the Beginning. Vertues in the beginning are like green fruits, sour and imperfect, but their Maturity is accompanied with sweetness and delight. It is hard to acquire a vertuous Habit at first, but when it is once gotten, it makes all Virtue exceeding Easie; nor Easie alone, but Happy and delightful."

If these *Meditations on the Life of Christ* were written when the habit was in the process of formation, it fully explains the greater proportion of those elements of difficulty which are almost imperceptible in the *Centuries*. Penitence for sin and asceticism are characteristic of all seventeenth-century literature except Traherne's; and it is their presence here, when they are so conspicuously absent in his best known writings, that might make the reader inclined to doubt at first that this is his authentic work.

What restores one's perspective, however, is the realization that penitence and self-discipline are by universal testimony inevitable concomitants of the Way, and of all religious life on Earth. "Our present Estate is not that of Reward, but Labour: It is an Estate of Trial, not of Fruition: A Condition wherein we are to Toyl, and Sweat, and travail hard, for the promised Wages; an Appointed Seed-Time, for a future Harvest; a real Warfare, in order to a Glorious Victory," wrote Traherne himself,[72] and with no real contradiction of his other teaching of the "Degree of Blessedness . . . transcendently Sweet and delightful" attainable on Earth, nor of his complete refusal to postpone Felicity to the other side of the grave.[73] No one can believe that Traherne attained his ultimate serenity and joy at little cost. He has indeed explicitly told us the reverse; and therefore it is no inherent contradiction of his authorship of a devotional work that the toils of the Way should have found expression in it. Indeed, once his authorship is proved, their expression here constitutes the particular value and interest of this group of devotions.

The style of these meditations strictly limits the commentary. There is therefore no opportunity for many of Traherne's favorite ideas to find expression here; as, for example, his loving use of the things of nature as symbols of his creed. There is room for very few indeed of his characteristic thoughts; but some of them—the glorious dignity of man, and the adorable excellence of love—make themselves felt; and whenever he thus escapes

[72] *Christian Ethicks*, p. 15.   [73] See *Centuries of Meditations* IV, 9, 10.

from the strict fetters imposed by the Gospel narrative and from the self-imposed form of these meditations, that strange force and fervor of Traherne is (at least to me) unmistakably perceptible—that "impetuous rush of a mind full to overflowing, strained, exalted to its utmost powers, yea, rather, lifted into ecstasy beyond itself," in the words of that quotation Bertram Dobell so aptly applied to Traherne. Who else among seventeenth century Anglicans, with their distrust of "enthusiasm," was writing like this?

And yet to give me Assurance that all that thou hast, is mine. O inexhausted Bounty! O Excess of Love! If all be mine, dear Lord, why then thy Grace is mine, thy Gifts are mine, thy Heaven is mine, thy Son, my Redeemer, is mine, his Righteousness mine, his Merits mine, his Satisfaction mine, his Life mine, and his Glory mine. O blessed be thy Name for this thy unbounded Love; for this thine unutterable, inexpressible Clemency to poor returning Sinners; let these magnetick Charms of Love draw all Hearts unto thee, and make us all remain in thee for ever.[74]

This is also the actual rhythm of one of his most famous passages in the *Centuries*: "The streets were mine, the temple was mine, the people were mine . . ."; a rhythm less subtle here in variation, but structurally identical, and identical too in its excited chant of possession.

Because of the fervent love of Christ by which these devotions are inspired, and because of that imaginative power of visualization which Traherne possessed, because in fact of those root causes which make these devotions so beautiful as devotions and so moving to those who share, even afar off, Traherne's passionate personal feeling for Jesus of Nazareth, it is impossible to quote much of them in a book like this. Criticism retires from the presence of a love so fervent and so all-consuming. The effect of spiritual drama, the effect of almost a hundred printed pages of intensest concentration on the suffering love of God and the seeking, self-abased love cry of a human soul cannot be con-

[74] P. 204 of these devotions.

veyed by quotation; to realize their power one must go to the meditations themselves.

The devotions which thus permit us to enter Traherne's most intimate Holy of Holies—whither, be it noted, we come quite uninvited—illuminate most vividly all Traherne's religious life. His ideal was to be "a philosopher, a Christian, and a Divine," as he has told us in the *Fourth Century* (3, 1). Of his "divine philosophy" the *Centuries* and the *Christian Ethicks* are the repository; of his Christianity, which is the root of it, and the secret of its quality, he has strangely little to say either in his poetry or his prose. Brief hints there are, which suggest the truth; but the portrait of Traherne as a Christian is painted at full length only in these devotions we are now considering; and that is part of the importance of their recovery.

Of autobiography in the narrower sense they also contain not a little, but one has to be on one's guard here more than in the *Centuries of Meditations*. These devotions were written particularly for Mrs. Hopton's private use; and occasionally the expressions of contrition are clearly a kind of general confession, applicable to all sinners, and with no particular personal allusion either to Mrs. Hopton or himself. On one occasion a passage occurs with particular personal reference to Major Hopton, and echoes Mrs. Hopton's own petition in *Daily Devotions*. Major Hopton's lack of any leanings toward the mystical and personally experimental in religion was apparently a secret grief to Mrs. Hopton and her friends; and Traherne does not hesitate to include on her behalf a petition which gives expression to feelings of hers which he shared or at least understood. It is part of a *Meditation on the Fifth Word from the Cross*:

O dear Lord, infuse this Thirst into those who have no Desire of thee, or heavenly things; encrease theirs who have it, and satisfy abundantly all their Longings. *Amen.*

By the Virtue and Merit of this Thirst fill me with it, and make my dear, dear Friends, who want it, to abound with this holy Thirst after thee. Fill that excellent Soul, my d. H. whom I most desire thou shouldst: O fill him, and all my other dear Friends, full of the Apprehensions of thy Divine Presence, and Affections answerable to those Apprehensions: Fill them and me with all thy heavenly Graces, give us all earnest Desires and earnest Endeavours to attain thee, and satisfy us all with the full Possession of thee. *Amen.*[75]

Yet the effect of writing these devotions for the particular use of another person is almost wholly discounted by Traherne's natural egoism, or whatever better name we should call that tendency of his to forget in his meditations the existence of everyone and everything else save his God and his own soul. The consciousness of Mrs. Hopton is very spasmodic, and being artificially induced, is soon swept away. It was not compatible with that intense imaginative effort, that intense spiritual apprehension after reality, which marks all Traherne's prayers. Thus when one finds certain faults and failings continually bewailed, one can be fairly certain that these were genuine faults and failings of which Traherne was himself personally conscious. As such, they are particularly interesting, and throw a ray of light on odd corners of Traherne's character and also on the difficulties of his life.

Make me industrious in whatsoever Life thy Providence shall place me, and never to be ashamed of poor Relations, nor of mean offices to them, when need requires.

That Traherne had an uncomfortable abundance of poor relations seems very probable by the existence of the numerous contemporaries of his name in Hereford alone. Traherne, "born to mean things," had by the good offices of those who paid for his education and by intense application risen to a new social level; and the lot of a man in these circumstances can be very uncomfortable indeed, and the temptation to snobbery very strong.

Another failing that is very frequently referred to is a hot temper and a quick tongue. No man of Traherne's fervor and energy of temperament could indeed be placid and phlegmatic

[75] P. 289.

of temper; it is quite easy to believe that he was exceedingly hasty by nature, and that the irony which to the end escapes into his writings might on occasion give an edge to his tongue, like Mrs. Hopton's, "as sharp as a razor."[76] So Traherne finds himself compelled to do somewhat frequent penance for the sins of his temper, a legacy perhaps from the pugnacious old innkeeper:

> I beseech thee to pardon and forgive me all my Offences I have done unto thee, in offending thine: Take away from me that Harshness of Nature, that Rashness and Inconsideration of Mind, and that Heat and contention of Spirit which I am liable to, and by which I have given Offence unto many; shew the wonderful Power of thy Mercy . . . by turning a Lion into a Lamb, a Child of Wrath into a Child of Grace.[77]

> I beseech thee, by this Example of thine, enable me to destroy that impatience of Spirit which I am so miserably inclin'd to, who cannot brook foolish and impertinent Tongues, much less willingly any Contradiction at all. . . . Make me henceforth . . . to digest all Injuries, to swallow down all Contradictions with Patience, and not to aggravate little Crosses with Violence.[78]

There is also one passage that seems to be an allusion to that period at Hereford in his adolescence before his religious life began. It occurs in the meditation on the events of Thursday night in Holy Week.

> I have often slept away and sinned away this Night of thy Passion, with carding, dancing, and vile Transgression, foolishly and vainly passing it away without any Reflection upon thee at all. But I earnestly repent. The Memory of these Sins of Idleness, of Vanity, of Vain-Glory, of Ingratitude, is grievous to me, the Burthen of them intolerable. Have Mercy upon me, have mercy upon me, most merciful Saviour.[79]

Spinckes, editing these devotions and probably not a little amazed to find the good Mrs. Hopton making these astonishing confessions, added a marginal note: "This passage is to be consider'd as not generally applicable." The truth and common sense of his remark emphasizes the particular applicability of the passage for the one who wrote it, whose prayers were rooted in his daily life.

[76] Ballard, *op. cit.*, p. 273.   [77] P. 206.   [78] P. 254.   [79] P. 257.

The still comparative youth of Traherne when writing these devotions is shown in other ways than by his consciousness of his unregenerate adolescence. There is the tendency to wit and wordplay, already noted in the *Hexameron*, which seems to be a youthful prelude to that control of language, that felicity of phrasing, he was to be master of in his later years. It is the same tendency that gives rise to one most terrible metaphor, deserving the ridicule Eachard has heaped on "indiscreet and horrid Metaphor-Mongers." "And I beseech thee give me as much Faith as a Grain of Mustard Seed. . . . Make me content to be ground by Contempt, bruised by Malice, mix'd with the Vinegar of sharp Reproaches, that I may by Humility, Patience, and Meekness, become savoury unto thee." It is but fair to add that the specimen is unique; but these devotions, from the occurrence of these elements in them, are of real value to the student of Traherne's prose style; and even as early as this he was capable of a prose as flexible and sensitive as the extracts have already demonstrated, and of so perfect a single sentence as the following, of the arrest of Jesus in the Garden: "Who, O Lord, could have bound thine ómnipotent Hands, if Love had not bound them first?"

These devotions also permit us to see more clearly than any other writing of Traherne's that his experiences in seeking a personal realization of communion with God were similar to those of all the other mystics who have sought and found that communion. One of the most extraordinary things in the history of mysticism is the identity of the intermediate experiences, as well as the identity of the great experience which crowns the adventure of the soul. Clothed in an infinite variety of symbol and metaphor, the essential experience remains unchanged.

As we have already said, the period at Credenhill was the period during which Traherne, in his·own favorite phrase, reached his "Journey's End." After reaching it, there were no more fitful burnings, but a steady radiance; no more spiritual hills and valleys, but an extraordinarily constant dwelling in high places. It is this serenity and harmony that his best known works reveal. The interest of these present devotions is that they give us a glimpse of the earlier days, the days of strife, and of moods of uncertainty and of but fitful peace.

The kinship of Traherne with all the great mystics is plainly revealed in such passages as these:

And I beseech thee, give me their Courage amidst all the Difficulties, Impediments, and Discouragements of the World, to pursue thee, in that right way thy holy Word and Ordinances do direct me; and even in the dark dismal Destitutions of all Light, teach me to depend on thee: And do thou illuminate my Understanding, and comfort me in all my Destitutions, with thy divine Consolations.

Make me rejoice at thy Visitations, and to correspond with them: and graciously vouchsafe thy Approximation, and close Adhesion to me.

And, I beseech thee, make me industrious in my Calling, and watchful over my Thoughts, and Words, and Deeds; that thy Visitations may comfort and illuminate me, direct and conduct my Soul unto thee, and with these Shepherds make me leave all to come unto thee.

Let all thy Returns be gracious unto me, that I may always go away comforted from thee. Take from me that fickle, staggering, paralytic Piety I am subject unto: make me strong and stable, reverent and serious in my Devotions; and be pleased to heal me of all my Instability.

O take from me all Bitterness of Spirit, and fill me with thy Meekness, by which only I can attain rest unto my unquiet Soul.

I beseech thee pardon me wherein I have been like unto these fickle People, magnifying thee one Day, dishonouring thee another; praising thee one Day, crucifying thee another. This indeed hath been my miserable unstable Temper: But O fix and rivet my Heart now fast unto thee. Deliver me from crucifying thee by my Sins, whom thou hast refreshed with thy gracious Visitation.

And I beseech thee give me that Humility of Spirit, that I disdain not to receive thy Mercies and thy Blessings from the meanest Creature of the World: And in all my Troubles, be pleased either to send thine Angels, thy Ministers unto me to comfort me, or else be pleased without their Ministry to vouchsafe me thine own blessed and divine Comforts and Visitations.

The essence of Traherne's mysticism is emphasis on the "personal and experimental," none the less real and vital because, in contrast with the Quakers and so many other of the spiritual sects of the time, it found no opposition in itself to the forms of the Church, but on the contrary support and control and inspiration in these very forms.

These passages that have just been quoted bring Traherne into the great company of all the mystics by the community of his experiences—a community that we have been able before only to surmise, and that has even, though surprisingly, been doubted. Taking Miss E. Underhill's well-known classification of the phrases of the mystical life, as explained in her work, *Mysticism*, we can see how each of these has its clear counterpart in the life of Traherne.

Miss Underhill gives as the first and second phases: (1) The awakening of the Self to consciousness of Divine Reality; (2) Purgation—the Self's attempts to eliminate . . . all that stands in the way of . . . union with God.[80] Since Traherne was a philosopher as well as a contemplative, his purgation was a two-fold one—a quest of knowledge as well as a quest of purity. His awakening and his dedication occurred, as we have seen, in two steps —that crisis in the lonely field, and that happier crisis in the quiet of the country, "seated among silent trees." The two-fold purgation, in its two aspects, occupied all the years at the University and at Credenhill.

At Credenhill, however, it was also merging into the next three stages of the Way: (3) Illumination—the "contemplative state" par excellence; (4) the Dark Night of the Soul—the most terrible of all the experiences of the Mystic Way, the final and complete purification of the Self; (5) Union—the true goal of the mystic quest.

Traherne's illumination is apparent both in his own autobiographical account of these years in the *Third and Fourth Centuries of Meditations*, which has already been given in preceding

---

[80] *Mysticism* (12th edition), pp. 169-70.

chapters, no less than in the fervor and joy of his *Contemplation* and the other writings of this period. The "Dark Night of the Soul," the oscillations of consciousness, the sense of divine withdrawal, are plainly evident in passages from the *Meditations upon the Life of Christ.* "My spiritual banishments," he calls them, "my Destitutions," "thy Delay." The terrible moods of doubt and uncertainty, the fear of self-delusion, the lack of peace, the consciousness of instability are no less clearly mirrored; and so no less is the certitude of union at times attained, of the reality and joy of "thy Visitations"; and there is a growing demand for uninterrupted unmistakable enjoyment of these.

The phase of union, the state of "peaceful joy, enhanced powers, intense certitude," is the state of Traherne at the end of his ten years' quest—the state reflected in *Christian Ethicks* and in the *Centuries of Meditations.* "The human instinct for personal happiness must be killed," in Miss Underhill's phrase; and the how and the why of this are the subject of Traherne's teachings on self-love, with their great conclusion: "Thus is God infinitely preferred by Nature above myself, and my Love to my self, being thoroughly satisfied, turns into the Love of God, and dies like a grain of Corn in the Earth to spring up in a new and better form."[81] "It was the actual knowledge of true Felicity that taught him to speak." Traherne says of himself with the dignity and simplicity of certitude; and the radiant peace and power of his consciousness of union gives to the great *Meditations* of the *Fourth Century* their beauty and their enduring truth.

With the *Centuries* and with *Christian Ethicks* in our hands, we knew that Traherne had arrived at the true goal of the mystic quest. We knew, however, almost nothing of the stages of his way; and thus it has been possible for Miss Underhill herself seriously to misjudge Traherne, and group him as a poet with Herbert and those who drew their inspiration from *The Temple.* It is a still more fundamental error to group him with

---

[81] *Christian Ethicks,* p. 529.

them as having the same attitude toward the religious life. No taster is Traherne, no manufacturer of secondhand Platonics, however charming, but, as his books beyond argument proclaim him, a great and strenuous and triumphant seeker after God, a mystic of the first order.

CHAP. XVII.

Poems, 1903, 1910, 1932.

WIth Traherne's poems, we come to the third group of his writings, those not published either by Traherne himself, as *Roman Forgeries* and *Christian Ethicks*, or by his friends, as the *Contemplation* and the others we have considered, but those which, left in manuscript, escaped the manifold ills manuscripts are heir to, to see publication in our own day.

There were at one time at least three manuscript volumes of Traherne's poetry—two in his own writing, one the selection Philip Traherne made. One of the former, as we have seen, came to rest on a secondhand bookstall in the East End of London, whence, after a few more adventures, it passed into the appreciative hands of Bertram Dobell. This is the volume now generally known as the Dobell Folio. Philip Traherne's copy, again by undiscoverable routes,[81a] made its way into the library of Charles Burney, and thus eventually into the British Museum. The third, frequently referred to in the annotations in the Dobell Folio, has not yet come to light. There is also a possible fourth volume, the book of poems which Mrs. Hopton's executor found among her papers and showed to Ballard as written by her. A slender manuscript of early work was found while this book was being prepared, and is discussed in the Appendix.

[81a] I failed to find any clue whatever to those Skipps of Ledbury who were believed by Bertram Dobell to have become the "owners and custodians of the poet's remains" (Introduction to the *Poems*).

As well as in the Dobell Folio and in the Burney manuscript, poems occur in most of Traherne's other writings; but the Dobell Folio is by far the most important single source.

Bertram Dobell published this folio in 1903, prefaced by the well-known memoir in which he told the story of the manuscript, of his long search for the true author, and his triumphant discovery of him in the long-forgotten Thomas Traherne. On their first appearance it was not possible for any critic to see these poems in the setting of their author's mind, or to know the philosophy of which they embody but detached fragments. That even with this handicap they called forth enthusiastic praise from Quiller-Couch, from John Masefield, and from other critics, is no small tribute to their quality and their charm.[82]

In the Dobell Folio, unlike the Burney manuscript, the poems are not arranged in any kind of sequence; but nevertheless they fall into three main groups, in accordance with the poet's pre-occupation with certain definite aspects of his philosophy. The ideas round which these poems group themselves might be summed up as the parable of childhood, the need of God for man, and the nature of mind.

The poems on childhood are professedly autobiographical; the experiences are related in the first person, and we have no reason to doubt are founded on actual fact. Yet, as in the *Centuries*, it is with the symbolic value of these experiences that the poet is most concerned. In the finest of these poems, there is a perfect fusion between literal experience and spiritual inter-pretation; in the less successful the ethical teaching is permitted to distort the literal picture and, in so doing, in part destroys itself.

It is easy to believe that the child who became the Traherne we know was unusually perceptive, and that he was deeply moved by beauty from the first dawn of consciousness. But it

---

[82] See *Times Literary Supplement*, March 27, 1903; Quiller-Couch, *The Daily News*, March 30, 1903; Masefield, *The Speaker*, April 25, 1903.

would be foolish to believe that as a child Traherne himself felt
and perceived all that the symbolic child of these poems is made
to perceive and feel. Indeed Traherne warns us in "The Improvement" against so literal an interpretation:

> But Oh! the vigor of mine Infant Sence
> Drives me too far: I had not yet the Eye
> The Apprehension, or Intelligence
> Of Things so very Great Divine and High.

At the present time one hears a great deal of nonsense about
the spiritual wisdom of childhood. And Traherne, as one who
has written so poetically of children, is in danger of being made,
indeed has been made, to sponsor a sentimentalism poles apart
from his real thought. What he does say is that a young child's
mode of awareness, beautiful in its happiness and harmony,
is akin to that ultimate mode of awareness attained by the man
who reaches full human stature, the mystic.

Traherne's poems of childhood are comments on the saying,
"Ye must be born again," and are not to be taken literally any
more than that saying itself. The child is unconscious of death
and mutability; the sage knows the meaning of eternity, that
"all transients are permanent in God." The child knows nothing
of sin; perfect manhood has attained freedom from its dominion.
The child sees perfection in the human beings of its world; the
man's vision pierces through all disguises to the potential
divinity of every human being. The child's delight in the sun-
shine, the trees, the shining fields of harvest is like the joy of the
man who has learned the "perfect story" of a grain of sand, and
sees the humblest thing of nature "clothed in endless glory."
Thus for Traherne the child is a living parable, an embodiment
of truth; but he is not the truth itself, as some would have us
believe. And there can be no doubt that the poems of childhood
wherever they occur in Traherne are the richer when we understand their symbolism. The delight of seeing the beauty and
wonder of the world through the eyes of a poetic child remains
unimpaired; and there is added the yet rarer delight of perceiv-

ing—and by their spell accepting—the radiant vision of life itself which they evoke.

Within this group of poems on childhood various aspects of the parable are brought into prominence. The opening poems, "The Salutation." "Wonder," "Eden," "Innocence," are all "songs of innocence," of joy complete and perfect. "The Preparative," "The Instruction," and "The Vision" reflect the sadder moods of one who seeks a lost childlikeness; "The Rapture" fitly expresses the joy of its recovery. In "The Improvement" and the succeeding poems, Traherne's thought dwells on childhood and its significance in the divine scheme of things, and depicts the happiness of childhood not only as a foretaste of ultimate happiness, but a foretaste deliberately devised by God to be an unforgettable memory impelling the soul to reject the lesser felicities and press on to its full satisfaction.

The poems "Dumnesse," "Silence," and "Nature" are also poems of childhood, but inferior on the whole to the rest. It is in these one feels that the symbolism becomes strained. In "Dumnesse," the infant who cannot yet speak or understand speech is said

> with Cleerer Eys
> To see all Creatures full of Deities;
> Especially Ones self; and to Admire
> The Satisfaction of all True Desire:
> Twas to be Pleasd with all that God hath done;
> Twas to Enjoy *even All* beneath the Sun:
> Twas with a Steddy and immediat Sence
> To feel and measure all the Excellence
> Of Things:

However just this may be as a description of the regained childlikeness, it is too great an exaggeration of the capacities of human infancy to satisfy the demands of art. The Divine in a poet's dress is here deserting Pegasus for the pulpit. But "The Salutation" and "Wonder" are pure poetry.

The most central of the second group are the poems "Amendment," "The Demonstration," "The Anticipation," and "The Recovery." They are surrounded by a number of others loosely linked to the preceding group as well as to this. Here the central idea is one we have already met with in the *Contemplation*—that man is an intermediary between God and the physical universe, and as such God has imperative need of his services. Man's physical joys are transformed by love and gratitude into spiritual joys; as spiritual joys they are communicable to spiritual beings. Only one who possesses the world in childlikeness can perform this office, for only he is capable of such love and gratitude. It is a special aspect of Traherne's thought on the magnificent part man is called upon to play in the world of eternity as well as in time; and it is developed at greater length in this little group of poems than elsewhere in his writings.

> And what then this can be more Plain and Clear?
> What Truth then this more Evident appear!
> The GODHEAD cannot prize
> The Sun at all, nor yet the Skies,
> Or Air, or Earth, or Trees, or Seas,
> Or Stars, unless the Soul of Man they pleas.
> He neither sees with Humane Eys
> Nor needs Himself Seas Skies
> Or Earth, or any thing: He draws
> No Breath, nor Eats or Drinks by Natures Laws.[83]

It is but another aspect of the same idea which is developed in "The Circulation," a Platonic tenet which was a favorite of Traherne's, that the whole cosmic movement is circular, an infinite series of circles within circles, that as seen in the physical world are parables of the movement of all energy outward from God to man, and back to God through man. All the poems named in this group, as well as "Another" and "Love" and those three exaltations of the human body—"The Person," "The Estate," and "The Enquirie"—express some aspect of this circular move-

[83] *The Demonstration.*

ment of the divine energy that is forever returning to itself by way of its similitude in man.

"Love," which belongs to this group, is one of the least satisfactory of all Traherne's poems. That is the more surprising when one remembers how favorite a theme it is with him, and how magnificently he has sung its power and beauty in his prose. The poem is frigid, and in its first stanza, with its string of fourteen vocatives, ludicrous. Divine love comes in "Golden Rain" to "Danae's Pleasing Fruitful Womb"; and with a still more unpleasant aura of association the soul is described in the next stanza as God's "Ganimede." There is nothing anywhere else in Traherne to approach this in frigidity and poor taste. The last six lines regain a measure of dignity and sincerity.

The remaining poems of the Dobell Folio, with the exception of "Desire" and "Goodnesse," make up the third group, where the poet is concerned with the nature of perception, the unfathomable mystery of mind. "My Spirit," which occurs earlier in the manuscript, also belongs here. Traherne is not attempting any solution of the mystery, but dwelling on the strangeness and wonder of the human faculty of thought, perceiving it as the infinite with the finite, and the one adequate symbol of deity.

Traherne's reflections on the operations and the capacity of the human mind occupy a considerable space in his maturest work, and have given us some of his most original conceptions. Bertram Dobell, indeed, claimed that Traherne was "a Berkeleian before Berkeley was born"; that "he had a clear prevision of that famous system which is known as the Berkeleian philosophy." That I think is true. But Traherne is chiefly concerned with the converse of the Berkeleian proposition that an object has no being, no existence until it is perceived; he sought to emphasize that there are multitudes of objects, material and spiritual, which a man can bring into being for himself if he chooses to exert his mental powers. Man, being the Divine Image in all respects, can create a universe; and this mind-created universe is for Traherne the real, the physical universe, the apparent. This for him constitutes the primary importance of thought. Thoughts, the product of the interaction of sense-perception, reason, imagination, and all the mental faculties, are endued for Traherne with a life of their own, and a nature of good or evil according to their origin. When they derive from a perfected human nature, they are the fine flower of all creation; and to produce them was the ultimate purpose of all creation.

All these poems on thought are extraordinarily interesting; both in matter and in the spectacle they afford of an acute and deeply penetrative mind doubling back to watch and record its own mysterious operations. The poetry, too, is not cumbered, but enriched, by the intellectual subtlety of its content.

Separating, and at first sight interrupting, two of the poems on thought, occurs the poem "Desire." It is one of the finest of all in this Dobell Folio. It is a passionate thanksgiving for that restless discontent, born of the memory of childhood's lost felicity, which did not permit Traherne to accept anything in place of the true and perfect felicity. "Dissatisfaction" in the Burney manuscript tells of the torment of that divine discontent; but in "Desire" the soul has seen the purpose of it.

> For giving me Desire,
> An Eager Thirst, a burning Ardent fire,
> A virgin Infant Flame,
> A Love with which into the World I came,
> An Inward Hidden Heavenly Love,
> Which in my Soul did Work and move,
> And ever ever me Enflame
> With restlesse longing Heavenly Avarice,
> That never could be satisfied,
> That did incessantly a Paradice
> Unknown suggest, and som thing undescried
> Discern, and bear me to it; be
> Thy Name for ever praisd by me.

This poem, by taking us for a moment away from the problem and mystery of thought back to the parable of childhood, subtly and I think deliberately suggests those hidden links whereby all these poems are bound into unity.

The Dobell Folio ends abruptly. One feels that it, too, like the *Centuries*, was interrupted by death. It does not allow us to see much of the poet's struggles with his Muse, but is on the whole a fair copy, written out very carefully, with remarkably few corrections. These are more numerous toward the end, and the sixth stanza of "My Spirit" gives a hint of difficulties encountered; but when Traherne wished to alter anything, it was his custom to erase the original completely and write over the erasure. So neither the critic nor the psychologist is permitted to draw deductions from his corrections.

Philip Traherne's practice—fortunately for us—was otherwise. He deletes by crossing through with a single line, and puts the new version above or below, so that one can almost always read the original clearly. By the courtesy of Mr. P. J. Dobell I have had full access to his Traherne manuscripts, and was thus enabled to discover in the Dobell Folio some corrections by Philip Traherne. Bertram Dobell had remarked on the existence of corrections in another and later hand; it has now been possible to identify them. The extent of these corrections in the Dobell Folio is but slight, only thirty-three lines being affected. But it is an interesting fact that this Dobell Folio was certainly used by Philip Traherne when preparing the *Poems of Felicity*. Whatever he has marked for omission in the Dobell Folio will not be found in the Burney manuscript; lines altered by him there never appear in their original form in the Burney manuscript and usually retain the Dobell Folio correction; and the order of the poems in the Burney manuscript is indicated in the Dobell Folio by inserted titles. Thus the Dobell Folio as we have it today has been worked over by two people—the poet himself, who copied into it the finished draft of his poems and made certain later corrections; and Philip Traherne, who used it when preparing the *Poems of Felicity* both for a revision of text and as a notebook for odd memoranda of arrangement.

The second important source for Traherne's poetry is the Burney MS. 392, a collection of fifty-nine poems, thirty-six of them occurring only here. These fifty-nine represent a selection made by Philip Traherne from the Dobell Folio and another original, now lost, and prepared by him for publication under the title *Poems of Felicity*, sometime between 1700 and 1723. Dr. H. I. Bell published these poems in 1910 in an interesting edition that reproduced not only the spelling and capitalization of the original but also its pagination. In his preface he proved that the handwriting in this Burney manuscript was Philip Traherne's, and furnished many hitherto unknown facts about this brother of Thomas's.

As is now established,[84] Philip Traherne altered the text of the originals as he thought fit, and is responsible for the numerous corrections in the Burney manuscript itself as well as for the readings there that differ from the Dobell Folio. The existence of these alterations, and the impossibility of recovering in many instances the original version, places this collection below the Dobell Folio for critical purposes. Yet it is a collection of importance, containing much fine material not occurring elsewhere.

Philip Traherne's alterations seem to have operated in two directions—toward a greater correctness of form, and toward a stricter conventionality of thought. One influence was probably beneficial, though many critics doubt even that; the other was certainly destructive and deplorable.

As regards the greater correctness of form, it will be noticed that Philip Traherne curtails the long lists; mends meaningless rhymes; lessens the frequency of the "Bower-Power" and "Treasure-Pleasure" rhymes; makes syllabically correct lines left too long or too short; occasionally improves the euphony; and sometimes mends a broken stanza pattern.

Of the three prefatory poems, two are by Philip Traherne, and do little either to increase our estimation of his poetical

---

[84] See the discussion in my Preface to the *Poetical Works of Thomas Traherne* (Dobell, 1932).

powers or to add to our knowledge of his brother. But the second, "The Author to the Critical Peruser," is by Thomas Traherne, and is of interest from several points of view. It shows by its very title that Traherne himself had prepared a volume of poems for publication. Other facts suggest that this was the volume that Philip used as his second archetype; that "An Infant-Ey" and "The Return," quoted in Philip's notes in the Dobell Folio as being on page 1 and page 2 of his original, were its opening poems; that the present title-page to the *Poems of Felicity*, with its subtitle, *Divine Reflections on the Native Objects of an Infant-Ey* was copied from the poet's own title-page, thus accounting for the description of Traherne as "Author of Roman Forgeries," with "& Christian Ethiks" an afterthought squeezed in by Philip.[85] If these inferences are correct, then Traherne prepared this volume between the publication of *Roman Forgeries* and his death; and it represents yet another literary activity of those crowded final years.

"The Author to the Critical Peruser" is also interesting for its distinct verbal echoes of Herbert and of Cowley, showing Traherne's interest in these poets. But it is most memorable as containing the only expression we have of Traherne's views on the craft of poetry itself. From his words here it is plain that for Traherne the true poet is he who has a vision of naked truth, and true poetry that which is a transparent reflection of the poet's vision. Vision is the primary essential of poetry, ease and simplicity of style the next. All the stock-in-trade of conventional poetical ornament is swept aside as worthless, as "gilded Scabbards sheathing rusty Swords."

> The naked Truth in many faces shewn,
> Whose inward Beauties very few hav known,
> A simple Light, transparent Words, a Strain
> That lowly creeps, yet maketh Mountains plain,
> Brings down the highest Mysteries to sense

[85] This title-page is reproduced in *The Poetical Works*, as it was also in Dr. Bell's edition of *Poems of Felicity*.

> And keeps them there; that is Our Excellence:
> At that we aim. . . .
> An easy Stile drawn from a native vein,
> A clearer Stream than that which Poets feign,
> Whose bottom may, how deep so'ere, be seen.

It is thus evident that the simplicity, almost naïveté, of much of Traherne's poetry is as conscious, if not as perfect, artistry as Blake's in his *Songs of Innocence.*

The first nineteen poems in this Burney manuscript are grouped to form two sequences, each telling of infant felicity, felicity lost and felicity regained. The second of these retells the story of the *Third Century*, often with additional particulars. "Dissatisfaction" in this second sequence is in many ways a companion-picture to "The Hound of Heaven." Traherne, though he sees himself as the seeker rather than the sought, travels on feverishly and foolishly, to discover, as that other who fled Him down the nights and down the days, that "naught contents thee." That experience of spiritual forlornness, of separation, of desperate need to escape from dissatisfaction, is curiously alike in the two poets.

Apart from the two sequences, the poems are not definitely grouped. As in the Dobell Folio, the poet's interest moves away from the parable of childhood to the nature of thought; but the fundamental unity is more strictly preserved, and the "infant-eye" consciously kept in mind.

Many of the poems in this collection are extraordinarily fine, giving us Traherne at his poetic best. Those poems in the second sequence—"The Apostacy," "Solitude," "Poverty," "Dissatisfaction"—are not only biography of the most valuable sort, with all the realism and sincerity of a personal record, but pure poetry, too. Perhaps the most magical lines in all Traherne are these from "The Apostacy":

> Drown'd in their Customs, I became
> A Stranger to the Shining Skies,
> Lost as a dying Flame.

Then there is the lovely "Shadows in the Water," richest of all in suggestion, which tells of a child playing by a pool with reflections, and delighted but puzzled by that other peopled world he can see below its shining surface. The symbolism, as in those poems of Blake which this so closely resembles, is triple or fourfold; and the child with his preoccupation is made a teacher of wisdom, a symbol of the sage who is preoccupied with another world than the everyday. The title, and part of the interpretation, probably came to Traherne from the following passage in Plotinus's *Enneads* (I.6.8.): "But what must we do? Where lies the Path? How come to the vision of the Inaccessible Beauty? . . . Those shapes of grace that show in body, let him not pursue. He must know them for copies, vestiges, shadows . . . like beautiful shapes playing over water."

The two dream-poems, with their interesting allusions to Philip Traherne, have the same blending of tender humor with delight in childhood's "sweet Mistakenness" that is yet so wise. There is no trace of grown-up superiority, but a reverence for these little living symbols of divine truth that is quite unlike anything in English literature before Blake.

A little child's idealization of humanity, and its love and trust and admiration, is often depicted by Traherne, who saw in it a parable of a deep truth; but he has rarely given a more attractive expression of it than in the two poems "Christendom" and "The City." That peaceful city of God he paints, with its walls and its fair prospect, its red clay soil, its kindly red-cheeked people, its prosperity, its tree-shaded houses and children playing in its streets and people sitting in their doorways—is not this an idealized Hereford? Does not the wistful beauty of the poem perhaps owe something to Traherne's own absence from scenes dear and familiar from childhood? It is possible; and "On Christmas-Day" certainly takes us to a country town and a country minster, where the air is heavy with the chiming of bells

and the streets are full of happy bustle. There are some delightful little pictures here of a seventeenth-century Christmas.

> See how they run from place to place,
> And seek for Ornaments of Grace;
> Their Houses deckt with sprightly Green,
> In Winter makes a Summer seen;
> They Bays and Holly bring
> As if 'twere Spring! . . .
> See how each one the other calls
> To fix his Ivy on the walls,
> Transplanted there it seems to grow
> As if it rooted were below: . . .
> See how, their Bodies clad with finer Cloaths . . .
> His gayer Weeds and finer Band,
> New Suit and Hat, into his hand
> The Plow-man takes; his neatest Shoos,
> And warmer Glovs, he means to use. . . .
> See how their Breath doth smoak, and how they haste
> His prais to sing
> With Cherubim;
> They scarce a Break-fast taste;
> But throu the Streets . . . to Church they haste. . . .
> The Sword, the Mace, the Magistrate,
> To honor Thee attend in State:
> The whole Assembly sings:
> The Minster rings.

As in the Dobell Folio, a considerable group of poems toward
the end are concerned with the living power of thought and the
comparative deadness of material things. Traherne took joy to
dwell on the infinite capacity of the human mind, and the infinity
of treasures bestowed by God to satisfy its insatiable desire. The
last poems in the collection, "Review I" and "Review II," must,
one feels, have been the concluding poems of Traherne's own
volume. They show that the movement of thought as we see it
in both the manuscripts was deliberate.

> Did I flourish or diminish,
> When I so in *Thoughts* did finish
> What I had in *Things* begun?

They sum up and round off not only the poems on thought, but the whole book, gathering into a unity the thinking man and the enjoying child, and showing the perfect circle of human life.

CHAP. XVIII.

Centuries of Meditations, 1908.

THe manuscript of the *Centuries of Meditations* was published by Dobell in 1908, five years after the poems. This edition of the *Centuries,* unlike the latest one of the poems, modernized Traherne's spelling, punctuation, and use of capitals throughout. The result is, I feel, a loss of color and liveliness; and when both the modernized prose and the unmodernized verse are freely drawn upon for quotation, as in this book, there is an unfortunate effect of discrepancy in Traherne's English. It is to be hoped that the present owners of the *Centuries* will some day let us have them in all their original subtleties of light and shade.

The manuscript itself is an octavo volume, leather-bound and in perfect condition. Whatever its history, it has been valued and cared for. There is no title, though a blank space has been left. This blank space and absence of any indication of authorship, is characteristic of Traherne.

The short prose passages are numbered in order. There are four complete hundreds, and ten of a fifth.

That a friend had given him this notebook in which they are written, the opening passage explicitly tells us. From the point of view of Traherne's biography, the identity of this friend of his has been of great interest. Bertram Dobell, and others who followed him, assumed that the friend was a woman, chiefly because of an inscription on the first leaf of the manuscript:

> This book unto the friend of my best friend
> As of the wisest Love a mark I send,

That she may write my Maker's prais therin
And make her self thereby a Cherubin.

I, too, believe that the giver of the notebook and the inspirer of
its contents was a woman, and that I have identified her in Mrs.
Hopton. But I think that these four lines have nothing to do with
her. I am quite sure that Traherne, who never uses words lightly,
would not apply the phrase "my best friend" to any human
being; and to God he has referred over and over again in these
very words. "God only is my sovereign happiness and Friend
in the World." . . . "There are some slight aims and adum-
brations of this Friendship on Earth; but the best and highest
degree of it here beneath is but a rude and imperfect shadow,
Only God is the sovereign friend: all adoration paid to anyone
beside is meer Idolatry." The feminine pronouns in the third and
fourth lines of this dedication refer, I suggest, not to a woman
but to "heavenly Aphrodite," the soul that in Plato and Plotinus, as in the commonest symbolism of the Christian Church, is
feminine. Traherne himself not infrequently follows this custom of feminine personification; an instance occurs in *Century
IV*, 82: "The soul communicates itself wholly by them. . . .
The harmony and joys of Heaven appear in Love, for all these
were made for her, and all these are to be enjoyed in her."

Again, read as a dedication to a woman, it hardly makes sense;
if Traherne is to fill its pages with those truths his friend loved
without understanding them, how can she be said to "write
therein"? and why "*my* Maker's prais" and not "*her* Maker's"?

But all is clear if we interpret the lines as meaning that he
dedicates this work to his own spirit, now purified and consciously
the friend of God, as a mark of that self-love which he has elsewhere defined and exalted as wisdom, in order that his spirit may
pour forth in its pages the praise of the Maker of his whole
self—of body and mind as well as spirit—and in so doing perform the office of the cherubin. "Cherubin" for Traherne, like
so many other words we use loosely, would have been an exact

term. I quote Aquinas's definition, and it will be seen that it implies an exceedingly apt description of these meditations and of that fullness of knowledge from which they spring:

"Cherubim" comes from a certain excess of knowledge; hence it is interpreted "fullness of knowledge," which Dionysius expounds in regard to four things: the perfect vision of God; the full reception of the Divine Light; their contemplation in God of the beauty of the Divine order; and in regard to the fact that possessing this knowledge fully, they pour it forth copiously upon us.

A perfect description of the *Meditations*—and their author.

The charm of these meditations, a charm they have exercised ever since their publication over an increasing circle of readers, has its root in the intimacy of the revelation we are privileged to share. In the beginning they were written solely for Mrs. Hopton, intended for no other eye than hers. They contain the most complete expression of Traherne's philosophy, because it was the purpose of their writing to present the unity and glory and reasonableness of that philosophy to one incapable of achieving it for herself. The lucidity and the completeness of the presentation are due in part to the limitations of the one who was to read them; the fervor and passion of it to Traherne's desire that she should share with him a "great enriching Verity."

As in quiet talk with a friend, the thoughts of the writer follow their own bent. There is not the slightest attempt at any formal exposition. None of the *Centuries* could be easily summarized. Yet under the control of two dominant ideas the current of thought for all its windings flows steadily in one direction; for all the diversity there is unity. Something is being presented from many angles; but the thing presented is always the same.

One of the dominant ideas is that Traherne's own philosophy should be set forth. Now one aspect of it, now another passes in review; now the nature of God, now the nature of man, now man's relationship to God and to his fellow creatures, or the mystery of God becoming Man in the person of Christ.

The other dominant idea is that the path for sinful and stunted man to the attainment of his full stature is found by opening the door of nature; that a serious reverent study of simple natural things, even the most ordinary, will lead him who follows it to the very throne of God. The *Centuries* are molded by the pressure of these two ideas, as they are quickened by emotion—by a companionable human love for a friend as well as by the still white heat of another passion that is the vital fire of all Traherne writes.

Since the *Centuries* are well known and easily accessible, there is no need here for description or quotations. I shall merely draw attention to some aspects of the *Third Century*, and of the *Fourth*, the two that from several points of view are of particular interest.

The *Third Century* may be roughly divided into two parts: the first, Traherne's own history, the other, confirmation and parallels from the Psalms. The first part is beyond a doubt the most perfect thing Traherne wrote, and constitutes Traherne's chief claim to classic rank in our literature. It is another *Pilgrim's Progress*, the story of one who in the beginning of life lived in an earthly Paradise; who was tempted, succumbed, and was cast out; who lived for a time "among dreams and shadows . . . feeding upon husks with swine . . . in a comfortless wilderness full of thorns and troubles"; but who after long travel and travail of spirit found again that lost country of the spirit and knew again its dear delights. And the one whose earthly and spiritual history is related is Traherne himself. We have thus an autobiography of the rarest kind; poor perhaps in common facts, since the friend had not our need to be informed, and since, too, these are relatively unimportant, but rich in vital experiences.

Yet this *Third Century* is not merely an autobiography. What Traherne has to say of his own life is to him incidental. He is not engaged in recording reminiscences. It is rather that in his own life he saw an allegory of all the lives of those who have lost and could regain a divinely intended state of well-being.

The emphasis is placed on this throughout; and the whole of the second half of this *Century* is written to show that Traherne's own path of experience, which as he first thought he had found by chance and trodden as a pioneer, was the selfsame path of the Psalmist, and the only way of return.

When I saw those objects celebrated in his Psalms which God and Nature had proposed to me, and which I thought chance only presented to my view, you cannot imagine how unspeakably I was delighted to see so glorious a person, so great a prince, so divine a sage, that was a man after God's own heart, by the testimony of God Himself, rejoicing in the same things, meditating on the same, and praising God for the same. For by this I perceived we were led by one Spirit, and that following the clue of Nature into this labyrinth I was brought into the midst of celestial joys: and that to be retired from earthly cares and fears and distractions that we might in sweet and heavenly peace contemplate all the Works of God, was to live in Heaven, and the only way to become what David was, a man after God's own heart.[86]

Traherne saw his life as a glorious triumph; and saw in his life the way to that triumph clearly mapped for Everyman. He was mapping it here for Mrs. Hopton. If she would find what he had found, she must travel as he had traveled; and Traherne's life was clearly to Traherne interesting and worth talking about only as an allegory.

Thus it comes about that what he writes here of the world of childhood is filled with the same tender radiance as his poems, and for the same reason. He was able to put before us himself as he was as a child, without egoism and without self-consciousness; with the realism of remembered fact and the bright light of vision.

The same is true of what he writes in this *Century* of the beautiful things of nature. He has seen and been moved by the wonder of a spire of grass or a field of red-gold wheat; but he has also seen beyond those wonders "Almighty Power wholly ex-

[86] *Centuries* III, 70.

erted." The "something Infinite behind everything" is a pervading presence, transmuting the ordinary into poetry.

With the *Fourth Century* the idea that what he had already written and was now about to complete might be of value to others beside his friend—the idea that he might therefore some day publish this work—began to take shape. It is possible that some interval elapsed between the completion of the *Third Century* and the beginning of the *Fourth*; it is certain that between the two Traherne resolved to finish for publication the spiritual history begun, and for this reason to change from the personal to the impersonal. The first version of the opening meditation of this *Century* read as follows:

> Since the Author in the last Centurie hath spoken so much concerning his entrance and progress into the study of Felicity, and all He hath there said pertaineth only to the Contemplativ part of it, I will in this Centurie supply his place and speak of the Principles with which he endued himself to enjoy it in the practical. For besides contemplativ, ther is an active happiness, which consisteth in blessed operations.

The designation of himself as "the Author" implies consciousness of an unknown reader, and the change from the first person to the third would avoid some of the embarrassments of autobiography. Yet, happily, the mood and tone of this record had been set by all that had been previously written, and the habit of intimate familiar self-revelation proved stronger than the new aloofness. Indeed, the pronouns are very thoroughly confused in this *Century*. Traherne at first decided to write of his own experiences in the third person and as though they had happened not to himself but to someone who was Mrs. Hopton's friend and who had described these experiences to Traherne. Thus there would be three people in the narrative—Traherne himself, Mrs. Hopton, and the imaginary third—as follows: "I will in this century speak of the principles with which your friend endued himself to eñjoy it. . . . He thought it a vain thing to see glorious principles lie buried in books. . . ." But in practice Traherne found this impossible to sustain. He is also somewhat self-conscious in his references to the supposed third, and as soon as he becomes absorbed in his subject he reverts to the familiar first person. Meditation 14 furnishes an instance of what is constantly happening:

> In order to this, he furnished himself with this maxim: *It is a good thing to be happy alone. It is better to be happy in company, but good to be happy alone.* Men owe me the advantage of their society, but if they deny me that just debt, I will not be unjust to myself, and side with them in bereaving me. I will not be discouraged . . . etc.

Had Traherne actually completed these meditations and sent them to press, these contradictions would doubtless have disappeared; but as we have them today, "your friend" and "he from whom I derived these things" as well as "I" all clearly refer to Traherne himself.

The purpose of the *Fourth Century*, as the opening meditation states, is to relate the actions of daily life to the contemplative quest of God. There is obviously a close connection in theme and purpose with *Christian Ethicks*. Both are a looking-backward by one who has arrived; but here the personal element is more defined. It is clear from many illusions that the background of the *Fourth Century* is the rectory at Credenhill. That was the laboratory of this experiment in living; and from the record of it we learn something of his daily life there, of his difficulties and consolations and ideals. But the personal element is here even more subordinated than in the *Third Century* to the presentation of his philosophy, which is restated in the *Fourth Century* from the viewpoint of the "glorious principles" that must govern every action when once a noble conception of life as a whole has been intellectually accepted. Some of Traherne's profoundest thought is stored in these meditations. And when, after the discussion of fundamental principles of conduct, and of the necessity of human freewill in conjunction with these, Traherne arrives at love as the universal principle of harmonious being, we shall not find in all literature the sublime beauty of "naked and divested Love in its true perfection" sung with greater wisdom or more moving power.

In that unfinished *Fifth Century* Traherne was essaying a still vaster theme, a contemplation of Divinity itself. That which is enjoyed in all beauty, that which makes of sun and stars and all things of nature the gate of the upward path, was for Traherne no less than God Himself. "God is the object, and God is the Way of enjoying." In this *Fifth Century* Traherne would contemplate all things as manifestations of the divine, and was beginning with the essential attributes of deity, omnipresence, infinity, eternity, omnipotency. But as we know, something intervened when only ten meditations were completed; and we surmise that it was the final fatal illness of September 1674.

When the *Centuries of Meditations* were published in 1908, they attracted widespread notice. Unstinted praise was given to the originality and loftiness of Traherne's thought, to the charm of his personality, and to the perfection of his prose. It is safe to say that nothing will ever in future be written of English religious thought or of English prose that will not take into account this book of Traherne's. His place as a thinker has already been considered by Dr. R. M. Jones,[87] his place as a mystic by Mrs. E. Herman,[88] to name but two of the more important; and he is in no danger of being overlooked by the compilers of anthologies.

One secret of the beauty of these meditations is that here, and only here in all that has come down to us, did Traherne find a literary form that perfectly suited his genius. In *Christian Ethicks* and to some extent in the poems the didactic purpose is a fetter, no less than the scientific framework of the one and the exigencies of meter in the other; and in both he is at his best when he is disobedient to his own structural law. These works in consequence have but imperfectly the delight which comes from the harmony, the organic unity, of form and content; but this har-

---

[87] *Spiritual Reformers in the 16th and 17th Centuries* (1914).
[88] *The Meaning and Value of Mysticism* (1915).

mony we do find in the *Centuries*. There is a didactic purpose in
them, but it is so fused with his tenderness to the friend for whom
he is writing, so integral a part of Traherne's burning desire to
share his joy, that it is perfectly a part of the content, neither
clogging nor distorting, but rather lending wings.

The form of these meditations exactly suited Traherne's quick-
moving mind; yet it exerted a necessary and perfective discipline.
A meditation might be longer or shorter, yet it must be comparatively short; there was not room in its narrow compass for
redundancies; words must be chosen with care, that rhythm and
richness be achieved with economy. This particular discipline of
form was exercised from the beginning, and in addition all these
meditations have been revised, the corrections for the most part
consisting of rigorous deletion of parallel phrases. It is interesting to turn from some passage of the *Centuries* to the *Serious
and Pathetical Contemplation of the Mercies of God*, where the
words tumble over one another and the synonyms are piled
high. Such a comparison reveals at once the nature, and the
virtue, of the control imposed by their form on these meditations, and the development in Traherne of a new insight into the
value of restraint.

Yet this discipline of form, effective as it was, was easy. These
loosely strung prose passages of variable lengths left his spirit
free to follow its own promptings. In this intimate talk to his
friend, he need obey no law but the law of association within his
own mind. The meditations are the moods of a sensitive mind;
and how varied are these moods as this spontaneous expression
reveals them! Prayers of adoration or of aspiration or of thanksgiving; sorrowful envisagings of the Passion or comprehension
of the eternal grief of God; repentance for personal sin; exult-
ings in the joy of felicity attained; gusts of anger at the "damned
folly" of men who perversely will not see God in the beauty of
the world; ironic humor; literary criticism; tender exhortation
of "my excellent friend"; rapturous exaltations of spirit; calm
exposition of subtle and exquisite perceptions, of profound and

original thought—there is room for all these and more in these *Centuries*.

Such a book as this has no literary ancestry. It has no traceable sources, as has *Christian Ethicks*. It is influenced by books because Traherne was influenced by books. If we find in its pages a multitude of reminiscences of reading, if we meet Plato and Seneca, Socrates and Cato, Pyrrhus and Alexander, Luther and Hobbes, Martial and De Mornay, Eusebius Pamphilus and Pico Mirandola, it is because these men and their words and their deeds lived in Traherne's own mind. The most formative literary influence was that supposititious work of St. Augustine, *The Meditations, Soliloquia and Manual*, from which Traherne copied into another manuscript a certain poem. Yet the differences between this work and Traherne's *Centuries* outweigh the few striking resemblances.

Because of the elasticity of the form, and because of the intimacy of the self-revelation intended only for the eye of a friend, this book is one of the most perfect expressions of personality in literature. It holds the reader by a twofold charm—the charm of what is written, the charm of the personality that could write it so. A poet's vision and exquisite perception, a pen gleaning the harvest of a richly cultivated mind—these have furnished the matter of the meditations; and as we read them, Traherne himself lives again and moves across their pages. Because we come to know him so well, we recognize how apt was Bertram Dobell's illustration of his nature by the poet and mystic and saint of James Thomson's "Open Secret Societies." "He was not more a Poet than a Mystic, nor more a Mystic than a Saint; but each at all times, and never one rather than the other." The poet, to whom "the universe is one mighty harmony of beauty and joy"; the saint, who is of them "who know, and live up to the knowledge, that love is the one supreme duty and good; that love is wisdom and purity and valour and peace, and that its infinite sorrow is infinitely better than the world's richest joys"; and the mystic, who is "the very flower and crown of the four already touched upon . . . the identity of the masculine ideal of Hero and Philosopher and the feminine ideal of Poet and Saint."

By the *Centuries of Meditations* we come into living contact with this rich and radiant personality, this joyous poet of God. We know his inmost self in a fashion it is given us to know very few on earth.

And, if we would but consider it, that is a strange and astonishing privilege.

CHAP. XIX.

Traherne's Prose and Verse.

FOr his verse, Traherne used only two forms—the heroic couplet and the stanza of varying complexity, both reflecting the fashions of his day. Toward the close of the third quarter of the century these two verse-forms were competing for future dominance, and at the moment their chances seemed equal. Cowley had raised to the height of fashion the irregular stanza; but he also practised the couplet, and chose it for his ambitious *Davideis*. Dryden, in whom the couplet found its first great exponent, did not neglect the complex stanza, as his famous Odes bear witness. Traherne's preference seems to have been for the stanza, though he continued to write the couplet; and his latest use of it, exemplified in "Thoughts IV" of the Dobell Folio, with its occasional enjambment, varied caesura, definitely emphasized rhymes, and excellent sense of form, reveals metrical skill of a high order.

But it was to fashioning stanzas of greater and ever greater complexity that Traherne bent his energies as a craftsman. There can be no doubt, as has already been remarked of the *Contemplation*, that he took pleasure in the pattern-making of these stanza designs; merely as design the pages of his manuscript are beautiful. Also he never repeated a pattern. He has all types, from the four-lined simplicity of "The Instruction" to the seventeen-lined complexity of "My Spirit." Many times he fails; indeed the heroic couplet was carried to its predominance by a tide of reaction against the jerky, chopped-up lines of prose into which the long irregular stanza tended to degenerate. With Traherne it did on occasion so degenerate. This stanza of "My Spirit" (note the rhyme-scheme and the intricacy of line arrangement, maintained for seven stanzas) shows Traherne defeated by his medium.

It Acts not from a Centre to	4	a
Its Object as remote,	3 '	b
But present is, when it doth view,	4	a
Being with the Being it doth note.	4	b
Whatever it doth do,	3	a
It doth not by another Engine work,	5	c
But by it self; which in the Act doth lurk.	5	c
Its Essence is Transformed into a true	5	a
And perfect Act.	2	d
And so Exact	2	d
Hath God appeard in this Mysterious Fact,	5	d
That tis all Ey, all Act, all Sight,	4	e
And what it pleas can be,	3	e
Not only see,	2	f
Or do; for tis more Voluble then Light:	5	e
Which can put on ten thousand Forms,	4	g
Being clothd with what it self adorns.	4	g

The stanza of "Desire," quoted in Chapter XVII, is, on the other hand, an instance of success. The stanza there has its own organic rhythm in which all the lines, long or short, play their contributing parts. The same is true of that poem as a whole, which has a unity Traherne does not always achieve. In the *Poems of Felicity* there is still greater complexity of stanza with, on the whole, increasing mastery. The long stanza of "Christmas Day" is limited to four rhymes, *abbaaaccddbb*, and the rhyme *b* is identical throughout all ten stanzas. It is an onomatopoeic rhyme, *sing, bring, ring, Spring*, etc., effectively employed to suggest the all-pervasive chiming of the Christmas bells. "Solitude," a long poem of fifteen eight-lined stanzas, is metrically one of Traherne's greatest achievements. The way the internal rhymes are used in the last couplet of each stanza is particularly skilful.

Traherne made use of only one rhythm—the iambic—and yet there is no monotony in his verse. Substitution is used freely, particularly in the first foot, to avoid too great a regularity of beat; as in the first line of "Wonder": "How like an Angel came I down!" or in the first line of "News": "News from a foreign Country came." The value of the stresses is also varied, as in the line "As if my Treasure and my Wealth lay there." These and other variations of the ground-rhythm Traherne on occasion uses very skilfully, and we may suppose not entirely by happy accident.

By modern pronunciation there is a large proportion of defective rhymes in Traherne's verse. Some of these, we can tell from their frequency of occurrence in all poetry of the time, were then true rhymes—such as "join" and "shine"; "regard" and "reward"; "are" and "compare"; "room," "presume," "perfume." It is also probable that seventeenth-century pronunciation of words of French origin made other pairs true rhymes. There is an interesting discussion of this, with its bearing on Traherne's rhymes, in *Notes and Queries* for March 25, 1911. Altogether it seems as if Traherne's practice was sufficiently strict.

Traherne has left us, as we have seen, a considerable body of poetry. In his mature work we find nothing trivial; no compliments, no miscellaneous or "occasional" poems, no fashionable flattery, no amorous verse. Traherne stands quite aloof as a poet from the social vices and political hatreds and religious sectarian strife of his day. The whole of his poetry is of high intellectual quality, warmed by the vision and eager with the enthusiasm of youth. "He comes to us in these latter days like the first of the larks in spring; like a bright dawn coming suddenly above solemn hills," as a fellow poet has written of him.[89]

Yet there is a "but" about Traherne's poetry. It fails somewhere. It is not of the first order. It is definitely inferior to his prose. Dr. Bell, in his preface to the *Poems of Felicity*, has well expressed this general opinion. He says:

Indeed, it is probably true to say that Traherne is not primarily a poet at all. His verse is full of the material of poetry; it is continually preparing (so to say) to pass into poetry, and here and there for a few lines, sometimes for longer, it does so; but for the most part it remains imperfectly fused; the lyrical impulse is insufficient to convert the thought into the fine gold of poetry, and we get the impression rather of imaginative thought turned into verse than of a naturally poetic inspiration finding its inevitable expression. . . . For the most part, as already said, his verse conveys the impression of a man writing in a medium not really natural to him. If we contrast his verse with his prose, we see the difference at once. As a prose-writer he has little reason to fear comparison with any writer of his age. His prose shows a simplicity and a lucidness of phrase altogether admirable; and it will indeed be wonderful if *Centuries of Meditations* does not become one of the classics of the language.

If Traherne had indeed been as great a poet as he was a prose-writer, he would have stood with Blake and Wordsworth. And he does not. Yet many of his gifts were not inferior to theirs; indeed he seems often astonishingly to have anticipated them, in phrase as well as in thought. Traherne had many of the essential gifts of a great poet. He had the greatest, for he had in the highest degree all that we mean by vision. No man ever lived in a vaster world than Traherne, or beheld more magnificent drama in the cosmos; no man ever saw beauty with clearer eyes, and beauty in one of its rarest forms; no man ever worshipped more truly the beauty he beheld, or served it with more complete devotion. He had passion and sincerity; he had culture and breadth of experience, access to all the treasures of books and contact at many points with the world of man; he had original-

[89] John Masefield, *The Speaker*, April 1903.

ity and intellectual force, so that nothing he wrote could be trivial or commonplace.

Yet he failed to be a great poet. Primarily, I believe it was because he never perceived the true function of poetry. He turned to it by a sort of instinct, and because his hero David was also a poet. Yet he did not ever perceive the creative power of the poetic imagination. He knew that the mind was a creative force, creating those worlds wherein it moves; but the function of poetry for him was but to comment on those worlds. He trusted reason too much, and imagination too little. Poetry for him "brings down the highest Mysteries to sense and keeps them there." But the highest mysteries are not to be so brought. He was not content to take us into his own fair worlds of vision, and to awaken in us his own emotion. The ethical teaching must be explicit, and the radiancy of his joy is clouded from us by the moral. So great indeed was the authentic fire in him that we do feel its heat and glow in spite of him; but we feel it most immediately when the didacticism is clothed in a concept that is itself lovely—as childhood or the beauty of nature. The greatest poets have succeeded in revealing to us the inaccessible beauty; they embody it in forms of words as strange and unexpected and inexplicable to reason as the magic of music; they speak directly to another faculty in us than reason; and they do not trouble to interpret their creation. Traherne all too rarely sings to that faculty in us; he all too frequently comments and interprets.

Another error followed on this first one—his misunderstanding of form. He saw, and rightly, that the vision of beauty is the essential quality in poetry; he saw that words misused can obscure the vision. That perception saved him from many of the faults of his age; and his "Author to the Critical Peruser" anticipates in many respects Wordsworth's famous preface. Where Traherne made his mistake—and Wordsworth was not quite innocent of it—was in thinking that one plain word was as good as another for the uses of poetry; that the function of words was negative, merely not to refract the visionary light. But as the greatest of poets have shown, this light will shine only through song. There is no virtue in mere plainness and simplicity.

Thus for Traherne there is not a vital connection between form and content; content may be the spirit of his work, but form is not the body shaped by that spirit, only a dress, embroidered and arranged with some care. The divine puts on the poet's dress, as Philip Traherne says, "to win Acceptance. For we all descry When Precepts cannot, Poems take the Ey." The precepts are the thing, the verse a concession to human weakness.

With no high conception of poetry itself, and with no understanding of the vital connection between form and content, it was not possible for Traherne to devote his energies to the mastery of his instrument, or to surrender all his being, as the poet must, to the shaping spirit of imagination.

The price of that error is Traherne's minor rank forever as a poet. To me that waste of spirit, that frustration of all those magnificent endowments for supreme poetic creation, is one of the tragedies of our literature. If only Traherne had seen the poet with Milton's eyes, as a chosen servant of God and man, what a "Paradise Regained" he might have written for us!

Writing of Traherne in his preface to the *Centuries of Meditations*, Bertram Dobell remarked: "His prose style, it seems to me, was entirely his own; for I know of no model which he could have followed or imitated. Certainly it was not the usual style of his own time, or of the Elizabethan period. It has not the least resemblance to the style of Milton, or of Jeremy Taylor, or of Sir Thomas Browne." Most critics have concurred in thus adding to their praise of the beauty of Traherne's prose the further praise that it is unique in this period.

This, however, is not strictly true. Milton and Taylor and Sir Thomas Browne were Carolines; and with the Restoration came new fashions in English prose as well as in so many other things. But changes of this kind are not made in an instant. The ears of men were tuned to the sonorous rhythm that the long sentence, with its delicate balancing of subordinate clauses, was capable of producing in the hands of its greatest masters. Modern prose style took fifty years to develop; and yet, as far back as Bacon, its essentials were already present in our language. It was a question of fashion; and while Traherne was writing, Cowley and Dryden were slowly making the new style fashionable. Dryden's masterpiece, the Preface to the Fables, was published only in the last year of the century, and marks the triumph of that new style. "The style is all Dryden's own—short and well-balanced sentences, restraint, lucidity, and precision, a tone of friendly intercourse with the reader, an ease which never becomes familiarity, and a dignity which never stiffens into pomposity," says the *Cambridge History of English Literature.* But Traherne had achieved this twenty-five years earlier; and not Traherne only, but a host of minor writers who made no great stir in the world of fashion and of letters, but who nevertheless played their part in creating the new taste.

The magnitude of the change which took place in our manner of writing English between 1660 and 1710 may be seen at a glance by comparing any passage from Traherne with, say, the following from the great Jeremy Taylor, who was Traherne's contemporary but belonged to the older school:

For as a Worm creeping with her belly on the ground, with her portion and share of Adam's curse, lifts up its head to partake a little of the blessings of the air, and opens the junctures of her imperfect body, and curles her little rings into knots and combinations, drawing up her tail to a neighbourhood of the head's pleasure and motion; but still it must return to abide the fate of its own nature, and dwell and sleep upon the dust: So are the hopes of a mortal Man; he opens his eyes and looks upon fine things at a distance, and shuts them again with weakness, because they are too glorious to behold; And the Man rejoyces because he hopes fine things are staying for him; but his heart aches, because he knows there are a thousand ways to fail and miss of these glories; and though he hopes, yet he enjoys not; he longs, but he possesses not, and must be content with his portion of dust; and being a worm and no Man must lie in this portion, before he can receive the end of his hopes, the Salvation of his Soul in the resurrection of the dead.[90]

The fashion that set in at the Restoration was a conscious reaction against the two chief elements of the older style, the long complex sentence and metaphors such as this just quoted—elements capable of great beauty and impressiveness in the hands of the few, but degenerating too easily into ungrammatical turgidity and far-fetched, intolerable conceits. In Eachard's *Contempt of the Clergy* (1670) there is an excellent contemporary account of the depths to which pulpit oratory had descended, "the intollerable fooleries of this way of talking." Eachard supplies lively and well-nigh incredible examples from the books and sermons of "these indiscreet and horrid metaphormongers."

The consciousness of the demand for simplicity and clearness is shown by this passage, written in 1664, concerning the new *Royal Society*:

There is one thing more about which the *Society* has been most solicitous; and that is the manner of their *Discourse*: which unless they had been only watchful to keep in due temper, the whole spirit and vigour of their *Design* had been soon eaten out by the luxury and redundance of speech. . . . And, in few words, I dare say that of all the studies of men, nothing may be sooner obtain'd than this vicious abundance of *Phrase*, this trick of *Metaphors*, this volubility of *Tongue*, which makes so great a noise in the World. . . . It will suffice my present purpose to point out what has been done by the *Royal Society* towards the correcting of excesses in *Natural Philosophy*, to which it is of all others, a most profest enemy. They have therefore been most vigorous in putting in execution the only Remedy that can be found for this *extravagance*, and that has been a constant Resolution to reject all amplification, digressions, and swellings of style; to return back to the primitive purity and shortness, when men deliver'd so many *things* almost in an equal number of *words*. They have exacted from all their members a close, naked, natural way of speaking, positive expressions, clear senses, a native easiness, bringing all things as near the Mathematical plainness as they can, and preferring

---

[90] Jeremy Taylor, *A Sermon Preached at the Funeral of the Lord Primate of Ireland* (London, 1668).

the language of Artizans, Countrymen, and Merchants before that of Wits or Scholars.[91]

The value of this work of the Royal Society in seeking a clear plain style for scientific exposition, and in roundly condemning as "vicious" the still prevalent fashions in language of the wits and scholars, can hardly be overestimated.

A reform of the abuses of pulpit oratory had already begun, though even by 1670, when Eachard wrote, its task was by no means accomplished. Tillotson, Stillingfleet, and South, all great and popular preachers, were of the new school, and so was Barrow, whose style at times so strongly resembles Traherne's.

Essays of Cowley's written in the last two years of his life, and enriched by all he had been taught by Montaigne, show how potent all these new ideas had become in the second decade after the Restoration; and by their charm and popularity and the influence of Cowley's great reputation, they set the seal of general approval on the new style. Cowley died in 1667, the year Traherne came up to London; his essays were published in the following year; and Traherne, who was deeply influenced as a metrist by Cowley, and who borrows from some of Cowley's poems interspersed in the volume of essays, was also as deeply influenced by his prose. In the personal element, the friendly intercourse with his reader, and the care in literary craftsmanship, Traherne follows Cowley as Cowley followed Montaigne.

Traherne is thus no brilliant meteor. He was caught by the strong tide of reaction that was to issue in the next century in the limpid impersonality of Addison; but he consciously approved of the reaction and deliberately surrendered his genius to it. Speaking of verse, Traherne wrote that "an easy Stile drawn from a native vein" was the style which he judged "fit to win Esteem"; and he has recorded his scorn of those "verbal Kings" that "Ransack all Nature's Rooms," and are given to "curling Metaphors" . . . "Pictures," and "painted Eloquence."

[91] Sprat, *History of the Royal Society.*

He has left us no theory of prose; yet from his practice we can clearly see that the transparency of medium he approved of in verse he no less emphatically approved of in prose.

The greatness of Traherne as a prose-writer rests in his ability successfully to combine the old with the new. The long complex sentence was gone; but that which had made the beauty of it, the delicate balancing of clauses, lived on as the more direct balancing of sentence against sentence, and of direct antitheses. The vigorous and effective use of antithesis, without that artificiality or predominance which was to mark its later abuse, is a feature of Traherne's style; and the sentence, freed from the cumber of complexity and unwieldy length, took to itself an immensely greater range of tone. It could still be stately and sonorous when occasion demanded; but it need no longer be pompous when the occasion for dignity had passed. The range of mood of Traherne's writing has already been shown; and it was the virtue of the instrument he used that it could furnish a fitting expression for every such change of mood. The "fit Temperance of words and materials" had been achieved.

The use of metaphor and of poetic imagery was also Traherne's inheritance from the past. He, and those of his temper, refrained from the far-fetched and erudite; they drew their comparisons from the simple and the ordinary; but they were not afraid, as those of Addison's day were afraid, of that high truth of poetry which is not the truth of fact. "You never enjoy the world aright, till the Sea floweth in your veins, till you are clothed with the heavens, and crowned with the stars." The time was coming fast when no English prose-writer would have so far forgotten himself as to use such "enthusiastic" expressions. But Traherne could do so with a glorious ease, because with one hand he touched the Carolines, and Donne, and Shakespeare himself.

Traherne also reaches forward to Addison, and the great prose-writers of the eighteenth century. Like these, he was master of the art of easy, friendly intercourse that yet is never undignified nor slipshod. He can mount the rostrum, but he can also occupy the armchair; and it is the perfect, equally unself-conscious command of the great capacities of both styles that gives to Traherne's prose its range and freedom. Cowley had much of this freedom; but his prose is inferior to Traherne's because his width of experience was narrower, and he did not need at any time a mighty organ to express vast imaginings of soul.

It was an auspicious moment in the history of our language, this close of the third quarter of the seventeenth century, when the grandeur of the old style was still potent to influence, and the freedom of the new style was already won; and, as so often, the beauty of Traherne's prose came of the fortunate coincidence of the man and the moment.

In consequence of this flexibility, Traherne has a variety of manners of writing—he has styles, rather than a style; and *Christian Ethicks* of all his works best exemplifies his range.

For straightforward narrative of fact, or for unemotional exposition, Traherne used a plain and simple style, the distinction of which is its appropriateness:

> Since the Consideration of the End is that alone which does animate a Man to the use of the Means, they that treat of Virtue do worthily propose the End in the beginning, and first shew the Excellency of Bliss before they open the Nature of Virtue. For it is a vain thing to discover the Means, unless the End be desired by those to whom the Nature and use of them, in their tendency to that End, is taught and commended; for if the End be despised, all endeavors are but fruitless which instruct us in the Means, and the Knowledge of them vain, if they never be used or improved.[92]

It is frequently said that it was the task of the eighteenth century to create this simple medium for ordinary intercourse; but as *Christian Ethicks* and other books show, it was already well-developed before that century began.

[92] *Christian Ethicks*, p. 2.

How vigorously Traherne used the short sentence and the simple style for argument is illustrated by the following:

> To love another more than one's self is absurd and impossible. In Nature it is so, till we are obliged; or perhaps till we see it our interest, and find it our pleasure. It is a surprize to an Atheistical fool that it should be one's interest to love another better than one's self: yet Bears, Dogs, Hens, Bees, Lions, Ants do it: they die for their young ones. Nurses, Fathers, Mothers do it. Brides and Bridegrooms frequently do it; and so do Friends. All Valiant Heroes love their Country better than themselves: *Moses* would have his Name blotted out of the Book of Life rather than the *Israelites* destroyed. *St. Paul* could wish himself accursed from Christ for his Brethren the *Jews*: and they both learnt it of their *Master, who made himself a Curse*, and even Sin, *for us*. And it was his interest to do it![93]

Christian Ethicks contains many similar passages; but *Roman Forgeries* affords us the best proof of Traherne's complete mastery of a clear and energetic style, excellently suited for vigorous argument; and in this book its effectiveness is further increased by the occasional use of irony.

Traherne used the short sentence with remarkable effectiveness for aphorisms—sometimes singly, to sum up an argument, sometimes in a succession, to clarify and illustrate. For instance:

> By giving me all things else, He hath made even afflictions themselves my treasures. The sharpest trials are the finest furbishing. The most tempestuous weather is the best seed-time. A Christian is an oak flourishing in winter.

> A Physician may kill a man with the best Ingredients, but good Medicines are those wherein every Simple hath its proper Dose.

The same choice of the neat and felicitous phrase points the wit of the but half-serious praise of temperance, from which the following is taken:

> A little Selfishness puts our Companions in mind of our own Interest, and makes them perceive that we understand it: which adds a lustre to our Self-denial, and renders our Liberality more safe and precious. Plainness without Policy is downright Simplicity, and Policy without Plainness

void of Honesty. The one makes us Crafty and renders us suspected; the other exposes us, and makes us *Ridiculous*; but both united are venerable and prudent.

In the chapter on meekness occur similar paragraphs of antithetical wordplay, and the chapter "Of Modesty" is almost wholly written in this tone and style. They are particularly interesting as revealing self-conscious craftsmanship in Traherne's literary art.

The personal note in Traherne's writing, and the delicacy and frankness of his familiar intercourse, have already been fully illustrated in the many extracts from the *Centuries of Meditations*, and need no further comment here beyond their recognition as attractive and characteristic elements of his general style.

Traherne's use of metaphor and simile is modern. Involved and sustained metaphors such as Jeremy Taylor's never appear; he is capable of the most magnificent use of poetic imagery; yet on the whole he uses metaphors of homely and concrete things as serviceable explanations of abstract ideas. Metaphor for him is not an extraneous ornament, but a swift summing up of the argument—something essential for its continued clarity in the reader's mind. Thus a discussion on humility and anger is crystallized in a metaphor: "If Wild-fire be thrown, I will put it out with my foot, and not by throwing it back, give my Enemy the advantage of retorting it upon me."

The following are also typical of his use of imagery:

To talk of overflowing in the disbursments and effusions of Love and Goodness, till our emptiness and capacity be full within, is as impertinent and unseasonable as to advise a Beggar to give away a Kingdom, or a dead man to breathe, or one that is starving to give Wine and Banquets to the Poor and Needy.

[Of a controversial writer obscuring the issue]

He Clouds himself, like the Cuttle, in his own Ink.
All inferiour felicities are but Miseries compared with the Highest. A

farthing is *good* and pleaseth a Beggar in time of distress: but a piece of Gold is *Better*. . . .

The World is not this little Cottage of Heaven and Earth.

Thy body . . . was given thee to be a lantern only to the candle of Love that shineth in thy Soul.

Metaphors so used are of the very texture of Traherne's prose. They are part of that image-making faculty of his which is his natural endowment as a poet. He could never, as we have seen, even in childhood, be content with half-seeing; his nature drove him on to seek full vision; and part of that more exquisite perception of all great poets and great philosophers has been the perception of analogies, the power to illuminate the abstract by the concrete, to see the material as symbol of the spiritual. Plato and Plotinus and the New Testament are full of the most richly suggestive use of such analogy; and it is not claiming too much to say that Traherne's use of metaphors is symbolism of their great kind.

So far the aspects of Traherne's style that we have been considering belong rather to new style than to the grander style it was supplanting. The fusion of the two styles is seen in such a passage as this from *Christian Ethicks*:

To shew that there is such a Goodness as that which infinitely delights in pouring out its Glory upon all Creatures, the Sun was made: which continues Night and Day pouring out its Streams of Light and Heat upon all Ages, yet is as Glorious this day as it was the first Moment of its Creation. To shew this the Stars were made, that shine in their Watches and Glitter in their Motions only to serve us. The Moon was made to shew this Goodness, which runs her race for ever to serve us. The Earth was made to support us, Springs and Rivers expend their Streams to revive us; Fruits, and Flowers, and Herbs, and Trees delight us. All corruptible Things waste and consume away, that they may sacrifice their Essence to our Benefit. . . . And if these (Spice and Odours) by Disbursing their proper sweetness, become more sweet and enlarge themselves, if they are made Bright and fair for our sake, if they enjoy any Light and Pleasure in their Service, as the Sun and Stars do, as Herbs and Flowers do, as Beasts, and Birds, and Fishes do; the Goodness of the Creator is abundantly more clear and apparent herein; for in all those Creatures that perfect themselves by the Service which they do, the Service itself is a sufficient Recompense, while those upon which we feed, being more Corruptible, are exalted in their Beings, by being turned into ours. And the Trade of Bees, in the Hony they make for us, and the Warmth of sheep, in the fleeces they bear for us, the Comfort of Birds in the feathers they wear and the Nests they build for us, and the pleasures of Beasts in the off-spring they beget and bring up for us, these things shew that *God is Good to all, and that his mercy is over all his Works.*

The carefully varied rhythm and construction of the shorter sentences; the reiterations, in *shew* and *do* and *for us*; the culmination of the short sentences in the three long sentences, those two long-suspended periods separated by a balanced antithesis; the whole rhetorical swell of it with its fervor and yet its restraint, belong to the great school of Caroline prose. We feel the same spirit at work in those yet greater passages from the chapters on courage and on magnanimity and "Of Charity to Our Neighbours" that were printed by Bertram Dobell in his introduction to the poems; and we meet it again in those exaltations of the love of God in the *Second* and the *Fourth Centuries*. It is a style of splendor, impassioned in feeling yet richly dignified, a perfect medium for the lofty themes to which it is wedded. In Traherne's hands it is strong-winged, rising with him effortlessly to the noblest heights of human vision.

Traherne's chief defect as a prose-writer is that the rhythm of his sentences tends to remain apart from the rhythm of his paragraphs; there is, in consequence, too often, no rhythm in the paragraphs. His unit is the sentence, or the little group of sentences; rarely the paragraph, and still more rarely the chapter. I have said of his *Roman Forgeries*—and the same is true of his *Christian Ethicks*—that it is not a book, but a collection of chapters; and within the chapters the same lack of organic unity is perceptible. At his best Traherne overcame this tendency; in those extracts quoted earlier in this chapter as exemplifying his rhetorical power, and in his most eloquent passages in

Christian Ethicks, he achieved this larger unity triumphantly; and *Christian Ethicks* owes no little of its beauty to the increasing power Traherne was manifesting towards its close of working on a larger canvas. There are unmistakable signs that, had he lived and continued to write, this defect would have been overcome. Then we should have had still greater works from his pen—works as perfect in structure as the present ones are perfect in detail. A critic[94] has said of the *Centuries of Meditations* that "only fifty out of the 410 paragraphs can satisfy the critical examination of English prose." His estimate is, I think, too low; but it is true that many of the meditations have no organic unity, whatever the beauty of their parts. The third meditation of the *Third Century,* which we shall consider directly, is one of those where the lovely rhythm of the sentences is part of the rhythm of the whole, to the immeasurable gain of both.

When Traherne died he was still perfecting his technique in the broader unities of construction; and this is also true of that smaller unit, the sentence. That the prose of the *Centuries* is so beautiful is due to the very thorough revision it received. A desire to accumulate detail was natural to Traherne; it was a consequence partly of his love of full knowledge, and partly of his energy and enthusiasm. He first acquired by study and by contemplation an extremely rich association for his favorite ideas, and then loved to pour it all forth copiously. The *Serious and Pathetical Contemplation* came of these complementary desires, and owes its curious beauty to their passion. An ear tuned to the rhythm of the Psalms, with their device of balanced and varied reiteration helped to determine his own favorite rhythm; and reiteration afforded an easy but extraneous method of securing that rhythm. By the time Traherne revised the *Centuries* and rigorously deleted its redundancies, he was

[94] *The Literary World,* September 15, 1908.

clearly aware of a new standard of perfection, and consciously striving to attain it.

It is evident that this same new "temperance in words" was exercised in *Christian Ethicks*; but the manuscript of the *Centuries* permits us to see Traherne actually at work in achieving that new sentence-rhythm which is organic and not extraneous. In the following, No. 51 of the *Second Century*, the words in *italics* are later insertions, the words in parentheses crossed through for deletion:

> Love is a far more Glorious Being than flesh and Bones. If thou wilt it is Endless (infinit and Eternal): and infinitly more Sweet (and Delightful) than thy Body can be to thee and others. Thy Body is confined, and is a Dull Lump of Heavy Clay, by which thou art retarded rather than doest move (and) *It* was given thee to be a Lantern only to the Candle of Lov *that shineth in thy Soul*: (It is that) by (which) *it* Thou dost see *and feel* and eat and drink: but the End of all is that Thou mightest (lov and) be (Lov) as God is: (and be like God) a Joy and Blessing by being Lov. Thy Lov is illimited (and unconfined). Thy Lov can extend to all Objects (in Heaven and Earth). Thy Lov can see God and Accompany His Lov throughout all Eternity (and Admire it). . . .

Yet the amount of these corrections is less than one might have expected; the restraint has already been largely exercised before the meditations were copied into this book; yet even this one example shows that its exercise was conscious.

The most famous passage in all Traherne's writings is the third meditation of the *Third Century* that begins, "The corn was orient and immortal wheat. . . ." People who know nothing else of Traherne are familiar with this. It is of course pure magic. And no analysis of content or of form will compel it to yield its secret. But because it is so famous, and so worthy of that fame, so haunting in its cadence, it challenges the attempt. I quote it in full:

> The corn was orient and immortal wheat, which never should be reaped, nor was ever sown. I thought it had stood from everlasting to everlasting. The dust and stones of the street were as precious as gold: the gates were at first the end of the world. The green trees when I saw

them first through one of the gates transported and ravished me, their sweetness and unusual beauty made my heart to leap, and almost mad with ecstasy, they were such strange and wonderful things. The men! O what venerable and reverend creatures did the aged seem! Immortal Cherubims! And young men glittering and sparkling Angels, and maids strange seraphic pieces of life and beauty! Boys and girls tumbling in the street and playing were moving jewels. I knew not that they were born or should die; but all things abided eternally as they were in their proper places. Eternity was manifest in the Light of the Day, and something infinite behind everything appeared; which talked with my expectation and moved my desire. The city seemed to stand in Eden, or to be built in Heaven. The streets were mine, the temple was mine, the people were mine, their clothes and gold and silver were mine, as much as their sparkling eyes, fair skins and ruddy faces. The skies were mine, and so were the sun and moon and stars, and all the World was mine; and I the only spectator and enjoyer of it. I knew no churlish proprieties, nor bounds, nor divisions: but all proprieties and divisions were mine: all treasures and the possessors of them. So that with much ado I was corrupted and made to learn the dirty devices of this world. Which now I unlearn, and become as it were a little child again, that I may enter into the Kingdom of God.

In this third meditation there is not a single deletion. There are two later insertions, both of them delicate improvements of rhythm: they are the "unusual" before "beauty" in the fourth sentence, and "again" in the final sentence.

The whole meditation is marked by straightforward simplicity of language, simplicity of sentence construction, and comparative rarity of epithets. "The dust and stones of the street were as precious as gold: the gates were at first the end of the world." The words have an air of inevitability, a fallacious air of being those that you or I must have used had we been writing this passage. There is no hint of art perceptible until we come to that reiterated "mine," "mine," "mine," whereby Traherne emphasizes his sense of possession. Yet even here, too, we hardly notice it, so natural does the cry seem, and so subtle are the variations. Yet supreme technical skill has gone to the framing of these sentences, with their emphasis now on the fact of pos-

session, now on the things possessed; with the variations between single subject and triple subject, between substantive and
substantive-with-epithet, between monosyllable and dissyllable,
between the monosyllabic beginning and the polysyllabic conclusion! There is no end to the hidden art of the form of this
whole meditation; and its very simplicity of words and structure
is not a little responsible for its magic suggestion of that simplicity of childlike wisdom which is its theme.

The opening sentence is quite perfect. Its beauty lies in part
in its rich suggestiveness of that mystery Traherne believed
to be a great truth, the mystery of the spiritual immutability of
mutable things, the permanency of all transients in God, a truth
seen by the child in sweet mistakenness, and not seen in real
truth save by the childlike soul in maturity. The poem "Shadows
in the Water" is another allegory of this idea. The whole meditation is an allegory, and however dimly we perceive its twofold
meaning, yet the richness and beauty of that deeper theme
determined the beauty of its external content and of its external
form as surely as the soul fashions the body.

The sentence rhythm throughout is that of advance and
retreat, varied continually by the length of the swing. It is
part of this rhythm that the epithets should be so often in pairs:
"orient and immortal," "strange and wonderful," "venerable
and reverend," "glittering and sparkling." Balanced pairs
occur continually, and are part of the inner movement of the
rhythm within its balanced swing: "everlasting to everlasting";
"dust and stones"; "transported and ravished"; "sweetness and
unusual beauty." Yet although the rhythm is strongly marked,
the effect is not that of a pendulum, but rather of the infinite
variety of breaking waves eternally advancing and retreating
on some wide sandy beach, now almost level, now swinging
strongly, now longer in the advance, now in the retreat. That
fourth sentence is like a great breaker, piling up and up and
crashing swiftly. And yet, as in all great prose, it is a rhythm
determined by fine shades of emphasis, of an emphasis in turn

determined by meaning. As a paragraph the rhythm is a gradual crescendo, culminating in the "The streets were mine, the temple was mine," and the rest of that rapid excited chant of possession, and then like a spent wave returning to the peace of the opening phrase in that final lovely close, "Which now I unlearn, and become as it were a little child again, that I may enter into the Kingdom of God."

Had Traherne never written anything but this one meditation, he would stand among the great masters of English prose; and how much more, almost as perfect, he has written, the readers of his *Centuries* know.

One wonders how much of this was conscious art on Traherne's part. It is difficult to say. Bertram Dobell believed it was all unconscious; but one rarely meets a master craftsman who is unfamiliar with the secrets of his craft. Dobell said of Traherne's prose that it was not in his opinion "the result of any conscious effort on the author's part to distinguish himself as a master of style. He wrote clearly, strongly and beautifully because his mind was full of his subject. . . . Whatever the worth of his ideas may be, it is certain that he fervently believed in them; and therefore his words still pulsate with vital force and still glow with the warmth of conviction." That is true. Traherne's sincerity no one can doubt; and it certainly to some extent controlled the form of his prose. It stripped off all falsities of ornament, it saved him from the pitfalls that always lie in wait for the insincere, never more so than in the seventeenth century. Traherne was not only sincerely convinced of the truth of his ideas, but emotionally stirred by their beauty and their poetry; and the strength of his feeling undoubtedly contributed to the formal beauty of his prose.

These two factors would operate unconsciously; but I find it difficult to believe that everything in Traherne's exquisite and subtle art is accounted for by these alone. In determining those gradations of rhythm, those shades of meaning and suggestiveness between word and word, those subtle varieties of sentence pattern, all those felicities of variation that we have seen in but one short passage, the judgment surely played its part in selecting and rejecting and bringing to the bar of the critical ear; and the ear, sensitive to the rhythm of prose by natural endowment and by culture, must have depended in turn on the conscious critical apparatus of the whole mind. If it be true of poets that they are neither born nor made, but made after they are born, it is no less true of the prose-writer.

PART FOUR.

Thomas Traherne the "Divine Philosopher."

"Since no man can be a man unless he be a Philosopher, nor a true Philosopher unless he be a Christian, nor a perfect Christian unless he be a Divine, every man ought to spend his time in studying Divine Philosophy."—CENTURIES IV, 3.

Christian, Platonist, Mystic.

IT is quite clear that Traherne believed himself to be a philosopher, and that the philosophy he practised, and preached in his books, was new no less than true.

Perhaps you will find some *New* Notions: but yet when they are examined, he hopes it will appear to the Reader, that it was the actual knowledge of true *Felicity* that taught him to speak. . . . He firmly retains all that was established in the Ancient Councels . . . only he enriches all, by farther opening the *grandeur* and *glory* of Religion, with the interiour depths and Beauties of Faith.[95] I will open my mouth in Parables, I will utter things that have been kept secret from the foundation of the World! Things strange yet common, incredible, yet known, most high, yet plain; infinitely profitable, but not esteemed. Is it not a great thing that you should be Heir of the World? Is it not a great enriching verity? . . . The thing hath been from the Creation of the World, but hath not so been explained as that the interior Beauty should be understood. It is my design therefore in such a plain manner to unfold it that my friendship may appear in making you possessor of the whole world.[96]

Again and again that note is heard—that what he writes, though "incredible" and "never so strange to our age" is exact truth, to be discerned by reason and tested by experience.

Was Traherne under a delusion in believing he had a message for his age? It is clear that much in his philosophy is not new. In its general web two or three borrowed strands stand out conspicuously; and chief of these is its Platonism. Moreover, we can detect the actual sources of that Platonism, and this is of interest; for the fact that Traherne, in that age and in the mental atmosphere of that age, was a Platonist, is indeed one of his major claims to greatness, and, in spite of the apparent contradiction, to originality.

[95] Preface to *Christian Ethicks.*   [96] *Centuries* I, 3.

Traherne was a Platonist first and chiefly because his Christianity was the Christianity of St. Paul and of St. John; and St. Paul and St. John were Platonists. As Dean Inge has remarked in his book on the Platonic tradition,

> Platonism . . . was Christianised long before the New Testament Canon was closed: and ever since the first century it has been an integral part of Christianity as an historical religion. . . . It is unquestionable that most of the canonical books of the New Testament, especially the epistles of St. Paul and the Johannine group, do not belong to the Palestinian tradition. . . . The whole doctrine of the Spirit in (St. Paul's) epistles corresponds closely to the Platonic *Nous*. . . . The words "The things that are seen are temporal, but the things that are not seen are eternal" are pure Platonism; and this is not an isolated instance. . . . In the Phaedrus as in I Corinthians, love is the great hierophant of the divine mysteries, which forms the link between divinity and humanity.[97]

One who had sufficient intellectual power might indeed build up the whole of Traherne's system on three texts: "God is Love"; "Ye are the sons of God"; "God so loved the World . . ."; as similarly all his ethical teaching is based on "We may be filled with all the fullness of God." It is noteworthy how frequently Traherne quotes these very sayings, and how much more frequently than anything else he quotes the Pauline Epistles. With a Christianity so based, Traherne, as Dean Inge has shown, could not be other than a Platonist.

But Traherne's Platonism was also reinforced by direct study of Plato—whom he quotes on several occasions—and of Plotinus. The teachings of Plato and Plotinus, in spite of their attraction for a group of the more spiritually minded of the time, were still "strange lore," "new Notions," to the many. As More wrote in his *Platonick Song of the Soul*,

> So of what's consonant to Plato's school
> (Which well agrees with learned Pythagore,

[97] W. R. Inge, *The Platonic Tradition in English Religious Thought*, Preface, and pp. 10-13.

Egyptian Trismegist, and th' antique roll
Of Chaldee wisdome, all which time hath tore
But Plato and deep Plotin do restore)
Which is my scope, I sing out lustily:
If any twitten me for such strange lore,
And me all blamelesse brand with infamy,
God purge that man from fault of foul malignity.

During the twenty years that elapsed between More's writing of these lines and Traherne's writing of his *Centuries,* the current of advanced religious thought had turned more definitely toward Platonism; but nevertheless the ideas so borrowed were far from being generally accepted; and this explains some of Traherne's comments on the strangeness of what he is saying. For Traherne was of the few in his deep study of Plato and Plotinus, and in his reverence for them as enshrining a great and divinely inspired philosophy of life. His books are full of images and ideas derived from this firsthand study—the World-Soul, the symbolic use of the sphere, the sun, the human eye, or mirrors, to name but a few. What I take to be an interesting example of this occurs in *Christian Ethicks,* page 71, where Traherne curiously sums up the beautiful effects of love in the human life: "These are the little *Cupids* that flie about this coelestial *Venus,* when it is what it ought to be, the Mother of Felicity and the Daughter of God." Is not this a paraphrase of Plotinus's "Heavenly Aphrodite, daughter of Kronos, who is no other than the Intellectual Principle, the Soul at its divinest" (*Enneads* III. 5. 2)? Such things, of course, were in the air, tossed about whenever men talked of religion and philosophy; yet we can be fairly sure, from their frequency, and from this easy familiarity with actual phrasing, that Traherne was not only at home in the works of Plato, whom he names and quotes and whom he summarized, but also in the *Enneads.* It is beyond doubt that Plotinus is the ultimate source of much that is of the essence of Traherne's philosophy.

A third and very powerful stream of Platonism came to

Traherne from his study of the writings of Hermes Trismegistus. The unquestioned opinion concerning these writings, as
handed down by the early Fathers, and endorsed by St. Augustine, Lactantius, and others, was that they belonged to the
remotest past, to the very dawn of history. It was long accepted
that the author was he who was afterwards deified by the Greeks
and the Romans, though Traherne himself reflects the doubt
of this which was growing up in his time[98] and which had first
been formulated by Casaubon. Traherne believed that these
writings, whatever their authorship, were certainly of immense
antiquity; that they enshrined "the philosophy of the ancient
heathen." He was quick to perceive and to welcome the correspondence between the teaching of Hermes and the teaching
of St. John and St. Paul; even the occurrence of the wording of
the Gospels and the Pauline Epistles and the Psalms would not
arouse in that age in the face of such strong authority, any doubt
of the genuineness of the supposed antiquity of these writings.
Such repetition merely emphasized the oneness of all truth; and
the absence of all reference to the person and life of Christ
effectively concealed from the seventeenth century their true
post-Christian origin. Traherne, and his contemporaries, gave
to Hermes the reverence they felt was due to hoary antiquity,
the reverence due to a revelation of truth by God earlier than
Moses, earlier than Plato; and that so much in Plato is to be
found in Hermes definitely enhanced the value of Plato.

The books of Hermes on these grounds enjoyed a considerable vogue in the seventeenth century. *The Poemander* was
translated into English in 1649 by Dr. Everard, and ran into
several editions.[99] Contemporary references are numerous—
Milton's in *Il Penseroso*, and More's already quoted, and the
many others well reflect this current of interest. Two groups of

---

[98] "Trismegistus (or whoever else was the Author of that Book) saw . . . etc.,"
Christian Ethicks, p. 454.

[99] Traherne, as it appears from *Centuries* IV, 74, used one of the many Latin
versions of Hermes.

students turned with eagerness to Hermes—those interested in magic, and those interested in Platonic philosophy: the Hermetic writings are indeed still studied seriously by modern occultists.

It was solely as a philosopher that Hermes influenced Traherne. Magic, and all the works of magic, are no part of his scheme of things. Traherne's chief debt to Hermes lies in the deeper and more spiritual conception he put forth of the nature of the Godhead, of its trinity and of its unity; and of creation as an eternal act of the Godhead; and still more markedly, in his teaching of the potential divinity of man. All this became an integral part of Traherne's thinking. It is in support of the latter contention, that man is no miserable worm but an incarnate angel, that Traherne devotes in the *Christian Ethicks*[100] some four whole pages to quotations from the *Poemander*, including the striking "Wherefore we must be bold to say, that an Earthly Man is a Mortal God, and the Heavenly God is an'Immortal Man." This is exactly Traherne's own belief; and a great deal of what Traherne constantly asserts of the infinite capacity of the human mind, of its power to know God, since like (and like alone) knows like, is based directly on the passages from Hermes quoted by Traherne himself in *Christian Ethicks*.

Platonism is a marked and constant feature of Hermes' teaching, following of necessity on his adoption of the Platonic *Nous*. Traherne, for example, quotes from Hermes: "And yet thou sayest God is invisible: but be advised: for who is more manifest than he? For therefore he made all things, that thou by all things mightst see him. This is the Good of God, his Vertue is this, to appear and be seen in all things": and characterizes the passage as "most divine." Not only the paragraph which immediately follows this quotation, but a great deal of what he writes elsewhere, is but an extended commentary on its central idea.

Thus Traherne, in being so deeply interested in Hermes—as

[100] Pp. 443-7.

the quotations in *Christian Ethicks* and the multitude of classified quotations in his commonplace book amply show—was brought into direct contact with yet another current of Platonism.

Yet Traherne's Platonism is strongly modified by his Christianity. His deity is a very different being from the Plotinian "Intellectual Principle" that "does not possess Being: does not know itself as Good" (*Enneads* VI. 7. 38), that does not act, because act is motion, and it is eternally unmoved. As we have seen, Traherne discards all these negative postulates of infinity for affirmations. His deity acts and suffers. The Plotinian Supreme is Father in being the source of all things; Traherne's is the Father whose sons have power to grieve and to rejoice his heart. The parable of the Prodigal Son cannot be written of an intellectual principle.

The Plotinian concept of evil is different from Traherne's: "Evil is of necessity: for there must be a contrary to Good" (*Enneads* I. 8. 6). "Evil cannot cease to be" (*Enneads* I. 4. 11). The Christian teaching of the Kingdom of God cuts diametrically across such a conception; and here, as elsewhere, Traherne is a Christian first and a Platonist afterwards.

The greatest debt of Traherne to Plato and his followers lies not in various ideas he borrows, important as these are, but in the support their philosophy afforded to his own experience that the religious life is the reasonable life: indeed, the only reasonable life; and that reason will guide a man right to the top of the ladder that leads to communion with God. If at the top there come experiences that are unutterable, these are not contrary to reason; reason is at its highest pitch when it ceases to be aware of itself as a distinct faculty of the personality, when it merges with all the rest into a mode of awareness for which language has no name. That harmonizing of the whole personality into a unity no longer conscious of its multiplicity is something all the great mystics have known. It is, they tell us, a mode of being akin to the divine. It is to be love: it is to be mind. "We shall be Mentes as he is Mens, we being of the same mind with Him who is an infinite, eternal Mind," as Traherne expresses it once. It is this belief in reason, this conviction that "the true exemplar of God's infinity is that of your understanding," that lifts Traherne's mysticism above emotionalism and sentimentality and makes of it the intellectual thing it is. To him as to Plotinus, it is by our power of knowing, by our reason, that we mount the rungs, and touch at the top the divine.

As a Platonist, and as an advocate of reason in an age that still distrusted it, Traherne takes his place in the little group of religious philosophers known as the Cambridge Platonists, though in reality its membership was by no means limited to Cambridge. These were the men whose intellectual power, spiritual insight, and moral quality were to free religious thought in England, and who individually were none the less original thinkers from the influence they exercised on each other, nor for the principles they held in common. As a group they proclaimed a new doctrine, a new outlook, and risked and indeed incurred the odium which seems the inevitable lot of the prophet. Traherne can hardly be called a "Cambridge" Platonist, yet it is obvious that he is of their school of thought; and thus the historical setting of the seventeenth-century Platonic revival and Traherne's affinities with or divergences from its leaders must be surveyed, however briefly, before we are in a position to estimate his own claim to originality and his status as "Divine Philosopher."

"Platonic Revival" is perhaps a misleading description of that powerful current of the intellectual life of that day, suggesting as it does a going-back to ancient viewpoints rather than the natural evolution it was, the rising to higher levels of perception and a wider vision of truth from the decay of outworn standards. The rediscovery of the Platonic philosophy was a most potent stimulus to the process, but its source was elsewhere.

The whole seventeenth century was rocked to its foundations by bitter religious strife; the first war of Protestant and Roman

Catholic had added to itself the wars of Anglo-Catholic and Puritan, and of Puritan sect and sect. But all this most earnest and unwearied conflict was fought on one common ground. It sprang from a common conception of the meaning of a church and the nature of religion. Roman Catholic, Anglican, and Presbyterian alike inherited from the Middle Ages, and fought to maintain, a conception of rigid uniformity in theology and ritual, an interpretation of Christianity which entailed strict adhesion to a definite ecclesiastical system, to be venerated as of divine origin. That differences of creed and practice should be permitted to exist, much less welcomed, was to all alike inconceivable: and we are apt to condemn with too easy superiority the intolerance of an age to which tolerance was but a synonym for the basest compromise. Religion was by their common consent a thing apart and external, an addition to other truths; and the knowledge of it was derived in other fashion than ordinary human knowledge. It had little to do with morality, and nothing to do with reason. It was an authority to be accepted and obeyed. Bacon's famous exclusion of reason from the affairs of religion, which is usually read as disingenuous if not cynical, only repeats what will be found elsewhere, and was probably quite honestly intended. It represents a genuine, indeed the orthodox, point of view.

Such a conception of the imperative need of uniformity as this involved, and of the supreme importance of dogma, steeled and embittered polemical theology throughout the seventeenth century and well beyond the era of Traherne and the others. Yet it was the very existence of this warfare, the impossibility of finding any basis of reconciliation for systems and dogmas so contradictory, that turned the most enlightened minds of the age to questioning the assumptions from which the unhappy state of affairs had arisen. Something was clearly wrong when a creed of love and brotherhood yielded in practice such hatred and violence; and those who were more deeply spiritual as well as more advanced intellectually were compelled to take the immense step of examining the universally accepted opinion of the nature of religion itself, and of the real basis of authority. The very spectacle of the state of Christendom provoked this reaction.

This desire for a more liberal interpretation of religion was powerfully stimulated by meeting in the middle of the century the strong and growing stream of genuine scientific inquiry, set in motion by Bacon. Already that spirit of impartial disinterested firsthand investigation had produced remarkable results; men had freed at long last the physical universe from the dead clutch of medieval theology, and had given it to human reason as its own to explore at will. But to many this was a disquieting thing. They foresaw that reason, grown conscious of power, would not leave long untouched the hitherto forbidden fields of religion.

The inevitable turning of the speculative spirit of the nation toward religion was hastened by the appearance of Descartes, who provided an example of a rational thinker interested in fundamental problems of religion. The English Platonists, despite More's period of enthusiastic admiration for Descartes, are not Cartesians. But apart from all results, the very spectacle of an orthodox Christian venturing to investigate the nature of spirit and of matter, and essaying to demonstrate by reason the existence of God, was a stimulus of incalculable potency to further adventurings.

In response to all these intellectual movements, and in conscious opposition to the new and powerful and attractive exposition of materialism provided by Hobbes, there came into existence an inarticulate, leaderless multitude who desired a restatement of the Christian faith more liberal and more spiritual than was then orthodox. The enthusiasm of the response at Cambridge—and far beyond Cambridge—once the leader appeared, is proof of this. For this desire produced the Cambridge Platonists, who in turn made this movement articulate and directed its development.

Before briefly considering Traherne's affinities with the more important of the Cambridge Platonists, it is interesting to note that he probably enjoyed direct personal contact with some of them. Sir Orlando Bridgeman was himself a Cambridge man; and Traherne's predecessor[100a] as his chaplain was Hezekiah Burton, a minor member of that group, and the friend and correspondent of More. Sir Orlando proved a generous patron to Burton, with whose views he thus apparently sympathized; and their friendship was not interrupted when Burton left his household. Burton and Traherne were both present at the ceremony of his will-making, and it is hardly likely that this was their only meeting. Through Burton, and still more probably through Sir Orlando, Traherne may have met all the more influential leaders of the movement. He certainly in that household came directly within their sphere of influence.

Yet it is true—and the fact is important—that Traherne is no mere disciple of that school, nor his writings mere echoes. Whichcote he may have heard preach at St. Lawrence Jewry; Smith's *Discourses* and Culverwel's *Light of Nature* he had probably read; but much that was most important in the work of these leaders was only being wrought out contemporaneously with Traherne's own writings. Whichcote's *Aphorisms* was not published until the middle of the eighteenth century; Cudworth's *True Intellectual System* appeared in 1678, four years after Traherne's death; More's most characteristic works, the *Divine Dialogues* and *Manual of Metaphysics*, in 1667 and 1671 respectively. Traherne's philosophy, mature and completely thought out some years at least before his death, is clearly thus not derivative, but itself an integral part of this whole movement. Only such independence could justify Traherne's own quiet confidence that he had something to say which had not occurred to the majority of his countrymen, and a power of saying it adequate to his stupendous aim of revealing to men as never before the grandeur and the glory of a living religion.

[100a] Or possibly colleague and co-chaplain. Dr. Hutchinson has drawn my attention to Wood's *Fasti Oxon.*, II, 186, which states that Burton was still chaplain to Sir Orlando in 1669.

That Traherne was a Platonist defines his position with regard to the general thought of his age; his relationship to the other Platonists can best be realized by a brief comparison of their views with his.

Of Whichcote[101] and Traherne not much need be said. Whichcote was of an earlier generation, and was already drawing crowds to his Sunday lectures in Trinity Church when Traherne was an undergraduate at Brasenose. He was still holding a faithful group in London for many years after Traherne's death. Whichcote's great achievement was that he reached a higher level of thought than any Protestant theologian before his day, and that by his power as a teacher and a preacher he enabled a host of others to make this advance. He saw reason steadily as a "candle of the Lord," a gift to be used without fear or restriction; and he proclaimed that religion was a unity of life, not a system of dogmas—that dogma was relatively unimportant and the essentials of a Christian creed very few.

How startling and how unwelcome such ideas were to an age that spent itself in maintaining the reverse, Tuckney's letters show. Tuckney was a lifelong friend of Whichcote and a colleague at Cambridge, and was moved to remonstrance by the highest motives. I quote part of Tuckney's second letter, as there could hardly be a better summing up of the early position of the Platonists and of the orthodox Puritan attitude towards this new thing in their midst.

Whilst you were fellow here, you were cast into the company of very learned and ingenious men; who, I fear, at least some of them, studied other authors more than the Scriptures—and Plato and his scholars above others—in whom, I must needs acknowledge, from the little insight I have into them, I find many excellent and divine expressions: and as we are wont more to listen to and wonder at a parrot speaking a few words than a man that speaks many more and more plainly, and all intelligibly, so whilst we find such gems in such dunghills, where we less expected them, we have been too much drawn away with admiration of them.

---

[101] Whichcote (1610-1683), Provost of King's College, 1644-1660.

And hence in part hath runne a vein of doctrine, which divers very able and worthy men—whom from my heart I much honour—are, I fear, too much known by. The power of nature in morals too much advanced. Reason hath too much given to it in the mysteries of faith—a *ratio recta* much talked of, which I cannot tell where to find—Mind and understanding is all; heart and will little spoken of. The decrees of God questioned and quarreled, because, according to our reason, we cannot comprehend how they can stand with His goodness. . . . Those our philosophers, and other heathens, much fairer candidates for heaven than the Scriptures seem to allow of; and they, in their virtues, preferred before Christians overtaken with weaknesses. A kind of moral divinity minted, only with a little tincture of Christ added. Nay, a Platonic faith unites to God. Inherent righteousness so preached, as if not with the prejudice of imputed righteousness, which hath sometimes very unseemingly language given it; yet much said of the one, and very little or nothing of the other. This was not Paul's manner of preaching.

And this in essence is the attitude of censure and of fear that for the whole century was to expose the Platonists to attack and to a fire of ignorant witticisms. Yet by Traherne, and by the other Platonists who followed Whichcote, the view of reason and of religion for which he fought is accepted so simply that it is not argued. Accepting it as axiomatic, they build on it their philosophies. That this is true of Traherne needs no demonstration here.

John Smith's *Select Discourses* appeared in 1652, and Traherne may well have been influenced by this most imaginative, deeply spiritual, and deeply thoughtful of all the Cambridge Platonists. In the blending of philosophy and poetry, in profundity of spiritual insight, in beauty and color of phrasing and warmth of feeling, Traherne has closer affinity with Smith than with any of the rest; and it is at least possible that Traherne had Smith, among others, in mind when he speaks of those he discovered, the "thousands in the world, that in . . . universities . . . enjoy felicity . . . who enjoy communion with God, and have fellowship with the Angels every day."

Smith was the first of the Platonists who was truly a philosopher. Whichcote, student of Plato though he was, and one who set the students at Cambridge on the study of Plato and Plotinus, remained rather the rational theologian. Smith, beginning where Whichcote left off, enlarged the scope of speculative inquiry and lifted the whole movement to more generalized, more truly philosophic levels. He was chiefly interested in a fundamental problem, the nature of knowledge, and whether it begins without or within, in sensation or in spiritual experience. To him the conflicts of religious dogma and the wars of religious parties were of little concern; and this was also true of Traherne, *Roman Forgeries* and sections of the *Book of Private Devotions* notwithstanding.

Traherne and Smith were wholly in accord in their conception of religion as life fully developed. Yet their way of intellectual approach to their rational conviction of this was very different. Traherne evolved man and the universe from the essential nature of God. Smith took as his bedrock truth the rationally demonstrable fact of an immortal soul in man; and thence arrived by induction at its divine origin and destiny. Traherne, too, had something of this, in his constant demonstration of how the glory of man and of nature proclaims the glory of God. Smith was more concerned than Traherne to authenticate human belief in the existence of a deity, and in presenting that deity as the generalization and archetype of human powers. Traherne rather sought an answer to the still vaster problem—why in the eternal scheme of things the phenomenon man has being at all. The difference is merely one of approach and emphasis, and is outweighed by their fundamental accord. Indeed, what was written of these *Discourses* long before the *Centuries* were discovered might well stand as a fine critique of the peculiar quality of the *Centuries*:

No spiritually thoughtful mind can read them unmoved. They carry us so directly into an atmosphere of divine philosophy, luminous with the richest lights of meditative genius. . . . We see a mind religious to the core . . . not only free from all pietistic weakness and dogmatic narrowness, but poising itself naturally at an altitude out of sight of them. . . . His mind . . . is fresh as a new-born life with open eyes of poetic wonder and divine speculation. He has not painfully reached the serene heights on which his thoughts dwell; but these heights are the natural level of his lofty and abounding spiritual nature.[102]

Smith, being more consciously, and as it were professionally, a philosopher, was led by his way of approach to explore many cognate subjects which Traherne, who was not writing a set treatise and was more concerned with the consequences of his theories for daily living, leaves untouched. Thus Smith compares in detail atheism, superstition, and divine knowledge; and investigates the nature and history of prophecy, and of authentic revelation. In so doing he compels his reader to go with him up mountains of erudition and through forests of classical quotation. Most of the Cambridge Platonists do this. It was part of the heritage of the dominion of tradition and authority that was to be broken by the new scientific spirit and the new speculative spirit of these Platonists themselves. But the process was gradual, and the fact that Traherne can be read with delight by a modern reader, to whom much even in Smith is wearisome if not unintelligible, serves to show, not that Traherne was less learned, but that he was more truly free from the fetters of the past.

A comparison of Traherne and Cudworth brings this into still clearer relief. Cudworth is preeminently the scholar of the group. Student, tutor, professor, in unbroken succession, his life and his outlook were wholly academic. He has in consequence all the strength and singleness of purpose of one whose energies have been bent only in one direction. He had at his command vast stores of learning, and a range of reading which both stimulated and enriched his own natural thoughtfulness. But as a writer and as a thinker he had also the defects of these qualities. In the expression of his thought the wealth of learning proved an encumbrance; and the academic habit of discursiveness freely

---

[102] Tulloch, *Rational Theology*, Vol. II, p. 186.

indulged has rendered his works well-nigh unreadable today. Their sheer weight and size, the massiveness both intellectual and physical, has won them a measure of respectful fame; but it might be safely assumed that *The True Intellectual System of the Universe* has not been opened by one in ten of those who are familiar with its title and its general purport. It is interesting to notice how Traherne's particular aim when writing each of his books, his desire to make his learning available for the unlearned, has accidentally preserved them from a most potent factor of decay. His scholarship was certainly not so profound as Cudworth's; yet he, too, had read widely and in the same fields.

Principal Tulloch has said of Cudworth:

> Like Smith, he quotes freely, not only from the Neo-Platonists and the Jewish schools, but also from such modern revivers of the Platonic spirit as Pico of Mirandola and Ludovicus Vives. . . . He draws at will from the most various and recondite authorities. We are pleased also to light upon an allusion to Bacon . . . showing that the most recent, no less than the most ancient, philosophical writings were known to so omnivorous a student.

It is the breadth of this reading that is here emphasized as remarkable, as indeed it was; but the reader of Traherne will remember that he, too, was familiar with Pico of Mirandola and Vives, and that he names Bacon in his commonplace book, quoting his theory of the nature of cold.

Traherne also resembles Cudworth in sharing that interest in early history, and particularly in the records of the early Church, which was part of the new spirit of rational inquiry. Traherne's *Roman Forgeries*, in its attempt at impartial and impersonal study and judgment, might from this point of view be regarded as a typical product of the scientific spirit of the age; and Cudworth, in what was also his first publication, investigates the relation of the Lord's Supper to the sacrificial rites of the heathens and of the Jews, and endeavors to determine its true origin and its true line of development from that origin; thus approaching one of the most bitterly contested points of dogma from a new and rational angle. All the Platonists share that spirit of rational inquiry into matters of religion and religious practice; and it is interesting that all of them stand in firm opposition to Roman Catholicism on this issue. The denial by that church of the validity of human reason was the challenge taken up by these finest thinkers of the seventeenth century; and in championing the claims of reason in religion—for the whole of the century in every field was dominated by religion—they were winning both for philosophy and for science their later unfettered scope.

Cudworth, unlike Smith, and like Traherne, came into conscious conflict with the philosophy of Hobbes. He was among the first to perceive beneath Hobbes's cloak of Biblical phraseology and conservatism in religion the existence of a profound scepticism, and to point out the precise nature of the danger. It is indeed no little to the credit of these Platonists as a group that they should have estimated so accurately an intellectual current of their own times. All of them, including Traherne, who wrote after the appearance of *Leviathan*, saw the need to expose this enemy and to attack him—and Traherne three years earlier than Cudworth.[103]

Henry More is the last of the recognized leaders whom we shall need to consider in our endeavor to define Traherne's relationship to the other Platonists of his time. With More Traherne has much in common, beyond their common Platonism; and even in the heightened degree of that Platonism they are akin. It is in charm of personality that these two particularly resemble each other, in loftiness and serenity of soul, and in a strange transparency in revealing without any egoism those experiences of the mind and spirit which most men hide from their fellows behind barriers of uncomprehension, inarticulateness, self-conscious reserve. From both More and Traherne we have a spiritual history of childhood and growth into manhood,

[103] *Christian Ethicks*, 1675; *Intellectual System*, 1678.

More's written after Traherne's and published in 1679.[104] There is no possibility that either was indebted to the other; yet at times they seem to echo each other, as when More writes, "Even in my first childhood, an inward sense of the divine presence was so strong upon my mind, that I did then believe there could no deed, word or thought be hidden from him."

For all More's entanglement by environment with Calvinism, one feels the essential similarity of their boyish and adolescent life, the identity of their young curiosity, their early fidelity to reason, their fall into the slough of scepticism, their emergence as mystics. With both, too, there followed on this a period of ardent search for knowledge of facts, succeeded by doubt "whether the knowledge of things was really the supreme felicity of man or something *greater or more divine* was: Or, supposing it to be so, whether it was to be acquired by such an eagerness and intentness in the reading of authors, and contemplating of things—or by the purgation of the mind from all sorts of vices whatsoever." So More also turned to the philosophers of old, the "Platonic writers, Marsilius Ficinus, Plotinus himself, Mercurius Trismegistus, and the mystical divines, among whom there was frequent mention made of the purification of the soul, and of the purgative course that is previous to the illuminative."[105] The final choice of both was that personal quest of spiritual wisdom, and both experienced the painful stages of self-discipline and were rewarded by attainment of felicity, "fix'd joy, winged might," as More phrased it.

More, like Cudworth, lived his life in the cloistered peace of a university college, steadfastly refusing all offers of preferment. There he lived, and there he died, enjoying an immense reputation, and influencing many by letters, by conversation, and by writing. Yet he, too, lacks the saving salt of direct contact with a many-sided world which quickens into enduring life the pages of *Christian Ethicks*; and for lack of this grip on mundane

[104] In a *Prefatio Generalissima* to his Works.
[105] *Divine Dialogues*, III.

reality, More's speculations drifted off, as he grew older, into aberrations of mysticism, his spiritual intensity developing those pathological conditions which, though by no means inevitable, yet only the greatest have quite escaped, as religious history shows. After 1668, he became increasingly absorbed in studies of the occult, of theosophy and the Cabala, and in attempts at interpreting such things as Ezekiel's dream or the visions of the Apocalypse. More's life thus presents a picture of gradual decay and of weakening allegiance to that power of pure reason he had professed and indeed proved in his earlier works.

It might be said that Traherne was saved from a like fate by the accident of early death; yet there seems to be in Traherne not only a balance derived from a greater breadth of actual experience, a richer emotional life, but also a solid commonsense, a grip of the concrete, which would have saved him always, one feels, from transcendental vagaries. More has as well, and for the same reasons, Cudworth's faults of prolixity and discursiveness. The result is that More, for all the charm of mind and personality he possessed, is unread today. He is far more interesting than his books; his writings have nothing of that which will make the *Centuries* something that men, having recovered, will not willingly lose again.

It is thus part of Traherne's greatness that while he was wholeheartedly of this Platonic movement he succeeded in escaping the dangers into which contemporary philosophers fell. The learning of the past was as potent an attraction to him as to the others, and it was adequately his to command; yet his pages are never a dead mosaic of quotation, nor does he stop to explore every bypath. His own ideal of life as awareness of and full response to all experience whatsoever—"We should be all Life and Mettle and Vigour and Love to every thing; and that would poise us"—did actually poise him; and nowhere more strikingly than in his subordination of learning to the greater end of living.

Having dedicated himself, as did most of the Platonists, to making a personal experiment of religious life, Traherne yet wholly escaped the pitfall of occultism in which so many of the finest minds of the time, deceived by its pseudo-scientific appearance, became engulfed. More, whom we have mentioned, Van Helmont, Lady Conway, Glanvil, Thomas Vaughan, are but some of the more prominent of those who wasted their energies on Hermetic and Cabalistic and Rosicrucian lore, and on incredible experiments in magic and necromancy. Traherne is perfectly free from any taint of this.

Of that other current of credulous thought of the time, the belief in the existence of witches and ghosts and supernatural apparitions, who thus constituted a most valid proof of the existence of God, Traherne's work again shows very little effect. It seems likely that he shared the general belief of his age that apparitions were a fact and that witches wielded evil powers. Aubrey's anecdote suggests the one and there is a reference to witchcraft in *Century* IV, 89. There is, too, in the *Book of Private Devotions* an occasional suggestion of overcredulous acceptance of ancient fable. Yet nevertheless it remains true that Traherne's allegiance to reason was remarkably constant.

Thus some of Traherne's strength is discovered in our realization of what in that age he might have been and was not; of what he was not, even in being a Platonist, and more particularly what he was not because he was a Platonist. He was not monastic, not ascetic; not as the author of the *Theologia Germanica* nor as Thomas a Kempis; not preoccupied with death and future torment; not one who crawls in self-abasement. Yet all these features of medieval Catholicism continued to pervade seventeenth-century Protestant thought. In the prayers of Jeremy Taylor, and the devotions of Andrewes, in Herbert's poems, in the multitude of sermons and devotional writings, one meets constantly and almost exclusively the old dualism, the old concept that the body is evil and that all its desires should be mortified, that the things of the world are to be shunned as a plague by the 'soul in quest of perfection. Against this tide of feeling, stronger far than the Christian Platonism of the few, Traherne stands in opposition, proclaiming the glory and the beauty of the natural world, the oneness of matter and spirit, the rightful possession of all things by joy.

That Traherne chose thus to be with the few against the many is one part of his originality. Here and there he has himself indicated points where his thought diverges from current opinion. One, already referred to, is his belief in the infinity of the soul; another is his teaching that the gift to man by God of free will is man's crowning honor, worth all it has cost the race; for without it man could not attain full spiritual stature. There are other divergences, as his readers will note. But his title to his own great claim "that he enriches all, by further opening the *grandeur* and *glory* of Religion with the interior depths and Beauties of Faith"[106] rests principally, I believe, on two striking features of his religious philosophy.

One of these is the extraordinary completeness, the thoroughgoing persistency with which he applies his philosophy to the everyday affairs of daily life. Everything must be seen and acted upon in the light of that vision. "Remember always that thou art about a Magnificent work!" No action, no thought of the soul is unimportant. Even an acorn or a grain of sand cannot be truly seen by the unilluminated soul. The striking effect of novelty that Traherne's own power of seeing all nature in this fashion gives to his writings has been remarked by many of his critics. His attitude toward nature is something new in our literature; and this is the secret of that strange effect of beauty. The part, every tiniest fragment of it, is for him flooded by the light of the whole; so that indeed his writings "put the earth and its wonders before us in a new and entrancing fashion: there is no one in the whole range of mystics who looks on nature just as Traherne does: we take a fresh breath, rub our eyes, and get our gratitude

[106] Preface to *Christian Ethicks.*

newly back again, as if indeed we were abroad with him in some sunlit down, seeing with him God's grace in every 'spire of grass' and in His 'orient and immortal wheat.' "[107]

To have attained such a sustained consciousness of the presence of God as this entails, is proof of Traherne's mysticism as well as part of his philosophy—it is the felicity man may regain if he will. "He thought it a vain thing to see glorious principles lie buried in books, unless he did remove them into his understanding; and a vain thing to remove them unless he did revive them, and raise them up by continual exercise."[108] Hence the vision must express itself continuously in the activity of thought; and that Traherne's own vision did so express itself gives us the unusual effect we have been noting.

It is not easily done. As he says, "Nothing is more difficult than to think well."[109] Traherne has indicated to us his own spiritual progress, how, beginning at the "gate of the senses" he studied "the most obvious and common things, . . . Air, Light, Heaven and Earth, Water, the Sun, Trees, Men and Women . . ." and how "to my unspeakable wonder, they brought me to all the things in Heaven and Earth, in Time and Eternity, possible and impossible, great and little, common and scarce: and discovered them all to be infinite treasures."[110] One is reminded of Tennyson, seeing just as clearly that his flower in the crannied wall held the secret of the universe. But Tennyson was baffled where Traherne goes joyously forward.

Having followed this path, and found it good, Traherne points it out to others as a way to blessedness. The first essential, he declares, is that a man must "believe that Felicity is a glorious though an unknown thing."[111] He must accept it as reasonable, and desire it; nothing else will set his feet on the ladder and nerve him for the climb. But to see and to long for felicity is not

[107] W. K. Fleming, *Mysticism in Christianity*, Chapter X, "Browne and Traherne."

[108] *Centuries* IV, 2.   [109] *Ibid.*, I, 8.   [110] *Ibid.*, III, 53-4.

[111] *Ibid.*, III, 56.

to possess it; the necessary spiritual discipline comes by this method of intense meditation of the common, visible things of earth, until the perception of their glory and beauty and exquisite interrelationship blends with the perception of their spiritual origin and operation. This for Traherne is the highway to felicity; this continuous, conscious perception of the essential beauty of the world is his *scala perfectionis*.

For those who persevere the end of the climb brings the power to uphold "Heaven and Earth, Time and Eternity, God and all things in our Souls, without wavering or intermission; by the perpetual influx of our life."[112] It is, at its highest, the joy of sharing with God the act of cosmic creation,

> The thought of the World whereby it is enjoyed is better than the World. So is the idea of it in the Soul of Man, better than the World in the esteem of God. . . . The world within you is an offering returned, which is infinitely more acceptable to God Almighty, since it came from Him that it might return unto Him. Wherein the mystery is great. For God hath made you able to create worlds in your own mind which are more precious unto Him than those which He created. . . . Besides all which in its own nature also a Thought of the World, or the World in a Thought, is more excellent than the World, because it is spiritual and nearer unto God. The material World is dead and feeleth nothing, but this spiritual world, though it be invisible, hath all dimensions, and is a divine and living Being, the voluntary Act of an obedient Soul.[113]

He who sees this inner world must see the outward one with different eyes; and to much of the outward world he will become blind—in the words of Traherne, a child, "a stranger to the thoughts, customs, and opinions of men in this world, as if we were but little children."[114] The room of these false things is taken up by a vision of truth, of God in all His works, even in the commonest and most ordinary-seeming. Since God is love, all these are love; and the soul that sees it is love also—the eternal trinity. The light of Traherne's exquisite perception of this love, the poetry of his own exquisite responsiveness, is shed on all he

[112] *Ibid.*, II, 87.   [113] *Ibid.*, II, 90.   [114] *Ibid.*, III, 5.

writes: so that, as W. K. Fleming has well said, "There is no one in the whole range of mystics who looks on Nature just as Traherne does."

The other outstanding feature of Traherne's philosophy, its other major claim to real originality, lies in the manner in which it combines vastness with unity and coherence. All his multitude of separate borrowings do not remain separate: they are worked over by that acute and perceptive mind, and welded into a unity. The whole, in truly creative work, is never the sum of the parts. Traherne, borrowing freely, as he himself admits, "taking out of the Treasuries of Humanity those Arguments that will discover the great perfection of the End of Man,"[115] creates out of this matter something new, something that is also a unity, a whole—that something we call his philosophy or his vision. And even though what, by a process of intellectual perception and spiritual experience, he discovered for himself and put before his readers, may not be the first discovery of that truth—if others before him have seen that love is the great principle of all things human and divine—yet this of Traherne's remains a real discovery, a new firsthand restatement, a great original vision of the unity of life, a vision at once luminous and logical.

Certainly, in Traherne's own age, the old and vaster conceptions had slipped from men's minds. It is their natural tendency to do so. The plain man prefers practice without theory; and the second half of the seventeenth century in matters of religion was an eminently "practical" age, welcoming rules of conduct, averse to that vision for lack of which a people perish. They were seeing fragments of life, not life. And the remarkable thing is that Traherne, who was of that age, was perfectly conscious of all this. None knew better than he the magnitude of the task of proclaiming the "grandeur and glory of religion" in Restoration England, nor the urgent need of this proclamation. "It was your friend's delight to meditate the principles of upright nature. . . . For now they are lost and buried in ruins,

---

[115] Preface to *Christian Ethicks.*

nothing appearing but fragments that are worthless shreds and parcels of them. To see the entire piece ravisheth the Angels. It was his desire to recover them and to exhibit them again to the eyes of men."

That he succeeded both in "seeing the entire piece," and in exhibiting his vision to the eyes of men, I hope the preceding chapters have made clear. One must go to Traherne himself to feel how he is ravished by the spectacle, and sings for joy like a morning star of old. Remembering what Traherne has written in the *Fourth Century* of the Divine Philosopher, and of the "riches of the full assurance" which are his, one sees how very near Traherne approached his own ideal, how fully he possessed those riches, how truly he was, as he claimed to be, the beloved friend of God. By the beauty of the vision to which Traherne attained, by its vastness and completeness, by his intellectual grasp of its meaning, by the joy born of it in his own soul, by the knowledge and joy communicated to others, Traherne is himself his own divine philosopher. And to be this is to be in no small measure his own description of that philosopher—"one of the most illustrious creatures in the world."

APPENDIX

PUBLISHED AND UNPUBLISHED WRITINGS

THe known writings of Thomas Traherne, in order of publication, are as follows:

1. *Roman Forgeries*, by A Faithful Son of the Church of England. 1673.
2. *Daily Devotions, consisting of Thanksgivings, Confessions and Prayers*, by an Humble Penitent [i.e. Mrs. Hopton]. 1673.
3. *Christian Ethicks.* 1675.
4. *The Soul's Communion with her Saviour.* The original, "reduced" by Philip Traherne, and published by him with that title. 1685.
5. *A Serious and Pathetical Contemplation of the Mercies of God, in several most Devout and Sublime Thanksgivings for the Same.* Published "by the Reverend Doctor Hickes at the request of a friend of the Author's." 1699.
6. *Hexameron* or *Meditations on the Six Days of the Creation,* and *Meditations and Devotions on the Life of Christ.* Published by Nathaniel Spinckes as Parts I and II of *A Collection of Meditations and Devotions in Three Parts.* Part II, *Meditations and Devotions on the Life of Christ,* is the original, unreduced, of No. 4 above. Part III of the collection is a reprint of No. 2 above. 1717.
7. *Poems of Thomas Traherne.* Published by Bertram Dobell. Contains the poems in the Dobell Folio MS. 1903.
8. *Centuries of Meditations.* Published by Dobell, from the untitled octavo Dobell MS. 1908.
9. *Poems of Felicity.* Published by Dr. Bell, from the British Museum MS. Burney 392, which is Philip Traherne's copy of a now lost original. 1910.

10. *The Poetical Works of Thomas Traherne.* Edited by Gladys I. Wade, and published by P. J. and A. E. Dobell. Contains the poems of Traherne from all sources. 1932.

In addition to these published writings, there are some works of Traherne still in manuscript. They include:

1. *The Book of Private Devotions.* An octavo Dobell MS.
2. A small collection of early verse. Also a Dobell MS.
3. A *Commonplace Book*, the second half of the Dobell Folio.
4. A student's notebook. British Museum Burney MS. 126.

Since these works are not yet available to students of Traherne, the following comments may be of interest:

THE BOOK OF PRIVATE DEVOTIONS

THE name *The Book of Private Devotions* was given to this important unpublished manuscript by Bertram Dobell, and so is usually referred to by that title. Yet, as a description of the contents, it is misleading. For the *Devotions* are not private or personal as are the *Meditations on the Life of Christ*; they have very little to do with the inner life of Traherne himself. Nor are they characterized by the range of revelation and the intimacy of the *Centuries of Meditations*. And the reason is not far to seek. For the manuscript shows unmistakably that from the beginning these *Devotions* were written for publication. In consequence, Traherne, particularly in the beginning, was self-conscious and somewhat stiffly formal; and there creeps in a note of didacticism which is not attractive.

The manuscript is a leather-bound octavo volume and the writing throughout is extraordinarily minute. On the eight-inch page there are on the average fifty lines of writing, with at least twelve words to the line.

In writing this book Traherne clearly had in mind a threefold purpose: to provide High Church Anglicans with information about the origin of certain church festivals and with the life history of certain saints so commemorated; to furnish suitable prayers and meditations for use on these festivals; and to attack the Puritans and Low Churchmen who opposed their observance.

The last element, though not obtrusive, is at times clearly perceptible. Perhaps the most significant of such passages occurs in the meditation, *How the Holy Ghost Descended upon the Apostles at Pentecost.* It makes quite clear the polemical aim of this work:

Nor can any object against the Holiness of Seasons with more Color than som against the Holiness of Places. For if such a Memorable Action as our Savior's Transfiguration upon Mount Tabor shall make it, even by St. Peter Himself, to be called in the New Testament The Holy Mount: well may such memorable and Divine Occurences as the Resur-rection of our Savior, and the Giving of the Holy Ghost, make the Times wherin they came to pass, both called and esteemed Holy Times. Since Times as well as Places are capable of the Impression of Holy Things.

O my God, Pardon and Accept the Zeal of thy Servant which breaketh forth against the Intemperance and Ingratitude of the World, even as it lies concealed under the Disguis of Holy but Ignorant Zeal. They would abolish Order and Beauty in the World, for fear of Superstition: Introduce Atheism by Degrees, and a Total Oblivion of thy Glorious Wonders: They would bring in a Publick Ingratitude and Deformity in thy Worship; and make that at no time to be don which they pretend should ever be don. They profane and Trample under foot the Days and Times, wherin thy most Signal and Inestimable Mercies were don, and wherein also they ought to be recorded. Fill them O Lord, with Light and Understanding, that they might be as Great in Wisdom as they think themselvs . . . that thy Praises may proceed in an undisturbed manner throughout all Generations for evermore.

The information concerning the origin of the festivals and the biographies of the saints reveals another side of Traherne's learning, and a breadth of reading well-nigh as extensive as that required for *Roman Forgeries.* The Life of St. James, for instance, is based on material derived from Baronius, St. Chrysostom, Durandus, Hegisippus, and Gemma, all of whom are quoted from and (let me hasten to add) named as authorities by Traherne. There is more than a suspicion in this part of the work of somewhat credulous acceptance of legendary matter as literal truth, but, on the other hand, one also meets with criticism of generally accepted theological tradition.

The general plan of these *Devotions* resembles that of the *Meditations on the Life of Christ*. Here, events in the lives of the saints replace the events of the Gospels, but are selected in the same way, and followed in the same way by personal applications, by contrition for shortcomings, and by prayers of consecration. As in the other, there is little scope for the exposition of Traherne's philosophy, though here and there, as before, certain features of it can be perceived, notably its characteristic exaltation of man.

The biographical interest is less than in his other writings; but even here there is a certain amount of self-revelation. For his consciousness of the general public for whom he was writing, and the formality arising from that consciousness, lessen very markedly as the work proceeds, as they do also in *Christian Ethicks*; and when Traherne has warmed to his subject, the detached expositor is apt to be lost in the wayfaring Christian, and the personal note is heard clearly in the prayers.

Thus one will find petitions for strength and guidance in his office as a priest "that I may win and save thy People"; that he may be "to those who are near unto me a Son of Consolation, and to those who dwell further off a Shining Light: a firm Pillar and not a Reed to my companion and friend, and an ornament to the Place in which I live." The allusions to Sir Orlando Bridgeman and the Bridgeman household, and to the friends in far-off Herefordshire, is sufficiently clear. One will meet expressions of contrition for "turbulency of spirit" and the faults of temper bewailed in others of his devotional works; and there is a prayer for chastity, afterwards crossed through for deletion. "I praise and magnify thy Name for the Hidden Use of thy unused Treasures. And for those far Greater Delights Thou hast given us to attain, by Denying the Powers Thou has given us for Delights. Oh, that I might Bury those

Appetites and Faculties Thou hast given me, rather suppress and conquer than to manifest; that in . . . [A short word, 3 or 4 letters, the last, *e* or *r*, not legible] Things also by not Sowing I might sow the more, and reap after a Time the more Glorious Harvest."

References to mysticism are numerous, the impersonal ones particularly interesting as showing a consciously held ideal of poise and balance. Thus, in the *Meditations and Devotions for Ascention Day*, on the words of the angel, "Ye men of Galilee, why stand ye looking up into Heaven?" Traherne has the following comment:

In which Words we have Three excellent Documents which we must learn: First, that Suspension, Admiration, and other Effects of Divine Contemplation are in this life to be taken with Moderation and Limitation, because they are not our last End, but only one Means to Atchieve it. . . . (It is) as if the Angel had said "You have looked long enough. Go and accomplish what is commanded." . . . Since Contemplation without Action is not sufficient . . . O King of Heaven, Grant that I may follow Thee not only with Desire but Obedience, not only with Contemplation but with Action.

Similarly, in *Devotions upon St. John Baptist's Day*, Traherne writes with characteristic common sense and insight into human nature:

Tho in Solitude, Pious Persons may go to Heaven in the Way of Prayer and Devotion, yet in Societie they go better in the Way of Mercy and Charitie. . . . Pride is apt to creep in to a Retired person, and to feed him so with Self-Complacency as to Poison his Spirituality. . . . A man long alone is apt to think all the World full of Ignorance in comparison; and that himself is the Sole Beholder of all Heavenly Perfections in the Mirrour of his Soul.

Traherne's personal mysticism is here subordinated, but colors his thought and influences his phrasing at times. Thus he will pray: "O Holy Spirit, fortify my weak Heart . . . that I may receiv the Illumination of thy Grace, being enabled thereby to Contemplat thy Perfections and to liv in Divine Union with Thee." There are no references in this work to any oscillations in his mystical state, to his "destitutions" and "banishments" as he called them in the *Meditations upon the Life of Christ*. But there is even more explicit acceptance of discipline. Mere discipline and self-mortification has no virtue in itself, he says; but of certain spiritual states it is the inevitable accompaniment. Mortifications are "holy revenges" practised of necessity by all saints. "Neglect of the Body and Corporal Austerities are nothing without Inward Indignation and Grief and Zeal: but accompany those as the shadow does the Body. The Body is a Carcase without the Soul: and these are the Body of true Repentance. . . . A Shell is worthless without a Kernel; yet a Shell preserveth a Kernel."

Of those other sufferings of the good, the sufferings to be joyously borne as part of conformity with Christ, there is in this work equally explicit acceptance. "The most intire friendship of Man with God doth not exempt him from the troubles and Disorders of this World. . . ." "From the beginning of the World, the Children of God have suffered Persecution: and to the end of the World in som kind or another must do so. . . ." "For through Tribulations we enter into the Kingdom of Heaven. The Saints before us found no other Way: nor can we." And there is full acceptance of the idea that the mystic, by his voluntary imposition of corporal austerities and by his joyful acceptance for love's sake of persecutions and involuntary afflictions, spiritually ministers to the spiritually poor.

These *Devotions*, and those on the life of Christ, seem in some ways to cast a shadow on the radiance of the *Centuries*. Solemn in tone they are, frankly accepting strife and pain and discipline as part of the mystic's lot in a disordered world; yet equally serene, equally untroubled by doubt, as passionately convinced of the supreme satisfaction of the religious life. The *Devotions* are in truth an exceedingly valuable complement to the *Centuries*, throwing into high relief the brilliance of their sunlight and the rare quality of their joy.

As literature, this book is not a success; and apart altogether from its more somber tone, most readers of Traherne would put it down with a feeling of disappointment. The polemical and didactic aims, the rigid form, proved too heavy fetters for Traherne's natural impulse to fly free-winged; and only occasionally does one meet with some passage worthy to stand beside the best in the *Centuries* or *Christian Ethicks*. The highest level is reached in the concluding pages of the *Meditations and Devotions for Ascention Day*. The style on the whole is simple. There are occasional displays of wit, as when virgins are described as "Angelical Bodies and Bodily Angels"; there are a few strange metaphors—"If Charity be the Milk and Nourishment of Souls, Devotion is the Cream," or Holy Days being "Market Days of Heaven wherin we traffique in Celestial Merchandise." There are also not a few excellent aphorisms; one has been already quoted, of penitence, "A Shell is worthless without a Kernel: yet a Shell preserveth a Kernel." The whole work has been carefully revised; and that redundancies, as in the *Centuries*, were now being consciously deleted, the following brief passage from the manuscript, where brackets indicate words crossed out on revision, plainly shows:

[Most] fit [indeed] also was it for Thee [O JESUS] to Ascend [far abov all Heavens] that Thou mayst receiv the Homage and Adoration of all the Angels [and Hosts of Cherubims].

As with all other books of devotion of the period, one is aware of a general indebtedness to the devotional classics. The devotional writings of St. Augustine, of John Hall, or of John Austin, were part of the substructure of all their successors. In this book of Traherne's there is also some particular indebtedness clearly to be perceived. To Daniel Featley, Traherne probably owes not only the prayer he acknowledges but the plan of commemorating in this fashion the festivals; for Featley in his *Ancilla Pietatis*[116] gave the outline of a similar scheme.

There is still more indebtedness to Bishop Andrewes. The

[116] 1626. Said to be the most popular devotional work of the day, and the one preferred by Charles I. Sixth edition, 1639.

Confession of Sins of this book, it is interesting to note, also appears in *Daily Devotions*, that work of Mrs. Hopton's compilation in which we know Traherne had some share, as also does the succeeding *Litany*, which is Andrewes's *Litany of Deprecation*. Close parallels to Andrewes's prayers in phrasing and arrangement occur throughout this work, as they do in *Daily Devotions*. There can be no doubt that Traherne was more influenced in his devotional writings by Andrewes than by any other one writer, and particularly by the *Institutiones Piae* (1630). In the *Institutiones* and also in the early editions of Andrewes's *Private Devotions* will be found the *Confession of Sins* and the *Deprecations* referred to above; and Traherne's subject matter, phrasing, and completeness of treatment in all his works, in the *Serious and Pathetical Contemplation* and the *Meditations on the Life of Christ* as in *Daily Devotions* and this work, owe not a little to the same source.

Jeremy Taylor's influence, though less powerful than Andrewes's, is also perceptible. The volume of his with which Traherne seems to have been most familiar is the *Choice Manual, containing what is to be Believed, Practised, and Desired or Prayed for.* From the *Litany for Deliverance from Evils* in this *Manual* is also taken part of the second prayer on page 20 of Traherne's *Contemplation,* and from the same source many of the petitions in all his devotions.

Yet it remains true that this particular book, like the rest of Traherne's writings, is Traherne's. Steeped indeed he was in great devotional literature no less than in the Scriptures; by constant use in his religious life they were, in his own phrase, as familiar to him as his walk and his table. But their wording and their meaning were no longer something external to him; what these other men of religious genius had written was not for him "words, words, words," but vivid embodiment of experiences of the religious life as he, too, had known them. Traherne poured forth his own devotions in response to the same impulse as they; and when the emotion is immediate, it matters little who first coined the phrases in which it finds its own expression.

There is, I understand, little immediate prospect that this manuscript will be printed. Its appeal for the lover of literature, for the general reader, and for the religious of our own day would certainly be less than the *Contemplation* and *Christian Ethicks*. Yet it is to be hoped that its turn will some day come. It is easily the most important of the works of Traherne inaccessible to the ordinary reader and even to the majority of students of Traherne; it has much in it of intrinsic value, and still more of critical importance for our understanding of Traherne.

A COLLECTION OF EARLY VERSE

THIS small but important manuscript came to light while these pages were being revised for publication. I have not had the pleasure of examining it myself; my account is based on information kindly sent me by Mr. P. J. Dobell.

The manuscript, he tells me, is a "fat little book, still in its original calf binding." Like the Folio, it has been used partly as a notebook, partly as a place for entering compositions in verse; and from many points of view it is very interesting.

The book to begin with was Philip's property. The young student proclaimed that fact very definitely on the first page:

Philip Traherne
is the true owner
of this booke.
Amen.
Año Domi
1655

(Philip was a "Traherne," we note, in those early days; the "Traheron" period came later.)

In 1655 Thomas was an undergraduate at Oxford.

Following that ascription of ownership is a collection of notes and extracts in the handwriting of Philip: fifteen pages headed "Ethica"; eleven pages headed "Geometria," with neat drawings; a number of extracts from the writings of Francis Bacon; and several others, some in Latin. What is interesting to us is that occasionally a few lines are added to these extracts in the writing of Thomas.

This points to a very close association in study between the brothers about that period; possibly during the Long Vacations from Oxford; possibly during the stay in Herefordshire that immediately preceded Thomas's ordination. We knew of the close intimacy between them from other sources; and this shared notebook is another interesting proof of their community of intellectual interests.

After the extracts begins a collection of short poems—all of them in Thomas Traherne's writing, and many of them signed "T.T." The notebook by now had apparently become the property of Thomas; and the verse it contains was probably composed and entered during the years 1655 to 1660. Mr. Dobell says of the collection: "It does not give anything that will add to Traherne's reputation as a poet, but is of great interest as containing earlier work than any hitherto known."

As early work, it is reflective of the youthful poet copying the poetical fashions of the day. There are types of verse here that will not recur again—for instance, four of the elaborate epitaphs so popular in seventeenth-century verse. One of these is dedicated to Anne Cholmeley, and has a title in an odd blend of languages: "Epitaphium Annae Cholmeley sacrum written on her gravestone." Research might discover who this lady was, and date this poem more exactly. (One remembers that a "John Chomley" signed one of Traherne's certificates for ordination in 1657.) This epitaph begins with a conventional conceit:

> Though stone I am, yet must I weep
> And sweat forth Teares of woe.

Another is called "In Obitum viri optimi J. C. Eirenarcha."
("Eirenarcha" I assume to be a young pedant's version of
"Justice of the Peace.") This is a poem of twenty-four lines, and
begins

> Heer lies pure and precious Dust
> Enclosed in this Urne.

The twenty-four-lined poem that immediately follows, with
the title "Job cap. 19 v.25,26,27. Memento Mori," may also
be dedicated to the same personage, or may be a separate
epitaph. It begins

> Beneath that Stone lies buried one
> Confin'd in narrow roome.

The fourth of this group of epitaphs is called "Night Meditations" and is of the same length, twenty-four lines. Mr.
Dobell remarked of this one that he thought it was of autobiographical interest. I am not sure on what he based that opinion;
the reference to a "mans owne House" in the second line would
be to clay, the grave, and not to anything more personal and
immediate:

> Here must Wee rest; and where else should we rest
> Is not a mans owne House, to sleep in best?

Of the remaining four complete poems, one is called "On ye
Bible," and the rest are untitled. The longest and most elaborate has four stanzas of eight lines each.

There are as well a few fragments. One, beginning "To bee
a Monarch is a glorious thing," suggests the Restoration or its
imminence; the others show the young Traherne experimenting
with the fashionable epigram, though with a religious turn.
One example is typical:

> Oh how injurious is this wall of sin
> That barres my Saviour out and bolts me in!

Students of Traherne will be interested to know that Mr.
Dobell will probably print this little collection of poems in the
near future. His present intention is to produce it as "a little

brochure which could be bound up with future copies of *The Poetical Works.*"

THE COMMONPLACE BOOK

THE *Commonplace Book* is part of the same manuscript as the poems, which occupy the first fifteen pages of the Dobell Folio. Then after a blank page or two, the alphabetical list of extracts begins, and continues for seventy-two and one-half pages. Like the poems, it is written in columns, two columns to a page; and by the extraordinary diversity of handwritings employed has raised the question whether or not Traherne wrote the whole of it.

On the flyleaf of this folio Bertram Dobell recorded his opinion of the handwritings both in the poems and in the *Commonplace Book*. I quote his remarks in full, partly because they have not appeared in print, and partly because they show the real difficulty of arriving at a decision on this matter. He says:

The poems in this volume are undoubtedly in the handwriting of the Author, Thomas Traherne. But there are a few passages of alterations which appear to be in a different and much later handwriting. Also the references to other poems which appear at the end of *Innocence, The Rapture, The Improvement,* and five others, are in the later handwriting. These references would seem to show that there is (or was) another MS. vol. of Traherne's Poems.[117] As to the prose passages at the end of the MS., it is evident that they are in two different handwritings— Traherne's and another. Who the latter was I cannot conjecture. Grosart had an idea that the writer was Theophilus Gale,[118] but I feel sure that it was not so. At a rough guess I should say that about one-third of the prose is in Traherne's handwriting, and the remainder in that of the unknown writer. There is a good deal of curious learning, and some good writing in the prose; but I hardly think, as Grosart did, that it is worth printing or publishing. However, I have not as yet examined it

---

[117] Written before Dr. Bell's discovery of the *Poems of Felicity.*

[118] Letters of Gale are preserved in the Bodleian. MS. Smith, f. 131, *et seq.* The writing bears no marked resemblance to this in the *Commonplace Book.*

with sufficient attention, and might alter my opinion on further consideration.

MARCH 12, 1900.   BERTRAM DOBELL

Later, he added a footnote to the sentence "about one-third . . . is in Traherne's handwriting," as follows:

Not so. There is really comparatively little of Traherne's writing in the prose. Probably less than an eighth of it is his. Yet it is possible (though not likely) that the whole of the writing is Traherne's. A man's writing often changes a good deal in the course of his life, and the differences in the two handwritings here are not so great that they may not be the work of one person writing at different periods of his life.

Throughout this *Commonplace Book* there are, as Bertram Dobell's remarks make clear, two main types of handwriting, which for the sake of convenience I shall call *A* and *B*, together with several varieties of both A and B. A is definitely Traherne's, since it and its varieties occur in the poems and in the *Centuries* as well as here. It is a small careful unhurried hand; but some idea of the degree of its variations may be gained by comparing the "Hymne upon St. Bartholomew's Day," reproduced in facsimile in the first edition of the poems, with the stanzas of "Wonder" reproduced in the latest. It is evident that for many letters, such as *e* and *r*, he used three or four forms; and that he had in fact no fixed hand. The evidence of the manuscripts is that while he could write a very small, very legible, indeed exquisite hand, in times of greater haste, or of fatigue, or of less concentration on the actual penmanship, a much larger and more uneven writing came natural to him.

Hand B, a type of printing, does not differ so completely from A as to rule out the possibility of its being Traherne's. Bertram Dobell found it difficult to make up his mind on the point; and after deciding, in that footnote, that what he had at first thought to be varieties of A were more probably varieties of B, he still added, "Yet it is possible (though not likely) that the whole of the writing is Traherne's."

And this I feel certain is the truth. It seems very unlikely to me that two people would use the same commonplace book simultaneously, or in the fashion we must suppose they did if we wish to maintain the Hand B is not Traherne's. For it is not as though B occurred later than A, or detached from A, or in such a way that the entries in this hand might be the additions of someone who owned the manuscript after Traherne's death. There cannot even be any question of the writings having been done at different periods in Traherne's own life. For the two hands are inextricably interwoven, the change from one to the other occurring sometimes in the middle of a sentence. For instance, in the entry headed *Intercession*, the title and the following are in A: "That Saints are not medial Intercessors for us with God Bellarmine proves by"; then B begins, and continues "places of Scripture . . . etc."; and in B is entered a long passage against Roman Catholic practice and teaching. Not only here, but in several instances, it seems clear that Traherne started off in his more usual hand, then realizing the length of the extract he wished to enter and the limited space, changed over to the more laborious but more space-saving type of writing. If all the work in B were really that of another person, then his writing not only bore a general resemblance to Traherne's, but he was constantly at hand, ready to act as amanuensis at a moment's notice—all of which seems highly improbable. The natural explanation is to suppose that Traherne, who displays many kinds of writing, adopted yet another for entering long extracts. Granted this, all the intermediate varieties are easily to be accounted for by circumstances of cold, fatigue, haste, and the like.

There is very little original prose in the *Commonplace Book*. As the purpose of the earlier notebook to be described in the following section was to classify and summarize the teachings of Plato, one might say that the purpose of this *Commonplace Book* was to classify the opinions and researches of Theophilus Gale. Gale, who had been a Fellow of Magdalen while Traherne was at Brasenose, had devoted the studies of a lifetime to elaborating his theory that all ancient learning and philosophy, and in particular the Greek, had come from the Hebrew Scriptures. The first part of this great book on this subject, *The Court of the Gentiles*, was published in 1669, the second in 1671, the third and fourth in 1677. This date of publication of Parts One and Two also determines the date of this *Commonplace Book*, again showing that it was not written at different periods of Traherne's life, but wholly between 1669 and 1674.

Gale's work was universally applauded as a marvel of erudition, and it is easy to see that Traherne, in spite of its Puritan bias, was greatly attracted by its major thesis of a Hebrew tradition underlying all that was fine in all the theology, science, political economy, and literature of paganism; and the corollary that the errors of Roman Catholic dogma were connected with the errors of pagan philosophy, having a common origin in a succession of apostasies from the first primal divine revelation of Absolute Truth. One element of the attractiveness of such an hypothesis for Traherne would be the insistence laid on the unity of truth, that being one of his deepest convictions.

It is not likely that the *Commonplace Book* will ever be printed. Its interest lies only in its revelation of Traherne's intellectual pursuits in the last years of his life. I can perhaps best indicate the trend of these by quoting his subject headings under one or two letters, with a brief commentary or quotation. Thus under B and C we find:

Banishment. The damned not banished from God's "essential presence," but from his "joyful presence."

Beatifick. Four quotations for Trismegistus on the Beatific Vision.

Beatitude. An entry of three and one-half columns from Gale (pp. 383-6). Quoting Aristotle on the Good and on Happiness. Several quotations in Greek.

Beginning. On the beginning of Being. From Aristotle, probably via Gale. A paragraph in Latin, and another in English.

Bounty. An extract from Barrow's Sermon, *On the Duty and Reward of Bounty to the Poor.* 1671.

Capacity. The infinite capacity of Mind. A long quotation from Trismegistus, part of which reappears in *Christian Ethicks*.

Cause. Aristotle on the First Cause, and on causation. Three separate entries, the longest in Latin.

Censure. An aphorism, "The corruption of humane nature makes it liable to censure and prone to censure."

Ceremonies. The symbolism of ancient religious ceremonies, "the first Documents and Instructions of the World . . . the A.B.C. of Mankind." From Gale. Traherne's interest in this symbolism is shown in *Christian Ethicks*.

Co-haesion. A scientific extract, with what is possibly Traherne's own comment. "There is nothing so unconceivable to me as that holding together of the parts of Matter; which has so confounded me when I have seriously thought upon it that I have been prone to think with myself that the Germs of the World hold together not so much by Geometrie as some natural Magic. . . . Particles so little that it implies a contradiction they should be divided into less, for they are truly indivisible, and impenetrable in like manner. And therefore they touch one another as it were in smooth superficies: now therefore they hold together or what is the Principle of their Union is inconceivable."

These entries are typical of the whole. The subject matter is mainly religion and science, and the former more than the latter; Gale predominates, with Trismegistus a close second. The entries show the debt to Barrow, and Traherne's interest in the history of mysticism and his acquaintance with its technical terms, though entries elsewhere bring this into greater prominence. There is very little, if any, original prose.

Under one entry, *Impossibilitie*, there is an interesting note: "Go on p. 239 to p. 240 Diary, p. 232 and page 236 to Merits." Thus we learn there was once in existence a diary of Traherne's, and of considerable size. Though in part a commonplace book, as this note shows, it may well have been in part a personal record, as the title suggests, of inestimable value for the biography of Traherne.

Much of the material collected in this *Commonplace Book* reappears in *Christian Ethicks*; and it seems likely that its decidedly laborious compilation was undertaken as a preliminary to the writing of that book. Whether that is so or not, it represents yet another task accomplished in the busy years in the Bridgeman household, and plainly reflects Traherne's interest in that period in the new ideas in science and philosophy, as well as his patience, his thoroughness, and his capacity for laborious toil in the harvesting of scholarship. It is the purely intellectual side of Traherne that we see in the early notebook, in the *Roman Forgeries*, and here; and since it is part of his real self, and no small part of his strength and greatness, it is well that this *Commonplace Book* has survived to prove that for Traherne mysticism, a quest for spiritual experience, involved no narrowing or neglecting of intellectual interests, nor any lessening of intellectual vigor and capacity.

BURNEY MS. 126

OF the four as yet unpublished manuscripts, three, *The Book of Devotions*, the collection of early verse, and the *Commonplace Book*, are in the possession of the sons of Bertram Dobell. The fourth, the Burney MS. 126, is in the British Museum. It has not hitherto been ascribed to Thomas Traherne. Dr. Bell discovered it, a slender octavo, and mentioned it in his preface to the *Poems of Felicity*; but supposing it to have belonged to Philip's son Thomas, he was not interested in the little volume, and dismissed it in a few lines.

Dr. Bell had not examined the other Traherne manuscripts and could not be aware of the extraordinary variety of handwritings they exhibit; but anyone thoroughly familiar with the Dobell manuscripts would recognize at once in this notebook the same variants of the one handwriting. Most striking of all, and most easily recognizable, is the printlike hand of the *Commonplace Book*; and the entries in this notebook in that hand are from the same work as in the *Commonplace Book*, Gale's *Court of the Gentiles*. That is conclusive. Here, however, these are later entries, not imbedded as in the *Commonplace Book*, but coming last, and in English when all the rest is in Latin.

It is pretty clear that the entries in this notebook belong to different periods; it is my opinion that all of them, except the extracts from Gale, are comparatively early—before 1661. Traherne has told us that he read widely in philosophy during his time at the university; and the facts that these notes are in Latin rather than in English, that they reveal the methodical student acquiring a knowledge of Platonism rather than one to whom it was a natural habit of thought, and that the valuable fifteenth-century folios of Ficino[119] he was summarizing would hardly be available to him outside the Bodleian, seem to suggest an early date, and the second Oxford period.

The first set of notes and summaries in this book are headed *Platonis Philosophii Speculationes practicae a Marsilio Ficino breviter digestae*; and eighty-six pages are filled with passages from Plato as translated by Ficino, classified under twenty-six headings. Further on, after some blank pages, come twenty-six pages of *Observationes . . . e Socratis vita (a Marsilio Ficino scripta) veraciter excerptae*; and there is one page on Trismegistus, also from Ficino. The extracts are interesting as showing Traherne's close study of Plato, the books he used, and the contact between the seventeenth-century English Platonists and the Platonists of fifteenth-century Florence. They are interesting also in showing how widespread was the revival of interest in Platonism at this time. The fame of the group known as "The Cambridge Platonists," discussed in Part IV, has tended to suggest that Cambridge University was the sole center of this English Platonism. Traherne's notebook shows that Oxford students were equally affected by this current. The Bridgeman circle in London was also sympathetic. Traherne's predecessor in the chaplaincy, Hezekiah Burton—who was present during Sir Orlando's final illness—was one of the Cambridge Platonists; and the connection between Sir Orlando, Burton, and Traherne is probably

---

[119] Marsiglio Ficino, 1433-1499. First to translate Plato from manuscripts; published his *Platonis Opera* in 1483-1484. Collected editions of Ficino's works appeared in 1516, 1561, 1641.

indicative of a much wider connection than generally recognized. But interesting as the contents of this notebook are in the glimpse they give of Traherne as a methodical student, and of certain studies that attracted him, the flyleaf is more interesting still. There is that tantalizing hint of an untold tale in the repeated "Elinor" penned at its foot; there is a conundrum in the words scribbled on its opposite page—"More especially in the Beginning God made. . . ." Made them what? Male and female?

But most valuable of all, a genuine find, is that this page contains one of the few autograph signatures of Traherne; the only others known to exist are the three I discovered on Sir Orlando's Will. This in the notebook is the only one to be found in any of Traherne's manuscripts.

BIBLIOGRAPHY OF CRITICISM

BY ROBERT ALLERTON PARKER

ANONYMOUS. "Thomas Traherne," *Contemporary Review*, Vol. 142. London: September 1932.

BEACHCROFT, T. O. "Traherne, and the Doctrine of Felicity," *The Criterion*, Vol. 9. London: January 1930.

BELL, HAROLD IDRESS. *Traherne's Poems of Felicity*, edited from the MS. Oxford: Clarendon Press, 1910.

BRADBURY, S. *Bertram Dobell: Bookseller and Man of Letters.* London: B. Dobell, 1909.

BULLEN, A. H. "Bertram Dobell," *The Nation*, Vol. 100. New York: February 11, 1915.

CHRIST, ERNST. *Studien zu Thomas Traherne.* Tübingen: E. Göbel, 1932.

DANIELLS, ROY. *A Serious and Pathetical Contemplation of the Mercies of God, in several most Devout and Sublime Thanksgivings for the Same. by Thomas Traherne* (reprint). Toronto: The University of Toronto Press (*Philology and Literature Studies*, No. 2), 1941.

DAWSON, M. L. Letter to *London Times Literary Supplement*, September 29, 1927.

HALL, REV. WILLIAM C. "Poetical Works of Thomas Traherne," *Manchester Quarterly*. October 1904.

HOLMES, ELIZABETH. *Henry Vaughan and the Hermetic Philosophy.* Oxford: Blackwell, 1932.

HOPKINSON, ARTHUR W. Letter to *London Times Literary Supplement*, October 6, 1927.

IREDALE, Q. *Thomas Traherne.* Oxford: Blackwell, 1935.

JONES, RUFUS MATTHEW. *Spiritual Reformers in the 16th & 17th Centuries.* London: 1914.

JONES, W. LEWIS. "Thomas Traherne and the Religious Poetry of the Seventeenth Century," *The Quarterly Review*, Vol. 200. London: July and October 1904.

LEISHMAN, JAMES BLAIR. *The Metaphysical Poets: Donne, Herbert, Vaughan, Traherne.* Oxford: The Clarendon Press, 1934.

LÖHRER, FRIEDA. *Die Mystik und ihre Quellen im Thomas Traherne.* 1930.

MARTIN, L. C. "Henry Vaughan and the Theme of Infancy," *Seventeenth Century Studies, presented to Sir Herbert Grierson*. Oxford: The Clarendon Press, 1938.

MASSINGHAM, HAROLD. *A Treasury of Seventeenth Century English Verse*. London: Macmillan, 1919.

————. "A Note on Thomas Traherne," *New Statesman and Nation*, Vol. 55. London: December 19, 1914.

MORE, PAUL ELMER. "Thomas Traherne," *The Nation*, Vol. 38. New York: February 18, 1909.

PARKES, S. T. H. "A Devout Hedonist: The Riches of Thomas Traherne," *Today*, Vol. 9. London: June 1922.

PRICE, C. Letter to *London Times Literary Supplement*, October 27, 1927.

QUILLER-COUCH, SIR ARTHUR. *Felicities of Thomas Traherne* (Chosen and edited, with an introduction). London: P. J. and A. E. Dobell, 1934.

SHERER, GERTRUDE ROBERTS. "More and Traherne," *Modern Language Notes*, Vol. 34. Baltimore: 1919.

SLATER, JOHN ROTHWELL. *Of Magnanimity and Charity—Thomas Traherne*, edited with an Introduction. New York: King's Crown Press, 1942.

THOMPSON, ELBERT N. S. "The Philosophy of Thomas Traherne," *Philological Quarterly*, Vol. 8. Iowa City: April, 1929.

TOWERS, FRANCIS. "Thomas Traherne: His Outlook on Life," *The Nineteenth Century*, Vol. 87. London: 1920.

WADE, GLADYS I. "St. Thomas Aquinas and Thomas Traherne," *Blackfriars*, Vol. 12. London: 1931.

————. "The Poetical Works of Thomas Traherne." Reviewed *London Times Literary Supplement*, July 7, 1932.

————. "Traherne and the Spiritual Value of Nature Study," *The London Quarterly and Holborn Review*. London: April 1934.

————. "Thomas Traherne as 'Divine Philosopher.' " *The Hibbert Journal*, Vol. 32. London: July 1934.

————. "Mrs. Susanna Hopton," *The English Review*. London: January 1936.

WAHL, JEAN. *Poemes de Thomas Traherne*. Paris: *Mesures*, April 15, 1936.

WATKINS, ALFRED. Letter to *London Times Literary Supplement*, October 20, 1927.

WHITE, HELEN CONSTANCE. *The Metaphysical Poets*. New York: Macmillan, 1936.

WILDE, HANS OSKAR. *Beiträge zur Englischen Literaturgeschichte des 17. Jahr-Hunderts.* Breslau: 1932.

WILLCOX, LOUISE COLLIER. "A Joyous Mystic," *The North American Review,* Vol. 193. New York: 1911.

WILLETT, GLADYS E. *Traherne.* Cambridge: W. Heffer, 1919.

WILSON, A. DORIS L. "Thomas Traherne: Poet and Mystic," *Poetry Review,* Vol. 16. London: 1925.

INDEX